ADVENTURES
WITH
CAMERA AND PEN

ANTHONY DALTON

BookLand
press

TORONTO, CANADA

Published by:
BookLand Press
6021 Yonge Street, Suite 1010
Toronto, Ontario M2M 3W2
Canada
www.booklandpress.com

Printed and bound in Canada.

Library and Archives Canada Cataloguing in Publication

Dalton, Anthony, 1940-
　　Adventures with camera and pen / Anthony Dalton.

ISBN 978-0-9784395-2-1

　　1. Dalton, Anthony, 1940- —Travel.
2. Photojournalists—Canada—Anecdotes.
3. Adventure and adventurers—Anecdotes. I. Title.

PN4913.D33A3 2009　　　　070.4′9092　　　C2009-902405-5

Mixed Sources
Product group from well-managed
forests, and other controlled sources
www.fsc.org Cert no. SW-COC-002358
© 1996 Forest Stewardship Council
FSC

*For Penny,
and for Pam and Chris*

TABLE OF CONTENTS

INTRODUCTION

My first published newspaper article was a short illustrated piece about the legendary West African town of Timbuktu in the southern Sahara. Since that first exciting publication, three decades ago, I've had the opportunity of travelling far and wide in search of stories and photographs by land, sea and air. As a result of my extensive travels, I have seen my usually light-hearted adventure articles published in magazines and newspapers in twenty countries and half as many languages.

The undeniable attraction of the world's wildlife has drawn me close on all continents and many islands. The rivers and seas of our world have provided me with much pleasure and the chance to cruise across their surfaces in an eclectic variety of craft, from dugout canoes in Africa to giant windjammers on the oceans. Deserts with giant sand dunes; mountains and glaciers; forests and open plains, have given me scenes for my cameras and grist for my literary mill. People of all colours, races, religious beliefs and economic means have inspired me with their lifestyles. I am blessed to have seen and experienced so much: I know it and I appreciate it.

This book contains a collection of my favourite adventures — all expanded from the earlier articles using my original notes. Although the collection might seem geographically random to some, I have, for the most part, placed the stories in a regional order. The book begins, however, with a series of tales about Canada, which I originally wrote for people in other lands. Canada has been my home for much the greater part of my life. It is a vast country with enormous scope for adventures of almost all kinds, and I have sampled many of them.

Each adventure journey represented here has added much to my knowledge and immeasurably to my life.

MUSK OX IN THE MIST

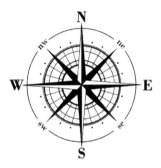

"Tony, there's two musk ox over by the radio towers. Meet me at the house."

"Thanks, Joe. I'm on my way."

That brief telephone conversation was all the incentive I needed to go out on a miserably wet Arctic day. Telephones simply cannot be trusted. If I had let it ring I could have stayed warm, dry and safe. Instead I answered its insistent ring and found myself face to face with a warm-blooded bulldozer. I grabbed my camera bag and parka and ran from the Ikaluktutiak Hotel to Joe Ohokannoak's home. He and Charlie Evalik were ready and waiting.

"Let's go."

Side by side we jogged through the rain to the shore. Getting in each other's way, we managed a mad scramble to push the boat out and clamber on board without getting too wet. Before I was properly seated Charlie had the motor

wound up and we were racing across Cambridge Bay to
the east side. The light rain and mist were cold. Our speed,
across an open body of water in sight of drifting ice, added
the wind chill factor to the equation. I pulled my parka hood
over my head and tucked my gloved hands in my pockets.
My eyes screwed themselves into wrinkled slits behind my
glasses.

Twice in the preceding few days I had seen musk
oxen. Each time I had been in a floatplane buzzing across
the tundra a few hundred metres above ground. From that
altitude musk oxen look no bigger or dangerous than little
brown mice. Coming back from a successful day's char
fishing, where the Surrey River pours out into Wellington
Bay, we had flown over five musk oxen feeding together.
They ran off at our approach, not knowing we couldn't land
anywhere near them. The weather had been fine and clear
that day, the way summer should be.

The Canadian Arctic can toss the most abysmal
weather around at times. I can handle winter blizzards.
In the Arctic, when the long winter months drain the light
from the sky, one expects a certain amount of snow, and
temperatures threatening to drop off the scale. The sea is
supposed to freeze over, creating an icy white traffic-free
highway between Canada's Arctic islands. Foxes and polar
bears wear their dress whites to render themselves invisible
against the snow. Even the Inuit, when he goes hunting,
wears white skins with the fur on the inside and out, as the
only acceptable camouflage and means of keeping warm
outdoors. As I said, it's supposed to be cold. It's expected
up north.

The summer should be different. Pleasantly warm
is ideal, with tiny tundra flowers, saxifrage and dwarf
willows carpeting the land. The birds come back for a few
weeks, after spending most of the year in southern climes.
Ptarmigans and loons arrive, as do swans and geese, a
variety of ducks, gulls and wading birds, and the fierce
snowy owl. The ice melts on tundra lakes and the trout pop
up to snack on winged devils. The rivers run free and the
Arctic char go with them in search of the sea. Summer is a

magical time. It can be damp though, extremely damp. The ground is usually soaking wet underfoot after the thaw. That's when the mosquitoes appear in squadrons so thick and deadly that they can be photographed as malignant clouds. Hats trailing fine mesh nets from wide brims have been known to offer reasonable defence against those miniature warriors. That's why I wear one.

All too often, when it's supposed to be warm and the skies should be clear, mists and rains descend. When that happens the Arctic is a wretched place to be, and the days are so long. Night, meaning darkness, just doesn't exist in summer, not as we know it. Mist and rain for twenty-four hours of daylight can send the most optimistic into bouts of depression. And then, in spite of the appalling conditions outside, a simple phone call telling of an unpredictable event happens along to liven things up a little.

Charlie swung the boat around a grounded ice floe and cut his motor. Silently, with only a hint of ripples licking the boat's sides, we ghosted to a stop in the shallows. We were some distance south of the towers. There was no choice of route. We had to trot inland against the wind and it was hard work. On a low knoll we crouched at Charlie's hand signal. Two hundred metres away, almost hidden in the mist were two large dark shapes. We edged forward cautiously. We were down wind so they could not catch our scent. That didn't mean they were stupid, or blind. We stayed low.

Musk oxen, scientists claim, are genetically more closely related to sheep and goats than to real oxen: nature just built them bigger and stronger. Fully grown they can weigh half a tonne or more. With a hump on their shoulders, long shaggy hair that looks as if it hasn't been groomed since the last ice age, and sweeping curled horns beginning at a parting on their foreheads and ending in wicked points, they give the appearance of being clumsy. Far from it. A musk ox is an amazingly agile creature, and can be extremely aggressive. In the summer rut the bulls have even been known to chase birds. In spite of the weather, it was summer. To be precise, it was August — the rutting season.

Joe and Charlie quickly briefed me on the typical warning signs leading up to a musk ox charge.

"When they get upset they paw the ground and shake their heads."

I looked at the vague shapes ahead. They stood perfectly still. They were watching us.

"Two young bulls," Charlie decided, although how he could determine their gender from so far away was a mystery. As far as I could see through my telephoto lens two unkempt coats trailed close to the ground completely obscuring their private parts.

Two young bulls, I thought, standing up there looking at us in the middle of the rutting season. Well, I hope for our sakes that they have really good eyesight.

"If they charge, run like mad and get out into that big pond as far as you can," came the next piece of advice. "Musk ox never run into water when they are charging."

I looked at the pond. It was more like a small kidney-shaped lake. The winter ice had gone, leaving a smooth surface trying vainly to reflect the sombre grey of the sky. It looked like a sheet of polished aluminium dropped on someone's badly cut lawn. I knew it would be cold.

Armed with valuable knowledge about the habits of one of the Arctic's largest creatures, and there were two in front of us, I crept forward with my Inuit companions. Charlie motioned us to spread out a little. I knelt and took a series of rapid-fire shots. Distant images, I told myself, were better than no pictures at all. Charlie and Joe remained parallel to me, one on either side. I noticed they had moved further away. I asked them about that later. Charlie had a brace of sensible answers.

"If you spread out you don't get in each other's way when you have to run."

And, "Keeping apart makes us less visible."

Joe, who had moved ahead of us, stopped and held out one hand.

"They've seen us," he whispered tersely. I had a feeling they'd seen us long before that but, as a visitor, I kept my own council.

"Be careful and remember what to do."

He was talking to me out of the side of his mouth. I had every intention of being cautious. The centre of the placid pond began to look relatively inviting. I believed I could put up with hypothermia for a while if it meant ultimate survival. Having a head on confrontation with a musk ox, and there were still two up there, was not high on my list of priorities.

Keeping low we continued our deliberate advance. The only sound was my breathing. It sounded like an over-worked steam engine. We got to within seventy-five metres, give or take a stride or two. Without warning one of the beasts charged.

"Where was the ground pawing? Where was the warning shake of the head?" I wanted to know. "Aren't there rules of engagement for this sort of thing?"

I flashed a look towards Charlie, expecting to see him halfway to the pond. He was rooted to the spot with his mouth wide open. Joe was like a statue too. Well, if they weren't going for an afternoon paddle, I sure wasn't about to get my lower person frozen. Not even for a charging musk ox. I stayed too.

The musk ox, watched by his mate on the hill and us some way down the slope, changed into high gear and sprinted toward me. I had an uncomfortable feeling that my life was due for a new experience.

"Turn, you big oaf," I prayed, aware that he had reached a point where he was between me and the water. He turned. I don't think he heard me. But he turned anyway. As if to prove my Inuit friends' wisdom for my benefit, he took the long way to the next hill. He ran right round the far edge of the pond. I began to feel better about the chances of immersion as a means of survival. On top of the hill the hairy ox nodded his head anxiously.

"You were supposed to do that before you charged," I complained from the doubtful safety of distance.

The three of us, much more confident now, moved slowly up the incline towards the remaining young bull. He knew the rules. He scraped at the ground with one paw and tossed his head the way he had been taught. We froze.

The bull snorted, sending twin gusts of snotty nasal steam at us. I took another pace forward. He tired of the game and charged. Not at us, oh no. This one had no respect for traditional values at all. He may have known how to thump the ground with a testy foot. He may have practised scaring other younger bulls with angry movements of his massive head. But, he didn't know much about ponds.

He thundered down the knoll without so much as a glance at us; towards the pond and the companionship of his pal on the opposite hill. He didn't hesitate at the water's edge. He didn't run daintily round it like the other wimp. This brash hairy bovine crashed headlong into the pond and swam powerfully across to the other side. He came out like an express train and pounded up the hill to his mate. At the top he turned, water streaming from his coat, and there they stood flank to flank glaring at us. I looked at the pond, which was still roiling in agitation, then at Charlie.

"Get out into the pond if he charges," I mimicked with an attempted laugh. Charlie and Joe ignored me. They were looking at each other in amazement. Finally Joe spoke.

"Musk ox don't do that," he said in awe.

"You won't find me running into freezing water next time I see a musk ox," I told them. "I'm gonna do what all cowards do. I'm gonna run like hell."

Not having my friends' deep knowledge of musk ox behaviour, I was determined to get close enough for more photographs.

"I'm going up there," I pointed to the hill where the shaggy ones waited.

"Be careful." The softly spoken advice reminded me of my mother. She used to tell me to be careful when I climbed trees as a boy. "You'll hurt yourself if you're not careful."

Even as a small boy I knew it was pointless reminding Mother that my intention was not to hurt myself, or that a tree could not hurt me. Gravity might when it slammed me into the ground at the tail end of a fall, but not the tree.

Being careful with a couple of healthy, ready to rut

musk ox considering another charge, was a wasted caution. If they charged any care I might take of myself would end the moment they caught me, whether out in the pond where they never go when charging, or racing across the tundra. My interest was in photography, not in being careful. I could have stayed in my hotel room in the dry and avoided the total experience if I wanted to be careful.

"Stay there," I told Charlie. I think that's what he and Joe were planning to do anyway. I walked on alone with camera at the ready. The two beasts paced restlessly back and forth, never taking their eyes off me. They moved closer together. Both heads began to shake. The great curved horns, which could inflict so much damage, framed their faces impressively. Front hooves pawed the ground aggressively. I stopped. My camera clicked a few times.

To my right the pond, which had settled back into mirror-like calm, beckoned. I thought about it fleetingly. The cold put me off: that and the short cut taken by one musk ox. Escape by pond did not seem a foolproof plan anymore. I backed off.

The musk oxen stopped acting tough and watched, wondering what I would do next. I took another couple of paces backwards. The two big fellas separated and turned broadside to me. They shook their great heads once in unison and bounded down the other side of the hill — out of sight. Three men exhaled noisily. Then, laughing with delight, we jogged back through the mist to Charlie's boat. We were still smiling as we stepped ashore and gave each other a big hug.

A day later, under a blue sky and with considerably warmer temperatures, I went fishing again with two other outsiders. Magic Pond is the local minister's favourite fishing spot. He thinks his supreme boss put it there for his and his associates' pleasure. We must have done something right because he allowed us to try it for ourselves.

Charlie Angohiatuk was our guide. He knew how to find Magic Pond. On the south side of Lake Ferguson, a few kilometres along a rough and rocky trail from Cambridge Bay, there is a spot avid fishermen dream of. As the ice of many long months begins to melt and the wind ruffles the water, hungry lake trout break out of their winter lethargy. At this time they will rise for almost any bait. For once the mosquitoes were a bonus. They kept the trout jumping.

We anchored our boat to an ice shelf in a large patch of open water. Using a simple homemade lure of polished red and silver metal (empty coke cans do have their uses) with a single barbless hook, I prepared to catch the big one.

The other three were visibly unimpressed with my cheap and cheerful attraction. They were about to learn that better is not always best. I dropped a long cast right on to the ice across the water. A snigger behind me suggested I didn't know what I was doing. Confidently, I gave one gentle clean jerk, whipping my lure into the lake with a satisfying 'plop' right beside the shelf where the trout hid when they weren't attacking flying pests. As the lure hit the water a trout struck hard, bending my rod double.

"Keep it away from the ice," came the cry as my reel screamed and the boat rocked under us. Ten metres away a sturdy silver shape leapt out of the water shaking its head in annoyance. The hook was well set. A few minutes later Charlie swung my catch aboard in his safety net. My homemade lure had been christened with a trout as long as my arm and weighing seven and a half kilos. There were no more comments about my equipment or my unorthodox angling style.

The fishing was intense. Most of the time we each had a fish to battle at the same time. Any thought of helping with a landing was forgotten. It was every man for himself. No wonder the minister liked fishing there so much.

In the heat of the action Charlie noted laconically, "There's a musk ox over there."

I looked around for an escape route. If that big burly beast came too close to the water I didn't want to be out there in a flimsy boat.

"We're okay out here," one of the visiting fishermen announced, remembering what he had been taught. "Musk ox never charge into water."

Right!

ARCTIC RAMBLINGS

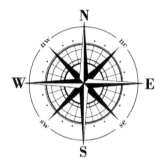

You would have to see it, as I did, to believe it. The Surrey River, where it flows out of Victoria Island into Wellington Bay, was thick with fish. Not just any fish, but Arctic char. The water churned with their life. If we had strung a net across the river's mouth we could have pulled in thousands of them in one haul.

With help from Adlair Aviation, six of us flew in to a landing on a patch of open but freezing cold water between ice floes. Our flight from Cambridge Bay in a noisy single-engine De Havilland Beaver, wonderful old aerial workhorse of the north, had taken a little less than one hour. Due to financial constraints, we had only chartered space on the 'plane for parts of the day. While we fished it was to continue south across the North-West Passage to Bathurst Inlet Lodge on the mainland. Much later in the day it would return and collect us and our catch, en route

back to Cambridge Bay. There was no time to waste. Fish
were waiting to be caught.

I had assembled my rod and line in the Beaver. As
soon as the floats touched shore and the propeller jerked to
a stop, I was out and ready for my first cast. It was so easy.
I swung the rod away to my right, snapped it back over
my right shoulder with a flick of my wrist and let the line
go. I must have hit a char on the snout because the barbless
three-pronged hook dangling under the silver lure caught
immediately. Before the rest of the guys had chosen their
positions and made their first casts, I had a plump nine-
pound char doing a sprightly northern version of the cha-
cha-cha across the backs of its multitudinous pals to land at
my feet.

I cast again with the same result. And again. And
again. The Beaver left while I was in action and I didn't
even notice its departure or hear it as it lumbered away to
the south. So, there I was fishing in the Surrey River. Only
it wasn't really like fishing. Okay, there were similarities. I
swung the lure and slightly weighted line behind me, gave
a sharp flick of my wrist and the line streamed out of the
reel on demand. The lure hit the water, or it hit a fish (it
didn't seem to make much difference), I pulled the line tight
and reeled a wriggling taste treat in to land at my feet. But,
as I said, it wasn't really like fishing. It didn't feel like sport.
It was, to my mind, more like wholesale murder.

Victoria Island is a vast barely inhabited barren
mass surrounded for much of the year by solid ice. At
almost 218,000 square kilometres in area (84,000 sq. miles)
it is Canada's second largest island (Vancouver Island is
the largest). There are only two permanent settlements:
Cambridge Bay (also now known as Ikalututiak) and
Holman (now Ulukhaktok).

Without doubt, Victoria is a fisherman's paradise.
Apart from the beautiful silver char there are large numbers
of lake trout waiting to be fed, or otherwise lured to the
table. But those Arctic char congregating at the mouth of
the Surrey River confused me. What were they doing there?
I wondered. Why did they mill around in such numbers

where the river runs out? Fortunately, one member of our group was an amateur naturalist. He spelled it out for me.

Arctic char (*Salvelinus alpinus*), related to trout and salmon, is both a freshwater fish and a saltwater fish and is native to the Arctic. In fact, no other freshwater fish is found as far north. The hundreds, maybe thousands, getting in each others' way on the Surrey River were simply trying to make up their minds whether to stay in fresh water or take the plunge, so to speak, and go exploring in the salty North-West Passage. Their indecision, as far as we were concerned, was their downfall.

I saved a few good sized specimens to take home for eventual consumption via the BBQ. After that I caught and released until I was tired of the game. In fact, I am convinced I kept hooking the same fish. Or maybe the others were cousins. One char looks very much like another to me.

By now it should be becoming obvious that I'm not exactly a dedicated fisherman. Don't get me wrong. I do enjoy it. I like the challenge of catching fish. But it has to be a challenge. Those char would snap at anything. I'll bet they would have had my finger if I'd waved it at them under water. So, that's by way of saying, I got bored quite quickly: but only with the fishing. The Arctic has much to interest me.

The Surrey River is shallow and fast. That means it has rapids. That means white water. Those two similarly related elements combined equal canoeing fun to me. I wished the guys a good afternoon's casting and wandered off alone to study the river and the tundra from different angles. The river is only about 150 kilometres in length as far as I can tell from my maps. Much of it seems to be short threads connecting a series of five long lakes. Idly I imagined being dropped by floatplane at the distant end of the most northwesterly lake and paddling the full distance. Those rapids would be fun and the wildlife-viewing opportunities had to be worth the cost alone. It had definite appeal for me; something worth considering for the future.

I walked for a couple of hours, escorted by the obligatory over-populated squadron of airborne Arctic pests. I was wearing a safari hat with a net that covered my hat, head, neck and shoulders. Still, more than a few mosquitoes fought their way through the mesh to get at my blood. I did my best to ignore them. The tiny Arctic flowers kept me enthralled with their beauty and occasional broken caribou antlers scattered on the tundra served to remind me where I was.

Because the land bordering the Surrey River is reasonably flat, except where the river has carved its channel, the vistas are huge. Distances are difficult to judge with the naked eye. I watched a distant white blob for a while, trying to figure out whether it was a rock, a white Arctic fox up close, or a polar bear far away. If it was the latter I was determined to show it how fast I could run. To be sure, I walked, with a certain sense of caution you understand, another hundred metres closer. The white blob, definitely no rock, proved to be less than a polar bear but somewhat more dangerous than a fox. As I got closer a pair of yellow eyes glared at me and a sharp curved beak began clacking ominously. The obviously angry snowy owl took off from its knee-high rocky perch and flew straight at me, although far enough above me to be out of my reach. Being a considerate wanderer, I retreated. The bird followed, making unpleasant gestures and unnecessary noises. I waved my arms, not at the owl, but to indicate the vastness of the land: more than enough space for both of us, especially as I was not hunting the owl's prey.

"Hey! There's enough room here for both of us, so piss off."

The owl ignored me, beating its wings over my head net, but still keeping its distance.

"Okay. Okay," I admitted defeat. "I'll go and you can be master of all the land you can see. And don't even think about..."

The owl must have understood because it was considerate enough not to expel its waste on my head. It did manage a reasonably impressive void, but missed me by at least an arm's length. A warning, or just a lousy shot? Only the owl knows for sure.

By the time I ambled back to the river mouth the fishing was over and my companions were eating sandwiches, drinking coffee and talking about, what else? Fish.

The Beaver came back about an hour later. Soon after take-off, en route to a stop at High Arctic Lodge to pick up another passenger or two, we passed over a handful of musk oxen. From the advantage of our altitude they looked tiny and benign. Close up, I knew from experience, they could be quite menacing.

Leaving the other guys to their own devices, I went fishing on the sea ice of the North-West Passage for a day with two Inuit adults and a child. I wasn't really interested in the fishing, you understand. The experience of wandering out on the ice of the historic waterway was uppermost in my mind.

The North-West Passage, a rarely open ice-choked waterway threading a torturous route through Canada's Arctic Islands, will forever hold a prominent position in the annals of polar exploration. For some three hundred years, from at least 1610 to 1906, explorers and adventurers vied with each other to be the first to find a navigable route through the Arctic, from the North Atlantic Ocean to the Pacific and beyond to the Orient. Although fame and considerable fortune was part of the attraction, the primary goal was an economic one: to establish the shortest sea route between the merchants of Europe and the riches of the east, specifically Cathay.

The list of those who failed and perished in the attempt is almost as long as that of the men who tried, failed, yet lived to tell about their adventures. It starts with the departure from London in 1610 of the enigmatic Henry Hudson and contains a sadly impressive collection of now historic names culminating with perhaps the most famous of all, Sir John Franklin — and his doomed coterie of 129 officers and crew aboard HMS *Erebus* and HMS *Terror*. William Cowper, 18th century English poet, pondered the apparent futility of Arctic exploration when he wrote:

Hard task indeed o'er Arctic Seas to roam!

Is hope exotic? Grows it not at home?

Despite the deaths, lost hopes and other failures, the North-West Passage was eventually successfully navigated. Between 1903 and 1906 a Norwegian explorer, the highly skilled and experienced Roald Amundsen, and his crew of six sailed *Gjøa*, a 72' long converted herring boat, from east to west. I know how rough the voyage is. I made a solo attempt on the passage myself in 1984 and nearly died in the attempt.

Back to the fishing. We didn't have a boat and we weren't planning to go far. Instead we wandered out onto the sea ice, jumping cracks and leads of open water where necessary, until we were farther from land than seemed safe. I commented on the distance. The answer I received was less than reassuring.

"If the ice suddenly breaks up any more, we can always run back to shore."

Having already suffered a long swim in the Arctic Ocean off the coast of Alaska the year before, I was not really interested in repeating the exercise. That northern sea water is very cold. With the break up warning in mind, I tested each piece of ice I stepped on by ramming my heel into it. If it squelched, or cracked, I quickly moved to stronger floes.

I have to say, the fishing wasn't as exciting as at the Surrey River. We didn't use fishing rods. An Inuit showed me how to jig a hand-held line up and down until it attracted a fish. It took him about five minutes to land two beauties. I tried to duplicate his feat for a couple of hours, unsuccessfully I should add. The other man and the child caught fish. I did not. There were a few raised eyebrows at my ineptitude. A few apparently funny comments in Inuktitut were aimed at me. I smiled back and jigged the line just the way they were all doing: nothing. Not even a gentle nibble. As the fish weren't biting, for me anyway, I amused myself by jumping increasingly wide leads. Before long, not paying enough attention, because I was too busy taking photographs of ice patterns, I had moved a considerable distance away from my companions. One of them called out to me.

"You'd better get back here. That wind's coming up and the ice will move."

I slung my camera around my neck and ran and jumped like a demented Arctic hare, following a confusing maze of my own footprints, until I was close to the Inuit trio. The lead between us had opened up to about five metres – much too wide to jump. One of the fishermen pointed to the east.

"Go that way."

He went back to his fishing. I ran as fast as I could on the slippery surface until I found a route to take me to solid ground. It took considerably longer than I would have liked under the circumstances. Later, as we were walking back to town, and I was being teased about my icy detour, I was told of a local who also ignored the signs.

"That guy could not get back to land. The wind blew the ice out and he went with it. He was out there for hours. We had to take a boat out later and rescue him. He caught some good fish though while he was waiting."

There was no obvious humour in the words and no sense of potential disaster: just the facts, nothing more. Then, a smile in my direction and…

"You didn't catch any fish, Tony. I guess we would have left you out there."

I really must learn to fish properly sometime.

REACHING FOR BUGABOO HEIGHTS

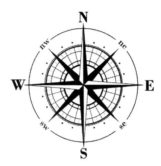

After a leisurely three-hour drive through increasingly stunning scenery from Calgary, it feels good to leave the car and stretch our legs. Even so, I remember from my first climbing expedition in the Bugaboos many years before, we have a long trek from the parking area up to the Conrad Kain hut at Boulder Camp. Actually it's only about five kilometres but there's a 700 metre altitude difference to take care of too. That's not so bad either unless, like each of us, you have a big and heavy pack on your back. We are starting with food supplies for four hungry guys for just over a week and enough camping and climbing equipment to hopefully keep us out of trouble every day.

As I shoulder my pack I realize it weighs about the same as the one I carried all those years ago when I first set off for the then relatively new Conrad Kain hut. In the mid 1970s, however, I was considerably younger and somewhat fitter than I am now, over a decade later. The shoulder straps fit comfortably and the pack frame is molded to the contours of my back. The weight, however, seems outrageously high. I grimace and grunt, something I know I will do a lot in the coming days, and look over at Christian. By far the youngest of our quartet, he's waiting impatiently for the rest of us.

"You are ready?" His slight Swiss-German accent and the toss of his head shows he's keen to be moving.

"Sure. We're ready." I mean it to sound positive. Instead it comes out sounding like I've just been tortured. Christian nods and sets off at a killing pace. We, the older guys, follow at a more leisurely stroll: Jim in the lead, Eric in the middle and me bringing up the rear. It looks as though Chris will get to the hut in less than two hours. I know my time will be over three hours. I'm happy with that. I want to enjoy the hike and savour the stupendous views as the mountains come in sight. I also want to have some energy left for the climbs we have planned.

We flew in to Calgary a few days ago: three of us from various parts of Canada and one from Europe, just to spend some time climbing and camping together. I haven't had my climbing boots on for over two years. I, and my tender feet, need time to adjust.

At first we ramble through a lush green forest. It's a pleasant walk but I'm looking forward to the moment when we step into the open and see the massive glacier tumbling down from the huge snowfield. When we sight the Bugaboos in all their glory, everyone stops, including Christian. He stands staring straight ahead for a few minutes then looks back at us. The expression on his face is that of a child on Christmas morning. His smile ranges from one ear to the other. He looks at me and gives me a thumbs-up. It's all up hill from here, but Christian doesn't seem to notice. Seconds later he's on the move again at his original pace. I look up, my eyes roaming from right to left, mentally naming the peaks I can see: some of them the granite spires I climbed long ago. There's East Post, Bugaboo, Snowpatch, Pigeon, the Hound's Tooth all by itself in the middle of the glacier, Marmolata to the left and off in the background, the formidable Howser Towers.

The fabulous granite peaks of the Bugaboos, in British Columbia's Purcell Mountains, are an exotic playground for serious climbers and a great outdoor school for novices keen to learn how to climb well and how to climb safely. Sandwiched between the Rockies and the Selkirks, they contain some of the most technically demanding peaks in North America. Scanning the familiar steep towers I can feel the adrenaline building in me. I'm keen to get higher, unload the heavy pack at the hut and start some real climbing again. I turn away from the spectacular view, cast my eyes a few paces ahead of me and continue the trek over a rocky field. By the time we reach the hut we are all soaked in sweat. Despite the groans we shed as we lower our packs to the ground, we are all smiling. Standing in the natural ampitheatre at just over 2,200 metres above sea level, we are surrounded by beautiful climbing routes up peaks reaching as high as 3,400 metres. It is a mountaineer's paradise.

The climbers' hut at Boulder Camp is named after the late great Conrad Kain, Austrian mountaineer and guide. Kain was born in 1883 and arrived in Canada in 1909 where he quickly established himself as the best alpinist in the Purcells and indeed in the Canadian Rockies. He is credited with the first ascents of Mount Robson in 1913, Mount Louis in 1916 and the imposing Bugaboo Spire in 1916. Those climbs are only three of some 60 first ascents he made in western Canada in his relatively short life. He also made 25 first ascents in the New Zealand Alps and summited that country's Mount Cook on two occasions. Kain died at the age of 50, soon after climbing Mount Louis for the second time.

Christian, ever the enthusiast, wants to attempt Snowpatch tomorrow. That is much too soon for us (well, for me anyway). We will go for the much easier East Post to get ourselves in shape for the harder climbs later. Snowpatch and its technical routes can wait until we have acclimatized. Christian will have to wait too.

East Post is not technically difficult or particularly

high, but it is a good wall on which to prepare ourselves. It's also an excellent way to stretch our muscles. Jim points out the route we took together a few years before. Three hours of near vertical ascent, partly on loose rock, will take us up 500 metres to the summit. We climb happily, chattering to each other and admiring the views each time we stop to rest. Most of the climbing is easy until close to the top. Then there's a bit of vertical exposure with a few hundred metres of open air between our feet and the boulders far below. Without wasting time, I lead the way, working up the sheer face by digging my hands and feet into wide cracks. Over the lip there's a shallow sloping area with a convenient rock for a belay. I secure a rope and call down to my companions.

"On belay. Come on up."

The response is immediate. I hear Christian's voice. "Climbing!" A few minutes later he hoists himself to safety and glances up and left to the summit. I know what he's thinking and make the suggestion before he does.

"Sure. Go on up. I can look after this."

By the time Eric joins me Christian is out of sight. Then Jim's head appears. He pushes down hard with his hands and almost vaults to a standing position in front of me.

"What are we waiting for?" he asks. "Let's go."

Christian is eating an apple on the highest point of East Post when we get there. Jim gives him a nudge.

"Move over, Kid. That's my spot."

Christian hurls his apple core into space and gives up his seat. Pointing at Snowpatch, just across the snowfield, he tells us he wants to climb it tomorrow. He can't wait any longer.

"Let's see what the weather brings in the morning," cautions Eric.

Our descent is considerably faster than the climb. Using our ice axes as brakes and our boots as skis, we crouch and race down the steep back snow-slope to the bottom. It's an exhilarating run and no one falls. Predictably, Christian is the quickest. Off the snow slope, as we contemplate a cold beer back at Boulder Camp (yes, we carried it with us from the car), Jim breaks into a trot. Christian takes off after him. Eric complains, "Oh, shit." He increases the length of his stride so as not to get left behind. I just shake my head in wonder and break into an easy lope. The race is on, sort of.

Later, relaxing in the late afternoon sunshine on the boulder-strewn field, Christian can't take his eyes off Snowpatch. The sky is virtually cloudless. The forecast for the next few days is good. He can almost taste that cold grey granite.

The morning dawns clear. Not a cloud in sight again. We agree to split up: a decision we had made before we left Calgary. Christian is concerned that the weather will change and his dream of standing atop Snowpatch will crumble. He and Jim, therefore, will tackle Snowpatch by the first ascent route to the south summit. They have climbed together in the Swiss Alps a few times and know each other's strengths well. We have no fears for their safety. Eric and I, not as experienced and needing a couple of easier rocks to climb, opt for the less strenuous but to me more picturesque west route up Pigeon. It means a longer trek up the glacier for us, but we're happy with that. We also know we should be up the spire, down again and back at the hut to rest long before the other guys return.

I have always enjoyed the exercise of cutting my way up steep snow slopes and wandering across glaciers. I am intrigued by the crevasses, although they scare me to a certain extent. I fell into one a long time ago in the Swiss Alps while crossing a weak snow bridge and did not enjoy the experience. To be honest, it scared the ...you know what... out of me. I do acknowledge, however, that the pastel shades of blue and green tinged with white reaching down into unfathomable blackness are beautiful in their danger.

Walking, and occasionally cutting steps, at a fairly relaxed pace, it takes us just under three hours to climb to the foot of Pigeon's west ridge by way of the Bugaboo — Snowpatch col and the Vowell névé. Once on the mountain, reaching the southwest summit is little more than a mad scramble up easy rock so we don't bother to rope up. As we share an energy-boosting chocolate bar on a broad sloping rock table, Eric comments we should be able to see our companions on Snowpatch from the main summit. That thought spurs us on. To get higher we must first descend a narrow chimney to reach the main route. We accomplish that without incident and get back on the ascent. Clean snow covers a sloping ledge and we work our way carefully across it to an obvious vertical crack. Up we go, with me in the lead, to a painful hand traverse which necessitates hanging almost the full weight of my body from my fingers. As I move sideways, desperately holding on by my finger tips and with my feet flat against the wall for friction, I slip a bit and the nail on my right index finger tears back to expose far too much quick. Blood flows down my finger and hand to my wrist. Dangling momentarily by the fingers and thumb of one hand, I let loose an oath.

"That was rude," says a quiet voice below me. "Are you planning to stay there all day complaining about a broken fingernail?"

I suck the blood off my finger, still swearing under my breath, and keep shuffling sideways to a safer position. A few minutes later as Eric pulls himself up beside me, I hear: "You left blood on the rock back there."

Eric loves sarcasm, especially when he's the one delivering it. "I thought you said something about us not leaving any signs of our climbs."

"Up yours," is the politest reply I can think of quickly as we scramble the last few metres to the summit.

From the top we can clearly see the sharply serrated Howser group in one direction and Snowpatch in the other. While I'm cutting off a lot of torn nail and wrapping a band aid round my finger to keep the tear clean, Eric claims he can see our companions on Snowpatch. I look but I can't locate them. His eyes are obviously better than mine. As we begin our descent he looks over the Bugaboo Glacier to the adjacent peaks.

"Did you and Jim climb Marmolata last time?"

"Yes. By the standard route it's quite a good climb: a good day out. We had some fun on that rock. From the summit there are a couple of long rappels down to a bergschrund, over there." I point across the glacier to the visible base of Marmolata. "That's not difficult to jump. After that it's a pleasant walk down the glacier and back to base."

We agree: Marmolata will be our target for the following day.

Christian and Jim stroll into camp just in time for dinner. It took them seven and a half hours to reach the south summit of Snowpatch by way of the south-east corner route. An excited Christian reported, "Fabulous views over the glaciers and other spires."

Jim's comment was somewhat more subdued and typically laconic. "It was a good climb."

That evening we sat chatting with three German climbers who arrived during the day while we were on the peaks. All in their twenties, Hilda, Maria and Kirsten are planning to take a good look at the Hound's Tooth for their first climb. It's close to our route so we agree to rope up with them to cross the crevasse-ridden glacier. We really don't need to be roped together. We were just flirting with them when we suggested it. And they were doing the same when, with happy smiles, they agreed. Not surprisingly, we stayed talking until much too late in the night.

I was still tired when we moved onto the glacier in the early morning. We hugged our new friends, because we could, near the Hound's Tooth and continued on our way without them to the southeast foot of Marmolata. Of the hugs Eric remarked with a rueful expression, "It's not as much fun with all this gear on."

Marmolata is a relaxing day out: at least, it is on the route I have chosen. There are a couple of very difficult routes which require serious technical abilities, above and beyond my skills. For today the guys are happy to practice their moves on a few ledges, a couple of cracks a long flake and a pair of chimneys to humour me. In three hours we are on the summit and enjoying a leisurely picnic lunch, followed by an hour's sleep in the warm sun. Christian, of course, sets the pace for the descent.

"Come on, you guys," he pleads. "Time to go down."

Eric has his own priorities. "Okay. Let's go see the girls."

He gets up and pulls on his pack. Jim and I have no choice but to wake up and go with them.

Getting off Marmolata is accomplished by a long rappel down a steep wall I would not like to climb, either up or down. The end of the rope lands us on a wide but unpleasantly sloping ledge. Christian stands close to the outer edge of our platform and looks up at the sheer wall; then to each of us.

"I would like to climb this now. I can see a good line." He points up; his finger tracing an imaginary route.

"Forget it. There's no time," Jim tells him.

I've looked at that wall from this ledge before and I have absolutely no desire to risk my life by climbing it. To make my point I head down the sharp ridge to the glacier. The bergschrund (a crevasse that forms where moving glacier ice separates from the static ice attached to rock) is wider than I remember it. I take a run at it and land well on the other side. Eric is not impressed.

"Nice jump, Tony. Smart people wear a rope."

Proving he's no brighter than I am, he jumps and hits the snowfield a metre to my left. Christian and Jim follow then, at Eric's insistence, we rope up and head down the glacier for home. Eric was right to insist. There are dozens of crevasses cross the glacier, carving deep jagged wounds into its heart. Each one is a potential deathtrap for the unwary.

That evening, while demonstrating my free-climbing skills on a huge boulder to an audience larger than I would have liked (yes, the German girls were watching too), I slipped and landed awkwardly, although on two feet. My wrenched knee screamed, "Enough!" and that was the end of my climbing for that trip.

I never did get back onto the granite that summer but, after resting for two days at camp, I did enjoy myself hobbling about on the glacier taking photographs of the

Bugaboos from all angles. Jim, Eric and Christian went on to climb Bugaboo Spire and a few more noteworthy peaks. They also spent a lot of evening leisure time with the girls instead of looking after their injured companion. But that, of course, like the risks inherent in the sport, is sometimes part of the fun of climbing.

NO POLAR BEARS FOR ME

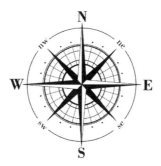

There's a plastic bubble at my feet. Beyond that there's nothing, only cold air and a strong gravitational pull, until the tundra calls a halt. The bubble extends in front of me too. If I look up I can see the outline of a rotor blade chopping purposefully at the air. Behind me Mark and Mike are looking for polar bears, beside me Steve is doing the same. I'm wondering how strong the bubble really is, because from where I sit it doesn't look too substantial.

Steve's voice whispers into my ears through the headphones, "I saw two bears out on the tundra a few miles away this morning, we'll see if they're still there."

I look sideways at him and nod in agreement. His eyes are busy, darting from left to right, searching for his quarry. A white beard disguises his chin. A few wisps of snowy hair stray from under his baseball cap. His hands looked comfortable and confident at the controls.

"Steve Miller will take us up for an hour or two," Mark had told me earlier as we walked across the tarmac to the helipad. "Steve's probably the expert on spotting wildlife in this region. He should be too. He's seen most of it."

Miller, I already knew, had an enviable reputation for his wildlife knowledge in general and his understanding of polar bears in particular. If there were any polar bears roaming the land near Churchill, or out on the ice floes close to shore on Hudson Bay, Steve would find them.

We ranged far and wide. Flocks of snow geese settled uneasily on melt-water ponds. Two herds of caribou on the move raised our enthusiasm for the chase. A square of white, on an otherwise barren patch of brown and green, caught Mike's attention. He tapped Steve on the shoulder and pointed down. Steve adjusted the joystick. We banked over so I could see the sky through the gap between my feet. I clamped my knees together and looked past Steve at Mother Earth, which was flying past the bubble over our heads. Steve's hands did something to the controls and the view changed abruptly. The ground rushed to meet us as if we were honoured guests. I pulled my feet up instinctively. That bubble certainly looked fragile to me.

The white was a sheet of plastic, blown in from who knows where by a strong wind. We took it with us: Mark had a place for it at the town dump.

"Let's try the ice along the shoreline," Steve suggested as the chopper lifted off again. Finding a white bear on white ice sounded like a tricky proposition to me, but, I was with experts, I trusted them to know what they were doing.

I was half expecting a great white bear to stand up and, shielding his eyes from the sun, shake a large clawed paw at us as we flew over the hummocks like a noisy dragonfly. There were no bears. No bears on the land, none on the ice, none swimming in the bay.

I flicked the switch on my microphone, "Maybe it's too early in the season."

"No, they're here somewhere. I've seen them for the

last couple of days," Steve told us.

On a spit of land, far in front of the bubble, the outline of a ship caught my attention. It looked as if it was under way, yet it couldn't be. It was on dry land. Steve circled it as Mark's tinny disembodied voice told me it was an old cargo ship and that bears often played on it. Not that day they didn't.

"There's a pod of whales," Mike's hand poked over my shoulder and stabbed towards the flimsy Perspex.

"They're adult males, feeding alone," Steve broke in as he hovered over the white whales.

Steve's got helicopter flying down to a fine art. He knows almost exactly the best altitudes to maintain when watching or photographing the wildlife of the region.

"I don't like to get closer than about four hundred feet above the whales," his voice probed my ears. "Any nearer than that and the belugas get really agitated."

The man's concern for the well-being of all the creatures he encounters showed in his actions and his words. He always does his best to avoid the helicopter's shadow passing directly over a whale.

"That drives them crazy," he said. "If the shadow touches them they spiral straight to the bottom."

Steve's a bit of a jack-of-all-trades when it comes to flying. Officially he's a contract pilot for a Churchill based helicopter outfit. He will fly anything his helicopter can lift: anywhere it has to go. Foremost in Steve's mind are those polar bears. He's been tagging bears for the Canadian Wildlife Service for many years. He claims to be able to process a bear in an average of twenty minutes. Once a bear is sighted, it takes less than two minutes from the time it is drugged by a dart fired from a special rifle until it falls. The bear is tagged where it stops. Steve stays with it until it begins to recover.

Polar bears are dangerous. There's a Nissen hut on the outskirts of Churchill known as the polar bear jail. Any bear making a nuisance of itself too close to town pays the penalty of incarceration. Notably curious and ever ready for a taste treat, troublemakers are lured to immensely strong bear traps on wheels. Rather like tubular steel paddy wagons, the traps are designed so as not to harm the bears just, perhaps, dent their dignity a little. Once trapped the offenders are towed to the jail where they are caged until the cells are full. Then Steve Miller is commissioned to fly the drugged outlaws far to the north.

Sitting in the bubble, with little between my under-protected butt and a long drop, I wondered about the wisdom of flying a helicopter with a polar bear as passenger. I know. I know...the bears are drugged and essentially harmless for a period of time. It's that period of time which bothers me. What happens if a particular bear has a stronger constitution than normal? When I was at school, one of my fellow students had to have an appendicitis operation. He woke up, and tried to sit up, during the process. If hospital staff could misjudge the dosage necessary to keep a teenage boy down long enough to perform an operation, couldn't wildlife anaesthetists make a similar mistake?

Can you imagine trying to fly a small helicopter, with nothing more than a plastic bubble between you and eternity, with a polar bear yawning and waking up behind you? I'd definitely be looking for a change of clothes when I got home from an encounter like that. I told Steve about my concern.

"We fly the bears in a strong net suspended under the helicopter," he explained patiently.

I don't know about polar bears, perhaps they've never learned to climb. There are not many trees where they live, that's for sure. However, I have seen a large number of the polar bear's darker cousins in the woods of western Canada. And those roughnecks have no problems climbing trees at high speed. If a black bear, or a grizzly, can climb a tree I think a polar bear could do the same. So, I reasoned to myself, with flawless logic, what's to stop the polar bear waking up and doing a quick hand over hand up the cable and joining the pilot?

A paw the size of a dinner plate comes through the oh so flimsy plastic, reaches down to the latch, opens the door, and a full size polar bear climbs in. Now I don't care how tough the pilot is, his nerves are sure to wobble a bit. He's bound to have some kind of sphincter reaction. It doesn't matter that the polar bear can't talk, the pilot would know the bear is looking at him and thinking, you're the son of a bitch who shot me with a dart. Just wait 'til we land.

My thoughts returned from the realm of fantasy when I learned it was impossible for the bear to escape the net: unless one day someone picks up a large, furry, white, monster reincarnation of Houdini.

Steve reckoned he probably held the record for bear flights. "I guess I've handled more polar bears than any other pilot," he admitted.

"How many? Any Idea?" I asked.

"Hmm. At a rough guess, about two thousand six hundred and ninety-eight in the last decade," he answered with a big grin.

The aerial expedition may not have produced the expected polar bears, it did, however, teach me much about the science of moving delinquent beasts from place to place. Determined to catch at least a glimpse of old *Thalarctus maritimus*, I went on an expedition of my own, by land.

"Try the dump," Mark advised, "but be careful."

Now the polar bears of Churchill are notorious for their love of sifting through the smouldering rubbish at the town dump. The smoking rubbish was there. Wisps of blue and grey curled up from particularly piquant sections. The cool wind, blowing onshore, dampened what could otherwise have been an exotic banquet of aromas. Still, I could recognize the gaminess of rotting food. For a hungry creature whose nose was a major part of its job description, the dump was pure temptation. All the sorts of smells one would expect a polar bear to find attractive were there. Heck, my dog would have considered herself in heaven at that over-sized, over-ripe pungent depository. How could a bear possibly resist?

They must have been on some kind of a holiday. They were nowhere near the dump. I broadened my horizons and went to check out the cargo ship we had seen from the air.

I parked Mark's van a few hundred metres from the rusting freighter. All was still. I scanned her decks through my telephoto lens. Not a soul in sight. My lens wandered over the bridge, round the funnel, from the bow to the stern. No bears, unless they were all playing shuffleboard out of my sight.

I thought about taking a stroll to get closer. With no one to watch my back it didn't seem like a good idea. I thought about driving closer. The ground was too soft and the tide had to come back at some point. That didn't seem like a good idea either.

"Maybe the bears are cavorting with Miss Piggy," I suggested to myself.

In November 1981 a C-46 cargo plane took off from the long runway at Churchill. She was carrying a load of timber, reputedly for a settlement in the north. It's not far from the airport to Hudson Bay. Not far at all. As the C-46 crossed the shoreline the pilot informed the tower of an engine problem. He circled for an immediate return to terra firma.

It has long been rumoured the plane was overloaded. In the event, as she came in, much too low over the power lines, her undercarriage caught on the wires. The combination of wheels and wires acted in the same way an aircraft carrier arrestor cable works. The crippled plane, now affectionately called Miss Piggy by Churchillians, was slowed in flight and deposited reasonably gently on smooth boulders almost in sight of the runway. The crew of two, it is said, walked away without much more than a couple of scratches. Miss Piggy sounded like an ideal playmate for bored polar bears. I went to see.

The aircraft was intact, more or less. It wasn't in flying condition, but most of its parts were still attached. Letters on the fuselage spelled, *LambAir*.

A name like that should attract hungry bears with no problem, I decided. I parked the van where it was close enough for me to reach without having to break the sound barrier. As a precaution I left a door open and the keys in the ignition. If there was a bear in the fuselage and it wanted to race, I had every intention of being first to the van.

"I'm here, Mister bear. I'm here," I called loudly. No answer. No cough. No growl. Not even a snigger of amusement. I rapped on the dull grey metal of one wing. The sound echoed briefly, then faded to nothing. Silence. I kept talking to the bears as I angled round the wreck. Having inspected it from all sides and found the open cargo door, I was convinced it was empty. Still loudly introducing myself to the bears, I banged my hand on the fuselage. A crow called raucously from atop the tail fin. My heart stopped.

I gave the inconsiderate bird my version of a murderous look. It guffawed at me and flew away. I banged on the metal again, sure by now that the derelict was empty. It was. My heart had re-started by this time and the beat changed from fear to disappointment. I wanted a bear to come out and greet me.

All the press releases I had read about Churchill spoke of the largest land-dwelling carnivore. Skilled hunters, they are called, with super-sensitive olfactory systems able to detect a scent from thirty kilometres away. Able to sniff out a seal hiding under a metre of snow and ice. One of the few creatures with no natural enemies and, consequently, a well developed superiority complex and no hint of fear. So why, I wondered, were they avoiding me? Didn't I smell right? Surely they weren't scared?

Normally, in summer, the bears wander about on the tundra south of Churchill. The males stay close to the water's edge, the females travel inland. In late October and November they all migrate north to the newly formed sea ice to hunt seals. As many as one hundred and fifty polar bears have been recorded passing by, and occasionally through Churchill on route to winter. There's an effective polar bear alert system in town. No bear gets far without being spotted and reported to the authorities. Everyone, from childhood, is taught how to steer clear of bears visiting the town. I got the impression the bears, in their turn, had taken lessons in avoiding itinerant adventure writers.

Steve couldn't find the bears for me. Mark hadn't come up with the goods. I went to chat with Len Smith, hoping he knew the answer. Len drives a Tundra Buggy: a huge box on enormous wheels. He has a fleet of them. When the snow covers the land and the bears are migrating north, the Tundra Buggies take sightseers out for face to face encounters with the 'Lords of the Arctic.' If a driver opens a window and waves a can of sardines, preferably an unsealed one, polar bears home in on the faint fishy remains floating on the airwaves. They drop whatever they're doing and cover the ground at a frantic lope. My mind wandered towards sardines as we talked.

Len's vehicles run on great balloon tires, big enough for two or three men to fit in at one time. Exerting little downward pressure, due to their size, the wheels are reasonably kind to the fragile tundra. The trucks are, without doubt, superb machines from which to watch polar bears in complete comfort and safety. Len hadn't heard any reports of bears in the neighbourhood that day. And, as it was mid summer, none of the Tundra Buggies were booked to go anywhere soon. In desperation I went to the store and purchased a bread roll and a tin of sardines.

Out by Cape Merry I had seen an attractive gathering of ice floes. Grounded by wind and tide, they were close enough to land to enjoy while I had a picnic lunch. The miniature icebergs were big enough for bears to relax on, or to use for spotting seals. And there were seals in the bay. To prove it a ringed seal popped its head up to see what I was doing, posed for a photograph, then submerged, leaving no trace.

I opened the sardines, half expecting to be surrounded by bears within seconds. Nothing happened. My fingers probed the oily fishes, selected one and raised it high. The breeze picked up the scent and ran with it. The fish dropped from my fingers to my waiting mouth.

"Not long now," I said, munching contentedly.

I'd eaten most of my roll and half the sardines when my first guest arrived for lunch. She tiptoed daintily over the glacial smooth rocks. Realizing that I was harmless and, more importantly, the owner of the deliciously fragrant fish, she rubbed her side against my leg.

"Meeow," she softly announced her presence in the manner of her kind.

A cat. Not a bear. My signal had summoned nothing more exciting than a common well-fed household cat with a nose for little fish: the kind of cat that curls up on its owner's lap to watch the news on television.

"Scram, I'm waiting for someone else," I told her sternly.

She rubbed herself sensuously against me, her tail straight up in the air and her nose trying to inhale my sardines.

"Those are for the bears; so will you be if you don't leave me alone."

She smiled at me and rubbed the other side of her graceful body on my arm. I gave her a sardine.

"So, where do you think the bears are, Puss?" I fed her another morsel as a bribe. She crunched and swallowed, licked her lips, looked at me expectantly and stuck her nose into the almost empty tin. I don't think she cared where the bears had gone. She was just using me. Once she had satisfied herself there were no sardines left and no oil either, she sat and cleansed herself. I didn't wait for her to finish. I pocketed the empty tin and went to find Mark. The sardine scent went wherever I went for the next few hours. No bears noticed.

Late in the afternoon Steve phoned Mark. "Tell Tony there's a bear over by the dump."

Like a racing driver on his last lap before the chequered flag, I accelerated the van to the outskirts of town. Steve flew overhead dangling what looked like a steel girder under his helicopter. I waved out the window and kept going.

There was no bear at the dump. He or she was back in hiding. I began to suspect a conspiracy. I held up my sardine can and waved it around, but it couldn't really compete with the other rubbish. In frustration I hurled it on a pile of junk.

"First thing in the morning," I vowed, "I will find a bear."

Up at the crack of dawn, I strolled to Cape Merry. A Parks Canada ranger asked me where I was bound. I told him and he advised against it.

"We haven't done our first bear watch yet this morning," he said. "It's better to wait."

I waited. In the estuary a rush of air attracted my attention. A pod of beluga whales moved up stream, their glistening white backs breaking the surface as they undulated past. The ranger came back to tell me there were no bears at the cape: just as I suspected — they were avoiding me.

Mike Macri offered me a chance to see the belugas at close quarters. There was just as much chance of seeing a bear from a boat as from land, so I went with him. A party of tourists from south of the border streamed on board as we stood talking.

Mike designed his jet boat, *Sea North II*, himself and had her built in land-locked Selkirk, Manitoba. She journeyed to Churchill on a flatbed railway car. Over a thousand kilometres and a couple of days from Selkirk, *Sea North II* finally slipped into salt water beside the massive grain elevator in the Arctic port of Churchill. She was ready for rough duty.

The passengers, clad in bright red rain ponchos supplied by Mike, clustered on the deck excitedly. Mike climbed up to his eyrie three metres above the water followed by me. From the bridge the view is spectacular. If there were any bears afoot, or out for a swim, I could hardly miss them from up there.

Mike eased away from the tidal pool. I stood beside him and shivered in the cold morning air. Delicately Mike conned his charge past two barges. We scraped between a pair of stranded icebergs nearby and into the estuary. Clear of obstructions he opened the throttle and raced across the wide Churchill River to the ice-choked jetty at Fort Prince of Wales.

Close in the ice proved to have enough open water

underneath for Mike to gently nudge the floes aside with his reinforced bow. One larger floe grounded abruptly as he moved it, stubbornly refusing all further attempts at relocation. Eventually it retaliated by leaving a small dent in the starboard side. Mike appeared unfazed. Later he commented, "That hurts worse than breaking my arm."

The passengers went ashore to explore the old stone fort under the guidance of a Parks Canada ranger. The line of red ponchos straggled inland looking like a line of embarrassed penguins.

"Just like a Little Red Riding Hood convention," Mike quipped.

We threaded our way back out into the drifting ice to open water. The twin jet drives proved particularly efficient at moving smaller floes away from the boat as we turned in our own length in front of the jetty. Safely in open water, mid way between the fort and Cape Merry, Mike shut down the engines.

"We'll just sit here until they have finished," he nodded towards the fort where the figures had shrunk to little red dots. "It's safer out here."

We drifted slowly with the current and talked about the boat and the wildlife of the region. Occasionally Barbara, Mike's only crew — also a qualified captain, fired up the engines and repositioned us in the estuary.

"A few years ago a polar bear dragged a beluga out of the water over there," Mike pointed to the south shore. "Someone saw it pick the whale up with one paw and toss it right up the bank."

I began to doubt the wisdom of a close encounter of the white kind.

A few seals inspected us, looking at the grey-hulled intruder curiously. Satisfied we posed no threat they went back to their eternal quest for food. After a relaxing hour we once again filtered our way back to pick up the red coats.

With all on board again and free of the constraints of the ice, Mike opened the throttle and raced up the estuary at over twenty knots.

"At any given time during July and August, there

could be as many as three thousand belugas in this estuary," he announced over the PA system.

It was mid July and we knew the whales were nearby. We had flown over them with Steve the previous morning. Mike eased back the engines and came to a complete stop over a submarine trench. The engines shut down and he lowered hydrophones into the water from the bow and the stern. We soon heard the high-pitched whistles and calls through the speakers as the belugas responded to our presence. It was easy to understand why they are often referred to as sea canaries.

Gradually a host of ghostly shapes, looking yellow in the brownish water, glided into sight. They rolled alongside and under the boat, showing interest but no fear. The adults, so yellow under water, proved to be creamy white when they broke the surface. The young calves, easily identified by their dull greyish colour, frolicked around us.

Mike told us the belugas spend six to eight weeks in the waters around Churchill each summer. Then, without warning, they go back to sea. No one knows for sure where they go for the rest of the year. Some are seen far to the north. Others show up in the St. Lawrence Seaway to the south. Their movements, generally, are a mystery. While Mike talked he constantly scanned the water and the horizon for any sign of danger to his passengers or to his boat. I did the same, but I was still looking for bears.

Cruising back to the dock Mike offered to take me out again in the afternoon in his inflatable.

"You can get closer to the whales that way."

We went back and we got close. Some local divers hang from the inflatable by one hand and cruise with the belugas. It was cold enough in the boat wearing a few warm layers of clothing. Even with a rubber suit on the Churchill River would not be a pleasant experience. I stayed on board.

One young beluga swam close to inspect the outboard motor's propeller, which was spinning at half revs. A whack on the nose from a rotating blade scared it into diving for the depths. Being so close, seeing a whale longer than the boat within touching distance, I wondered at the phenomenal strength of a bear which could toss a beluga over its head.

It was no surprise to learn, when we returned to shore, that there had been two bears at the dump that afternoon. Another one had been seen out by the *Ithaca*, the beached cargo ship I had visited the day before. They were definitely avoiding me. And my allotted time was up.

As I left Churchill, soaring over the town in a floatplane, en route for more adventures on inland lakes, I looked down. The white bears of the sub-Arctic couldn't even give me the satisfaction of a glimpse as I left. To this day I believe they huddled out of sight, waiting until the drone of the plane's engine faded. Then they got up with supercilious smirks and a collective, "Okay he's gone. Back to work guys."

MANITOBA'S HOT FISHING SPOTS

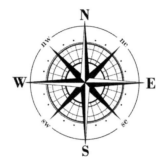

Stu McKay didn't look much like a fisherman. He collected me from my Winnipeg hotel wearing a white Panama hat, a bright red v-necked sweater and denim pants. For a moment I thought someone had made a mistake and sent me a golfer for the day. Stu soon set me straight. He stuck out a big hand and introduced himself with a question, "Hi, I'm Stu. You ready to go fishing?"

I was wearing old and slightly torn blue jeans, running shoes, a faded denim shirt and a green baseball cap. For a moment I debated whether to run back in and change into something a little more elegant to match my guide. There was no time for that.

"Let's go. Those fish are waiting."

As soon as Stu caught his first fish of the day I understood the reason for his colourful outfit. He held up a big channel catfish and posed with it.

"That will look good on the front cover of a magazine," he announced. "That's why I wore red. Sure stands out well in photographs."

He was right. The red did stand out, both on the river and in my photographs.

Two major rivers converge in Winnipeg and they are both noted for the size of their fish. The Assiniboine River begins its journey in Saskatchewan and flows over 1,000 kilometres to reach Winnipeg, where it meets the Red River at The Forks, a pleasant garden-like environment in the heart of the city's downtown area. The Red River, by contrast, begins its 885 kilometre run across the border in North Dakota. Once it crosses into Canada it flows almost due north to Lake Winnipeg.

For our purposes, Stu had chosen the Red River. It's not actually red, I noted. More like a dirty greyish brown. We were going after big channel catfish: not exactly the most colourful species of fish either. It was obvious that, no matter how big they were, with water that colour we wouldn't be able to see them until they were almost in the boat with us.

I have to admit, I had never seen a really big catfish. Stu told me a couple of tales as we puttered along the river in his boat. I listened with a reasonably open mind, but I did wonder at the size of the fish he talked about. Could they really be that big? I was soon to find out.

For the next few hours as we drifted along the river, Stu cast his line one way and I cast the other. When I felt the first strike, I thought I'd hit a whale. There was an audible shock up my arm and the line twanged taught like an over-strung guitar.

"Don't let it get away," Stu cautioned.

Let it get away? Did he think I was in charge or something? Okay, I was the guy holding the fishing rod. I was the guy standing up and straining. I was also the guy being towed upstream by a monster. I was not in charge, the fish was.

"Reel it in, Tony. Reel it in."

I tried to crank the reel handle and almost broke

my thumb.

"Give it some slack. It'll come up."

I slackened the line a fraction. At least that was my intention. I think a couple of hundred metres shot out immediately.

"Reel it in!"

So, I reeled in again. I slackened off. I reeled in. I slackened off. It became a contest to see who would tire first. I had my concerns about that but was not ready to give in. Suddenly I wanted to see that catfish close up. I put extra pressure on the line and gradually pulled it in for a confrontation. When the fish finally broke the surface it was angry and it showed. It twisted its head from side to side and up and down. It threw itself out of the water and it raced under the boat. When it did eventually appear out of the murky river beside the boat, I don't know who was more surprised, me or the fish. It gaped at me. I gaped back. One thing struck me immediately: although I was taller and weighed quite a lot more, that fish had a mouth twice the size of mine.

Stu collected the wriggling beast in a landing net and brought it aboard. A few seconds later I was cradling it in my arms for the obligatory photograph. It wasn't quite as romantic as it sounds – the cradling in my arms, I mean – this 'thing' was slimy and more than a little smelly.

The first fish of the day for me weighed 28 lbs (12.73 kgs). Oh, yes. They sure could be that big. It was heavy, the biggest fish I had ever caught and it was, without doubt, the ugliest creature I have ever hooked. And that catfish, as Stu pointed out, was not a really big one. The record for Manitoba, I learned, was in excess of 36lbs (16.5kgs) and it was caught right about where we were. Heck, with fish that big, maybe I could become a real angler.

Keeping my hand away from its mouth, which looked as though it could swallow my arm, I carefully lowered it horizontally back into the river with a succinct warning.

"Stay away from hooks. They are bad for you."

We spent a pleasant few hours playing with big

catfish. None of them weighed less than 20lbs. We hooked them, fought them, landed them, weighed them, and released them to fight another day. The thought of eating them did not enter my mind. With their grey skin and distinctly sinister facial features, none of them had the kind of looks that deserved to adorn a dinner plate.

In the middle of the afternoon Stu suggested we move to a different part of the river. He wanted to pick a fight with some wild carp. The record weight for a carp caught in Manitoba was actually higher than for the big cats, so it seemed like a good idea. I had heard of carp in Africa that weighed upwards of 100lbs (45+ kgs). We fished for a while and caught a few carp: not as big as their African cousins, or even the local catfish; not as much fun to play either, but definitely better looking. Time for me, however, was running out. I had an appointment 1,100 kilometres to the north.

From Winnipeg I flew to remote North Knife Lake Lodge in a private plane. I had proven myself in battle against the denizens of the Red River, now it was time to see what I could do with the more elusive lake trout. Doug and Helen Webber were my hosts for the few days I stayed at their magnificent rustic wilderness lodge and I could not have been more comfortable. The food was excellent. The evening conversations in front of the log fire were stimulating; and my bed was comfortable. Oh, yes, then there was the fishing.

Expressing admirable consideration for his regular employees, Doug assigned his son-in-law, Mike, as my fishing guide. Was 'Amateur' written on my forehead? If it was, I certainly proved it correct as I managed to create an incredible tangle with a lot of monofilament fishing line on the first morning searching for lake trout. Mike was patience personified.

"I think we'll just cut that mess away," he said quietly as he reached for his knife. His eyes, however, flickered from contained amusement to cleverly disguised concern. I knew he was thinking, what have I got here? Fortunately, I did better with my next attempt at sending a lure out into the lake. I did my best to hold the rod properly and look as if I actually knew what I was doing, at last. Then I got snagged on something.

"Mike, my line feels like it's wrapped around a tree trunk which I'm dragging through the water. I think I'm caught in a patch of weeds."

Mike looked from me to the end of my rod and answered, "I think it's much more likely that you have a large lake trout on the end of that line. Reel it in and we'll take a look."

Well, that was a surprise. I couldn't feel any wriggling, or any motion at all. There was just this sluggish drag. To keep Mike happy I started to reel in. It took a while as my line had been slowly disappearing off the reel for a while, completely unnoticed by me. I have to admit, I thought Mike was wrong. I have hauled in long-sunken logs instead of fish many times. You could say I am something of an expert on the topic. Whatever was on the end of my line was, I knew, not a fish. Mike reached for the landing net as the point where my line entered the water came closer to the boat.

"There it is," Mike said as he scooped the fish into his net.

I wanted to ask, "How did that get there?" But I stayed silent, looking at Mike in amazement as he held up a lake trout big enough to feed a reasonable sized multitude.

"Hmm. Nice fish," I said knowingly, nodding my head and pursing my lips in exactly the right way. I still couldn't figure out how a log that had been stuck in the mud of a lake bed for eons could metamorphose into a fish at the surface.

I always thought trout were fighting fish. The few I had caught in the Arctic had lots of fight in them. If the ones in Knife Lake were all like that recently caught and released dullard, I wanted to try something a little more sprightly. I'm sure that lake trout specialists will hate me for this but, after bringing in a couple more trout, I was ready for some different action.

"Where can we find some big northern pike," I

asked Mike.

Without questioning my interest, he started the outboard motor and raced towards a part of the shore where the reeds waved like welcoming wands. Stopping a few metres away he cut the motor and we sat there in silence, apart from the sound of water lapping against the gull.

"We'll try here."

Northern pike are such voracious eaters that it doesn't take an expert to catch them. Heck, even from my limited experience, pike will attack almost anything that moves. No, all it takes to hook pike is the basic fishing equipment with enough strength in the line to hold a powerful fighter, that and the knowledge of where they like to feed best. I really enjoy battling pike of all sizes. I like eating them too: pan fried, for lunch preferably.

Knife Lake's pike lived up to my expectations. Oh, yes. They waited among the reeds for me, their menacing teeth bared ready for prey. They lurked in the shallows, tails moving lazily, until a vague movement spurred their tails into action. Then they thrashed the water and attacked with a speed and viciousness hard to comprehend. For me, the good part is, pike strike ruthlessly and, I believe, indiscriminately.

I cast a red and white spinner to land just beside the reeds about fifteen metres away. Casually, acting as nonchalantly as I could, I reeled it in keeping it away from the reed bed. The first cast was a non event, although a sinister shape rocketed towards the lure as I lifted it dripping from the water. I cast again, dropping the lure in almost exactly the same spot and began reeling in again.

I had the spinner revolving at medium speed halfway to the boat when its colours disappeared. My line went taught and the rod bowed. Strike! I was happy. I played with that fish for a while, seeing what tricks it would get up to. It tried a lot I had seen before racing for the reeds, tossing its head, shaking its body until it blurred with the vibration, racing towards me then away as fast as it could. By the time I landed it in the boat and removed the hook from its jaws, it was visibly tired but still had enough anger left to snap at my hand. I let it go. It deserved to live to fight another day.

That evening I sat in a large armchair by the fire, a book in one hand and a glass of single malt Scotch in the other. There was a quiet buzz of conversation. Everyone was relaxed. I guessed there were a lot of fish stories involved in the conversations. I was well into the latest Wilbur Smith novel when Doug Webber came over.

"Tony, how would you like to go fishing for brookies tomorrow?"

I looked up at him and gave my best quizzical expression. It said, I hoped, rather eloquently, "What's a brookie?

"A couple of the guys are flying down to the Churchill River for the day. There's room for one more. The seat's yours if you want to go."

I still didn't know that 'brookie' was a cute term for a brook trout. That knowledge would come later. To be honest, I don't think I had ever heard of a brook trout anyway, but I was not about to admit that gap in my education in front of other fishermen at a notable fishing lodge. But, an offer of an adventure? Heck, I would go anywhere I hadn't been before. An excursion to the Churchill River, far from civilization, sounded tailor made for me.

With pilot Djerzy at the controls, Mike beside him and me in the back with another guest, Graham, the Cessna floatplane dashed across the lake and soared over the trees heading south. Somewhere along the way Mike had the pilot drop down to take a look at a lake which, he thought, might prove to be ideal for fishing. He was probably right. As we flew low over the lake a bald eagle flashed out of the sky to our left and hooked a large trout.

"That looks good," Mike said. I assumed he was talking about the fishing potential, not the eagle's aerial skills, impressive though it was.

The Churchill River had its own attractions. As we came in for a landing we passed a cow moose and her calf standing on a small barren low-lying island in the river. They pretended to ignore us.

On a previous visit Mike had stashed an inflatable and outboard motor in the bushes. While Djerzy stayed behind to look after the plane, we retrieved the boat and motor and set out for nearby rapids. Mike skillfully took the boat down an easy chute before putting us ashore on a series of flat rocks, there to whet our fishing appetites by casting for a few walleyes in the eddies. It was fun and we could have taken a lot back to the lodge but Mike had those brookies on his mind. He secured the boat and told us to follow him.

A small shallow side stream led us on foot through dense undergrowth. In case any resident bears were, well, in residence, Mike announced our progress loudly with each step.

"We're here, bear. We're here."

About 100 metres up stream he found a bit of a clearing with enough room for the three of us to stand and cast without hooking each other. Opposite and conveniently sited was an obvious pool where the stream had carved its way into the bank.

"Drop your lure into that pool," Mike advised me. "There will be a brookie or two in there for sure."

He knew what he was talking about. I flicked my line in the suggested direction and hooked a brook trout within minutes. We were all successful that afternoon. The bears stayed away. We each caught four or five trout on barbless hooks. I photographed them. Mike measured their lengths; then we carefully placed them back in the river to live some more.

On the way back to the plane, just above the rapids, I flicked my line overboard and a fighting northern pike snapped. Our departure for the lodge was delayed a few more minutes while I toiled with my catch. It proved to be half as long as me and with teeth almost as big and infinitely sharper. We returned it to its element with my thanks for the sport. My fishing for this Manitoba trip was over. I had had fun. I had learned a lot and I had caught some big fish.

A few weeks after I arrived home I received a pair of certificates and two medallions in the mail. Those souvenirs proclaimed me a Channel Catfish Specialist and a Master Angler. As a fisherman, despite my incompetence at times, I had made the grade at last. Thanks, Stu and Mike, you were great hosts and fun to be with, but I still like fishing for northern pike best.

OUTRIGGING WITH INNOCENCE

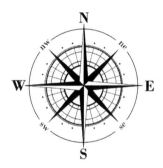

If you want a boat and can't afford to buy one, there are only three options left. One is not recommended, one is a cop out and the other requires considerable effort. Theft, the first possibility, makes no sense. Forgetting the idea is for wimps. Building a boat at home is the only answer.

That's more or less how my reasoning went. I ordered a set of plans for a small yacht, tacked them on the wall in my workshop, and there they have stayed. I wanted to build a boat but, even with the plans in front of me, I had doubts about my ability. We went on vacation to French Polynesia instead.

The peoples of the immense Pacific Ocean, particularly the Polynesians, Micronesians and Melanesians, discovered all of the habitable islands between the Tropics of Cancer and Capricorn. Some Polynesians voyaged even further and settled in the land we call New Zealand. Others travelled from New Guinea in the west, all the way to Easter Island — 100 degrees of latitude to the east. Those intrepid sailors explored thousands of islands and atolls. And they did it all in canoes. Hand-carved from their native trees, the hulls were stabilized by long outriggers lashed on with ropes of coconut fibre. As propulsion they had paddles and, for when the winds blew, they had sails carefully braided from tropical leaves.

3,000 years ago, many centuries before the arrogant Vikings set off across the Atlantic and long before Europeans ventured out onto the oceans, Polynesian navigators went out on a dangerous and unpredictable ocean in small boats.

Today's Pacific islanders, from Vanuatu to the Tuamotus, from the Cook Islands to Hawaii, still use outrigger canoes. In parts of Vanuatu, dugout canoes are hand-carved on the beach, while in Port Vila — the capital, an entrepreneur manufactures fibreglass equivalents. In French Polynesia sheet plywood is employed to build sleek modern versions. Powered by outboard motors, they are fast and efficient for travel from motu to motu.

On the wondrously beautiful island of Bora Bora, three hundred kilometres northwest of Tahiti, I sat on a pristine white-sand beach. Out on the iridescent blue lagoon the long red hull of an outrigger canoe raced across the water towards the coral reef.

"I want to go out on one of those," I told Penny, my wife, as I pointed seawards.

Perhaps the germ of an idea was digging at my mind. Later we cruised on that same outrigger from the lush greenery of the main island to tiny uninhabited motus. Suspended over submerged reefs, where millions of multi-coloured fish live out their short lives, stopping to watch a manta ray and a dolphin competing for attention, the germ became a vague plan.

"This is what we need at home," a thought spoken out loud.

"Well, why don't you build one? You're good with your hands." Penny's reply showed confidence. She'd apparently forgotten the plans on the workshop wall and my complete lack of boat-building experience.

About a year later, at home in the Gulf Islands, I looked out to sea and thought of that red outrigger again. As a boy I had designed and built my own model aircraft and taught them to fly. Could I build a real boat and make it float? The answer, of course, was simple: give it a try! I reasoned that, if the ancient Polynesians could put together boats to cross vast oceans, then surely I, with my well-equipped workshop, should be able to fashion a reasonable likeness.

Without benefit of plans, only a few photographs I had taken on Bora Bora and a simple sketch made at the same time, I really did not know where to start. Scanning boat-building books helped enormously. Two directives stuck in my mind: set up a form of some kind and build the boat upside down.

I built the boat on our sun deck. Penny absorbed as much of the sun's rays as she could on one end while I turned the other into a boat yard. Our dog came to help. She, the dog, stole my wood, sunbathed against fresh paint, left her paw prints all over wet varnish, and generally took an interest. Once she finally figured out what I was making her enthusiasm for the project knew no bounds. She tried to help at every possible occasion. The work did not always go well.

Three months after I laid the first strip of wood my prized creation slid into her natural element for the first time. Penny exhibited a certain uncomplimentary surprise.

"It floats!" She said in wonder.

"Of course it floats," I replied, with more than a hint of pique. "It's a boat."

A boat needs a name and this one, my boat, needed a special name. I had once owned a boat named *Audacity*. I wanted to use a variation of the same for my new craft. As the boat was of Polynesian design, based on centuries of experience, I passed the question over to some Maori friends living in Vancouver. They came up with *Niwhaniwha*, a Maori word meaning cheeky, or audacious. It sounded right to me.

With an outboard motor clamped to the stern we were able to go anywhere in the Gulf Islands. Few people in our part of the world, we discovered, had ever seen a real outrigger. Running *Niwhaniwha* up on to a beach far from home one day, a sun-tanned young man came over for a closer inspection.

"Wow, man, where d'ya get a boat like that?" He asked.

"I built it," I answered. There was undeniable pride in the answer.

Most of the time we stayed well clear of busy shipping lanes. Inevitably in our somewhat busy waterways, we occasionally had to cross known ferry routes. We followed our course carefully and, usually, at high speed. When the lumbering car ferries rumbled past, between terminals on the mainland and the various islands, the passengers pointed to us and waved. We waved back while mildly cursing the rolling wake trying to swamp us. But it was always fun.

Tavi, the aforementioned dog which helped my construction work, was the product of a union between a black Labrador and a pitbull. She loved the sea. From her favourite vantage point amidships she peered over the sides in search of marine mammals. From the foredeck she searched for other wonders of the wild. Together we encountered seals and sea lions. We greeted cormorants drying their wings on floating logs, paid homage to the magnificent bald eagles and nearly abandoned ship together when a baby killer whale got too close.

On a week-long camping cruise with a friend I learned how resilient my boat was. At the northern extent of the Gulf Islands, where Vancouver Island and Gabriola squeeze the sea through a narrow channel, we ran into trouble. Much of the water contained in the Gulf Islands tries to get through that gap — all at the same time. Spring tides can whip the current up to a frantic ten knots. Even with a current running at half that speed, the danger is there. On the flood a standing wave rears up in Dodd's Narrows.

It is a challenge for boaters, most of whom sensibly avoid the problem by waiting for slack water. I was in a hurry and, it's true — I like a challenge.

Bruce sat in the bow with paddle in hand. I stood at the stern holding the outboard's control arm. A paddle was in reach.

"You okay up there?" I shouted.

Bruce didn't look back. He was too busy studying the confused seas piling up ahead of us. A thumb appeared pointing skywards. He was okay and ready.

"Don't do anything unless I tell you to."

The thumb came up again. I slowed the motor and studied the white water. There was not a lot of room. Normally, in any other kind of boat, I would have aimed the bow straight at the centre of the wave. With an outrigger, which is essentially a twin-hulled vessel, I had to try something different.

My problem was to get the hull and the outrigger over, or through, the wave without breaking the outrigger struts. My eyes told me I could point the bow at the right shoulder of the wave, then the outrigger would miss the rock wall on the other side by a coat of paint. As the current swept us towards the big wave, I told Bruce what I intended. The thumb came up again. Then the engine stopped. My stomach lurched.

I pulled hard on the starter cord. Nothing. I looked over the side. The painter, or bow mooring line, was wrapped around the propeller. Bruce had let it slide over the side past him. He looked over his shoulder at me in alarm as the wave got closer.

"Ready to paddle," I roared, waving mine in the air. Our only choice was to paddle directly at the wave. If we tried to turn and got caught beam on the wave could roll us over. I steered Bruce at the right shoulder as planned. He sat perfectly still, with paddle across the thwarts, looking up at a monster.

"Dig left. Dig deep," I bellowed, thrusting my own paddle in on the right side. Bruce responded, driving the boat with the current, heading straight for a wall of water.

"Keep going. Dig, dig, dig," I shouted. With my rear end on the steering arm to keep it central, I stuck my paddle in and we drove *Niwhaniwha* up the wave. There was a moment when I had the distinct feeling she wanted to slide back into a watery grave. She didn't. My stomach felt as though it was trying to turn itself inside out. For a fraction of a second we balanced on top, with the outrigger just skimming the rock, I leaned forward as Bruce drove his paddle hard and down the slope we went. Our stomachs caught up with us a few moments later.

"Left, Bruce," I called, pointing to a safe shore with my paddle. We nosed the bow onto a flat rock and I swung the stern in close.

"That was hairy," Bruce grinned at me. "What happened?"

"You let the (old Anglo-Saxon expletive) painter fall in the water. You can untangle it from the prop."

On a subsequent stretch of water, in a storm, we snaked between half-hidden rocks as waves broke over us both. Some pinnacles were sharp enough to unzip the hull as we passed. Bruce redeemed himself by keeping his eyes open and alerting me to all dangers. We suffered no further mishaps, apart from getting terribly wet and experiencing a few close encounters with immovable objects.

On the return journey we had to negotiate Dodd's Narrows again. We were looking forward to it. We had surfed through using paddles. Under full power, I did not anticipate having any trouble this time. Unfortunately I forgot to check the tide tables. The passage was an anti-climax. Dodd's Narrows whimpered as we approached. The standing wave was gone; only a few lazy whirlpools of little velocity remained. We drove through without a drop of spray coming over the side.

On Bora Bora I was told that fast outriggers do not like rough water. They may not enjoy turbulent seas but, as *Niwhaniwha* proved, even with two relative innocents aboard — she could handle anything.

GREEN FACES AT THE OLD MAN

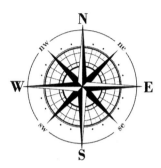

"What're you doing?" The disembodied voice, with a thick Scottish accent, bellowed from the open car window. I looked up from where I sat, obviously unemployed, on the cold concrete.

"Waiting for the ferry."

"Where are y'going?" The voice, emanating from the weather-beaten face of an old man, asked.

"To Orkney. Where else?"

"Why're you going to Orkney?"

"Because we've never been there." The conversation, such as it was, could have gone on for hours in the same vein.

"Why do you young people always want to go somewhere else?"

"Curiosity."

The inquisitive one changed his approach. "D'you

know anything about diesel engines?"

"Some," I replied cautiously. "Enough to keep them running anyway."

He went off at a tangent. "So, if you're going to Orkney, you won't want to come and work for me?"

"What do you do?" I asked, more out of politeness than interest.

"I'm a farmer."

I shook my head, "Sorry, I have no interest in farming."

"What about boats? D'you like boats, laddie?"

At last he had my undivided attention. "Yes, I like boats. What are you getting at?"

"See those two over there," he pointed to the harbour. "They're both mine. I need a deckhand who's useful wi' tools and machinery."

I stood up and looked at the two boats. Both converted MFVs, they looked strong and seaworthy.

"How much are you paying?"

"Thirty pounds a week, all the food y'can eat and live aboard. If y'stay all summer I'll gi' you a bonus at the end."

"Do you need a cook as well?"

"Is she any good?"

"I can cook anything anywhere," Mac stirred and stretched herself. My partner and travelling companion in those days, Mac was the kind of girl the editors of Playboy magazine recruited for its centrefolds. When she stretched all men within range stopped whatever they were doing and watched. Their breathing changed involuntarily. When Mac stretched, or walked, or was just there, the world was a brighter place.

"We're a team," I explained. "We work together. Take one, you take us both."

"Aye," he looked Mac up and down approvingly. She gave him her most dazzling smile. Dark brown eyes, under a mop of tight brown curls, sparkled at him. I could almost hear him melt, or perhaps the sound was that of his rich highland blood beginning to boil.

"Aye," he repeated. "Thirty pounds each then. The same for y'both."

I shouldered my bag, shook his hand through the open window and we went to work. "The captain's name is Hugh," our new boss called after us. "He's the dark haired laddie on the *Pentland Firth*, that's the first boat."

Instead of paying to visit the Orkney Isles we would be paid to go there. Instead of sleeping in a pup tent we had the luxury of a bunk. The summer was definitely looking exciting.

Captain Hugh was younger than me by about five years. In his late twenties he was about mid way between Mac's age and mine. He gave us the captain's cabin, right behind the wheelhouse. Mac got the single bunk and I got the floor. Sometimes, as the weeks went on, we shared the bunk. At other times we shared the floor. Once, when only the two of us were aboard, we experimented on the wheelhouse floor. Captain Hugh went home each night, unless we were in another port. On those occasions he made himself comfortable below decks.

"You can have the night off," he told us. "I'm away to my home. I'll see you in the morning."

Mac and I had spent months working two jobs each for the chance to go travelling. We'd enjoyed a few weeks in Spain and Morocco, and a week or so with friends in London. After a short stay in the Orkneys we had planned to wander through Europe for a while. Our plans, that summer of 1975, were quite flexible.

Saturday morning Hugh came aboard and gave Mac a wad of money and a list of needed provisions. She went off to get the supplies while Hugh showed me around the boat and explained my duties. Simply put, I was to keep the boat clean, make any necessary equipment repairs, assist the cook, and help look after the passengers.

"What kind of passengers?"

"This week we have a group of anglers from Yorkshire," Hugh told me. "They'll be here early this afternoon. We'll take them out for an hour or two to get some live bait."

The motor vessel *Pentland Firth*, named after the body of water which separates the northern tip of Scotland from the Orkney Islands, and its sister, *Pentland Wave*, had dual values. Half their income came from sports fishermen, the other half from SCUBA divers.

The waters of northern Scotland were rich in cod, pollock, ling-cod, halibut, haddock and mackerel, among others. Mackerel were used as bait and, when we got the chance, as a tasty meal for the crew.

That first afternoon we watched in amusement as hardened Yorkshire fishermen, supposedly used to rough North Sea waves, began to turn green the moment we left Scrabster's harbour. Out in Thurso Bay a lazy swell soon had us rolling casually from side to side. Hugh cut back the engines and called, "Okay."

Over the side went the lines, most of which had eight or ten baited hooks attached. The fishermen jigged the hooks up and down. *Pentland Firth* rolled lazily, in tune with the sea's rhythm. A first face peered over the rail and threw up. A second soon followed. I leaned my back against the wheelhouse and watched. In the galley Mac sang happily as she made sandwiches and tea. Hugh looked out the window, grinned down at me, "It's always like this the first day."

A sudden oath and a little impromptu dancing on the swaying deck caught my attention. One of our guests had been a little less than careful in pulling up his line. The hooks, which were there to catch fish, had allowed one of their number to draw first blood. With barb still attached it was embedded in a thumb. The owner was not a happy man.

"Let me see," I commanded. He'd done a good job. If the intention was to hook something well, he had achieved his objective.

"I'll bet that smarts," I told him cheerfully. Taking a pair of needle-nose pliers from my back pocket I held his injured right hand in my left. "This will hurt even more," I added.

I nipped the shank of the hook with the pliers and

forced the hook to continue the path it had chosen. The owner of the thumb yelled and tried to pull away.

"Keep still, you'll rip your thumb." I held on tightly, keeping up the pressure until the hook's point and barb broke the surface again.

"There it is, now keep still." With that I snipped both off and pulled the now harmless hook back the way it had come. "You'd better put some disinfectant on that," I suggested.

My ears may have played a trick on me but, I'm sure I heard him say something like, "Sadistic bastard," as he wrapped a cloth round his hand and went in search of a sympathetic ear. She was busy but, being a nurse as well as a cook, she cleaned his hand and gave him a soothing cup of tea. He stayed far longer than necessary for such a small wound.

We took on a good load of mackerel that afternoon. Enough to keep the anglers busy for days. Once they were satisfied, Hugh took us back to our berth.

Most Saturdays were like that. The fishermen came on board. Hugh asked me what I wanted to do, with a smile on his face. I answered, with a matching grin, "Let's take them out and get them sick." It wasn't really as heartless as it sounds. The sooner they got used to the motion of the boat and their stomachs, the sooner they would begin to enjoy themselves. On Saturday nights they went to one of the local pubs. We usually went to a different one.

We had a routine for the week, which depended to some extent on the weather. Sundays we fished in the Pentland Firth off Dunnet Head, the most northerly point on the Scottish mainland. At night we returned to Scrabster. Monday morning we crossed the Firth to the island of Hoy. It's a short voyage, no more than ten nautical miles. A little more than an hour at our cruising speed. Both shores can be clearly seen from the middle, unless it's raining as it so often does. The problem with the crossing is that the might of the Atlantic Ocean, and the slightly lesser power of the North Sea, chase through the Firth twice each day. It can, and does, get extremely rough.

George Bernard Shaw wrote that there was enough power in the Pentland Firth to provide all Europe with electrical power. He must have crossed on a really wild day.

The island of Hoy is blessed with magnificent cliffs on its western side. Sheer precipices of red, orange and white, topped by a cap of green, rise out of the sea. There's the Kame of Hoy, St. John's Head, Rora Head and the old sea stack known as the Old Man of Hoy. We fished along the coast, under the shadow of those cliffs, down past Rackwick to Tor Ness. Our guests hauled in catch after catch. Everyone was happy.

In the late afternoon Hugh took us past Flotta Island into Scapa Flow. The barren hills are lower there. Hoy tapers off toward Scapa, sloping gently to the sea. The islands of Fara and Cava, like green and brown bumps on leaden water, rise up out of Bring Deep to port. Off Graemsay Island, with Stromness dead ahead, Hugh lined *Pentland Firth* up with the markers — one on the shoreline and one on the hill behind.

"When they're in a straight line you have the middle passage into the harbour," he explained. He left unsaid the fact that any helmsman who failed to line up on the marks was asking to run aground. Minutes later we tied up at the grey granite stone wharf in Stromness. Against another wall an old wooden Norwegian whaler rested. Mounted on the bow was a wicked looking harpoon gun. The Norwegians were still active whalers in those days. We considered sabotage but rejected it as highly illegal. Silently we prayed for many unprofitable voyages for the modern-day Viking.

Norsemen have been visiting the Orkney Islands for centuries. Vikings settled Scotland's northern islands as long ago as the ninth century. The islands remained under Norse rule for five hundred years, until Christian I of Norway handed them over to Scotland in 1469. Legend tells that the islands were pawned in lieu of a suitable dowry on the occasion of Christian's daughter's marriage to James III. Norway's loss became Scotland's gain.

There are sixty-five islands in the Orkneys, of

which thirty are sparsely inhabited. It's an ideal spot for archaeological island hopping. Some islands have remnants of settlements dating back to 3,500 BC, in the Neolithic — or New Stone Age. In the history of the Orkneys, the Vikings were recent arrivals.

The two interconnected homes of Knap of Hower, on the little island of Papa Westray, are the oldest known domestic dwellings in northern Europe. Roughly four hundred years later a complete Neolithic settlement was built at Skara Brae. Thanks to the necessity of building with stone, due to a complete lack of other durable building materials, the site is in a remarkable state of preservation. And it's been through the worst weather nature could throw at it.

Six hundred years after Skara Brae was built, a tempest of gigantic proportions buried the site under a huge layer of wind-blown sand. The accumulation of sand added to the site's natural defences, ensuring its salvation for future generations. The inhabitants of Skara Brae, according to specialists, had little or no warning of the coming disaster. One woman lost her necklace in the rush for safety. The beads were scattered to lie untouched until another, similarly violent storm blew the sand away again in 1850.

In addition to sturdy settlements, chambered tombs and giant standing stones bear silent witness to little understood cultures. The Ring of Brodgar, which predates the far better known Stonehenge by centuries, once consisted of sixty-six monoliths. Today thirty-six survive, some intact, others little more than stumps.

The ancient granite rock, which stone-age men carved for dwellings, tombs and monuments, is still in use today. Houses are built from granite blocks, as are the stone wharfs and jetties jutting into Stromness Harbour. The narrow lanes through the town are paved with flat rocks polished and smoothed by time, and the passing of countless feet.

We went ashore in Stromness and scuffed our soles on the timeless stones. While Mac shopped in the bakery, savouring the warm heady aromas of dozens of loaves and bread rolls, I talked with old fishermen on the wharf. Their speech was slow and deliberate. The strong Scottish accents, tinged with echoes of the Norwegian fjords, took time to understand. I asked about the Hudson's Bay Company, knowing many young Orkneymen had signed on to work as factors in the Canadian wilderness.

The old ones spoke of the company, and the early explorations to discover a route through the North-West Passage, as if it had happened but days before. They all knew someone who had sailed away for a long stint in some remote Canadian outpost. One talked of Franklin's expedition of 1819 as if he had been personally involved. The time passed swiftly. Soon Mac returned laden with groceries. There was work to be done. I thanked my impromptu history teachers and went aboard.

We fished for giant skate on Bring Deep. The reward was a great flesh-coloured triangular fish weighing in excess of fifty-seven kilos. Out in Pentland Firth one of the anglers spent the better part of an hour coaxing another heavy mass to the surface. Eventually a flat dark green back came into view. Bulbous eyes looked up at us in surprise. The mouth, still undergoing some interminable evolutionary process, was in the wrong place. Or maybe it was the eyes. Either way, the big fish did not look as if it had been put together correctly. If the eyes were in their correct position, then the mouth definitely needed moving.

"It's a BUT!" the happy fisherman yelled as we hauled the monster over the boat's rail.

The 'but' was a halibut: a big one for that area, over a metre in length. Stretched out on the deck it was easier to study. There was definitely a design fault. One side was white and the other, which I first thought was the back, was green. If one ignored the eyes for a moment, it looked like a normal fish. Mother Nature had obviously not completed her evolutionary task on the halibut. The eyes had migrated from one on either side of the head to both being on the same side: the dark side. This enabled the fish to swim along the sea bed on its side, in search of food, without getting dirt in one eye. The drawback was that the mouth opened sideways from that position, which must have caused the fish some difficulty in feeding. I assumed that, eons in the future, if the ocean's bounty lasts so long, the halibut's mouth will also change position to match the eyes. Then only the tail will be left to rotate through ninety degrees and stand vertical. One day, if all goes well, halibuts all over the northern seas will look like real fish again. No longer will they be the 'butt' of other marine creature's jokes.

Sailing back to Scrabster after one fishing cruise we ploughed through a Force 9 gale. As soon as we came out of Hoy Sound, with Stromness behind us and the Old Man of Hoy standing sentinel to port, the storm hit. It was rougher on the open sea than Hugh had anticipated. We were still towing our large inflatable dinghy so the storm chastised us for being careless. It snapped the towing rope and whisked the dinghy away. Our stalwart fishermen, all seven of them, stayed below in the warm passengers' quarters. Hugh, determined not to lose a valuable dinghy, turned us through 180 degrees while I stood on the foredeck. *Pentland Firth* rolled off a wave and slid into a trough as the dinghy crested another white cap. I signalled the direction to Hugh and went below looking for help.

"I need four strong guys on deck right now," I bellowed, forgetting to add the all important 'please.'

Buttoning coats up to their necks and grumbling about being used, the four biggest followed me on deck and leaned into the wind beside the wheelhouse.

"What's oop?" one asked in a broad Yorkshire accent.

"We have to catch the dinghy and get it aboard. It won't be easy," I shouted in return. "Follow my orders and try not to fall overboard."

Hugh missed the dinghy on the first pass. Even with the help of a long boat hook I couldn't quite reach it. We went round again. My four stalwarts looked at the waves breaking above us and tried to keep their stomachs in check. On the second pass Hugh put me in a perfect spot to hook the dinghy. Had I been two and half to three metres tall I could have done it from the deck. Being less than two metres, from the tip of bare feet to the top of a bald head, I had to resort to drastic measures. I hooked one foot over the rail and stood upright, with the boat hook just skimming the water.

"Hold my belt and each other," I yelled. My left foot stepped over the rail to join the right. Praying my belt would hold and that the fishermen really did like me, even though I hadn't said please, I leaned as far out from the prancing boat as possible. In relation to the sea I was about horizontal for a few seconds. I hooked the dinghy and held it fast.

"Pull me up," the intended shout was more like a scream once the wind had finished ripping it apart. The stalwarts dragged me to safety. So then we had five of us on the foredeck, and an extremely heavy dinghy hanging off one side of the boat with half its length trying to get under our keel.

"We have to pull it straight up," I pantomimed the order, "then haul it over the rail to the deck."

Eight eyes looked at me as if I was crazy. Hugh kept *Pentland Firth* as steady as possible under the conditions while I tied the dinghy to the rail.

"Now then," I croaked into the wind. My voice was getting hoarse from shouting. "We have to pull it up and over in one motion. You got that?"

Four heads nodded. I looked back at Hugh, he had the wheelhouse window open for a better view in spite of the rain. I explained my plans in rapid sign language. He understood.

"Okay, guys, get ready. When we go off that wave the dinghy will be lifted up above the rail for a second or two. That's when we pull it aboard."

They lined up, two on each side of me. "Don't get trapped underneath it. It's bloody heavy," was my final order.

Hugh slid us neatly off the wave and the dinghy rose with the foaming crest. "Now," I screamed as I pulled on the boathook with all my might. Eight additional arms pulled with me. The dinghy let go its grip on the wave and flew to join us. My brave assistants ran for cover, leaving me in the dinghy's path with only the boathook for defence. I tried to out run the black rubber invader. It was too fast for me. With a thud that knocked all the wind from my lungs, the dinghy embraced my body and threw it to the deck. I was trapped, but at least I was out of the wind and the rain.

After a while, fingers probed under the inflated sides in front of my nose. Slowly the dinghy was lifted until I could see the storm.

"Are you all right?" a voice rasped in my ear. I don't think my answer was heard. If it was, or if one of my rescuers could read lips, they would surely have recognized the sexual implications of my two-word answer.

I scrambled free and ordered everyone off the foredeck. One, hanging grimly to the windward rail, was too busy trying to decorate the waves to take any notice. I watched him curiously from the shelter of the wheelhouse, thinking that the ancient sailors of old Skara Brae never had to put up with such foolishness.

"Why can't they learn to throw up with their backs to the wind?" I asked myself as the lone hero collected a sudden return on his investment.

FJORDS AND FERRIES TO HELL

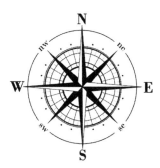

"Kick out further from the cliff, if you can," I called to Grunjar. He responded, urging his body out into space. As he put a metre or two of air between himself and the rock face I took a series of shots.

"That's great," I called. "Now abseil slowly."

"This is ridiculous," I moaned to myself as I aimed my camera at the climber. "I'm hanging on to a sea cliff with my right knee jammed into a crack, my left foot in another and my body leaning at forty-five degrees. I have no ropes and my hands are too busy with a camera to hold on."

"You don't look comfortable," Grunjar called back as he descended the cliff the easy and safe way — at the end of a rope.

"I'm not," I muttered. "I'm too bloody busy defying gravity."

My knee hurt, my foot hurt, my back ached and I

was only too well aware that, if I slipped, everything else on my body would suffer pain too. Grunjar reached the rocks on the shore and waved up to me.

"It's okay?"

"No, we need to do it again. I want to get closer if I can."

Grunjar, unhampered by photographic equipment, free-climbed back up the cliff. I slung my cameras behind me, found a solid grip for my right hand and eased my knee from the crack. It was sore. Suspended by one hand and one foot I scanned the cliff face nearer to Grunjar's rope for a comfortable spot. There wasn't an obvious one. Grumbling to myself about the agonies I put my physical self through at times, I took a hesitant step sideways. My foot found a nub of rock to keep it steady. My free hand wandered over the cliff face, caressing, searching, until it found something to cling to. Acting like a crab with a suction cup on the belly of its shell, I edged sideways. The only crack big enough to accept any part of my limbs was just wide enough for the fingers of one hand. I stuffed my bare right hand in and tried to make a fist. It hurt.

"Okay, let's try it again."

Grunjar's long legs, faded red parka, and reddish-blonde hair swung into view. He glided over the rock with the grace of a ballet dancer. I braced one side of the camera against the cliff, held my breath and pressed the shutter. The motor drive did the rest.

Back up on the cliff, overlooking the rolling waves of the North Sea, we packed up the climbing gear. Phase one of the shoot was completed. Phase two meant a trip on the water. In a nearby harbour a fishing boat waited for me. Beside it bobbed a long slim brown kayak.

Grunjar insinuated himself into his hand-made skin craft. I boarded the fishing boat. We tossed Grunjar a line and towed him slowly through a channel bordered by rounded boulders on one side and the cliffs we had so recently climbed on the other. As our bow responded to the first swell Grunjar set himself free. His double paddle flashed in the sunlight as he turned seawards, powerful arms driving his kayak onwards. Eventually he swung his bow around, facing us. He waved once then urged himself to pick up speed. He and his fragile boat rode the incoming waves with style. Up and down he went, visible one second, gone the next. On the fishing boat I could not get a clear shot at him.

"I'll have to sit on the bow," I told the boatman. He pursed his lips and raised his eyebrows in one motion. Then he shrugged his shoulders. I understood the gestures to say, "It's your life."

The bow deck was small, about one metre long and the same at the widest part. Like most boats it narrowed to a point at the front. In essence it was little more than a small triangle, rounded in the centre. Standing, while the boat rolled in all directions at once, was out of the question. I tried kneeling, so I could pray while I worked. My knees complained that they had been tortured enough for one day, and I still couldn't grip. I changed position, parking my rear as close to the windshield as possible, bracing my back against the glass and my feet against the raised stem on the bow. No matter how I tried I still couldn't get a decent shot. I needed a series of wide-angle pictures. My feet managed to sneak into the viewfinder each time.

"You hold my belt," I instructed the bored boatman, as I stood up.

Grunjar came in from the sea riding a breaking wave. Directly in front of him jagged rocks lined up to rip his kayak apart. With perfect timing he corrected his course at the last possible moment and rode the wave through a narrow gap. There might have been a few centimetres of water under him, but no more. It was a spectacular feat, one which would have looked so classy on film. Unfortunately my boatman, concerned about our proximity to other rocks, chose that moment to let go of me and spin his wheel. He dropped us into a trough. The boat fell away from under me and, for a second — which lasted an hour or two, I was airborne. Then the bow came up and collected my feet again. Instinctively I swayed with the boat's motion, my index finger still on the shutter. I have an excellent series of images of a wall of water; up in the top right hand corner is part of the kayak and flecks of white water.

"I want you to go to Norway and photograph it through your own eyes," Per Holte, director of the Norwegian Tourist Board's London office, told me. A simple and enjoyable assignment, travelling the fjords from Bergen to Kristiansund, photographing anything and everything: whatever attracted my attention. There was nothing in my brief that said I had to hang precariously from rocks, or bounce around on a slippery deck on the open sea. Those things just sort of happen to me.

At Rosendal, where I was photographing the magnificent old 17th century Baronial Manor from the ground and briefly from the air, I met a trio of fjord horses. More importantly, I met two beautiful flaxen-haired Norwegian girls. The girls and the horses were together. They were a stunning combination.

Fjord horses are strong, thick in body and sturdy in the legs. In the mountainous fjordlands of western Norway strength and stamina are necessities. The horses are the colour of clean sand with dark brown, almost black, tails. Their manes are two tone. Lighter than the rest of their body, as seen from either side, the perfectly trimmed manes have a central spine which is the same colour as the horses' tails. Equally at home pulling carriages or carrying a rider, the horses matched their attendants for beauty.

"I need to photograph you separately, and together," I told the flaxen goddesses. One of the horses began to toss its magnificent head and pawed the ground impatiently. Spring was over, but the memory was still in its blood, and in mine.

"I know what you mean," I told the horse confidentially. "If she was sitting on me, I'd be feeling the same way."

Both girls got the giggles.

"Thank you," one laughed. "That is a nice compliment."

"It's a nice thought too," my brain replied. Fortunately my tongue kept still, as did my right foot although it did have a barely controllable urge to paw the ground.

"Now," I took command of the situation, "walk the horses slowly across the bridge as soon as I'm in position."

I ran down the hill a way. The grass was slippery and a few rocks lurked half hidden, in wait for the unwary. One foot caught on a large stone sheltering behind green camouflage. The other kept running until it skidded out of control on the wet ground. With style, and a certain precision, my body somersaulted. One hand swung my open camera bag in an arc, attempting to keep it upright and hold the equipment in place. My head watched with interest as my feet left the earth and spun wildly skywards. I landed heavily, square on my back on a mossy bank. A glacial stream gurgled beside me in amusement. I coughed to see if my chest still worked. Nothing came out.

Acting as if acrobatics were a normal part of a photographer's daily work, I got to my feet and forced a smile to my face.

"Are you ready?" I tried to call.

My voice, usually fuelled by my lungs, was lacking a fundamental known as air at the time. It went on strike. I wheezed asthmatically, the sound carrying just beyond my lips and no further. One hand clutched the camera bag, the other, to my surprise, was in working order. I could feel my fingers. Cheerfully I waved to the girls, in lieu of verbal instructions. They smiled and waved back, then burst into a spontaneous round of applause. I bowed deeply from the waist, sucking air into my lungs as I did so. I felt as though I'd gone ten rounds with Rocky I, II, III, and IV.

"You are so energetic," Ingrid told me later as we walked back to the manor with the horses. "Do you like kayaking?"

I recounted my adventures with Grunjar off the Bømlo islands. "It is calm here," she pointed to the smooth fjord. "I can borrow another kayak and we could go out this evening."

The temptation was strong, so very strong. It tugged at my self-imposed discipline. One foot began to scrape the ground. The professional side of me explored the photographic opportunities. The masculine side, much baser, could only imagine how pleasant it would be to spend an evening with such a lovely young lady. With a sigh of regret and, no doubt, a rueful expression on my face, I thanked her politely.

"I would love to, but I can't. Unfortunately I have to be in Ulvik before dinner."

As I declined the invitation my mind flashed Napoleon's regrets to his mistress after a hard day at war: "Not tonight, Josephine!"

Ulvik was kind to me. As if to reward me for my moral fortitude, the small town at the head of an arm of Hardangerfjord, introduced me to two more of Norway's inexhaustible supply of lovelies. One was a teenage model, the other the head of the local tourist board. I posed them individually, and as a pair, among the blossoms of an apple orchard overlooking the fjord. They were charming and easy to work with. I began to feel less disgruntled about missing the kayaking evening.

Travelling the fjords is a bit like island hopping, even when on the mainland. Without the excellent car and passenger ferry service linking opposing sides of fjords, island to island, and island to mainland, journeys by road would take infinitely longer. A short saltwater cruise every hour or so is a wonderful way of relaxing between drives.

Norway's most westerly mainland mountain is Vestkapp. Rising 496 metres above sea level, the flat-topped promontory, known as Kjerringa — or — the old wife, is an ideal spot for sunset photography. Vestkapp overlooks the Stad Sea, one of the most feared stretches of water along Norway's jagged coast. It's a windy spot and, as the sun goes down, the temperature goes with it. In preparation for the sun's departure I anchored my tripod, using weights to eliminate wind vibration, at the edge of the cliff. My hands spent much of the late evening in my pockets, only appearing to press the shutter release at appropriate moments then plunging back into the warmth again. The sea was quite calm, although a steady stream of rollers flowed in from the North Atlantic to spend themselves on the rocks at the foot of the cape.

In stormy conditions, I was told, the seas and the cape are merciless. At one time sailors, including the Vikings, preferred to drag their boats overland across Dragseidet, from the area of Leikanger to Drage, to avoid coming into contact with the ferocious Stad Sea. If the Vikings preferred to avoid the Stad, it must be wicked when it's bad tempered. Most of the sea stories I heard centred on bad weather conditions, all along the coast.

Runde Island is probably visible from the highest point of Vestkapp on a clear day. It's to the north, across the Stad Sea. Its rocky shores are eroded by that same body of water. I went out in a small fishing boat to see Runde's birds.

Runde is the southernmost of the renowned bird islands of western Norway. Hundreds of thousands of birds, perhaps as many as half a million, annually lay their eggs on Runde's mountainous terrain. Over twenty different species of sea birds and more than two hundred types of birds in total can be seen on the island in summer.

Norwegian fishermen have to be superb sailors. I couldn't imagine the taciturn Olav, who took me around Runde, being awed by the Stad Sea. He took his small boat to within a metre of the cliffs at times, just so I could get a close up shot. Seeing a grotto, carved by the constant action of the sea, I said I'd like to get closer. Olav's facial expression remained fixed. No smile, no twinkle in hooded blue eyes, no apparent emotion. He nodded. With a deft movement of the wheel he turned his boat to face the opening. Watching the incoming waves over his shoulder, he held us steady until he judged the sea to be exactly right. As a wave picked us up he opened the throttle a little, keeping us at the same speed as the sea. With the grotto entrance less than half a boat length away he slid off the back of the wave and into the cave. Had I wished, I could have touched the walls on either side as we slipped through the opening. That was seamanship of the highest order. Getting out again was simply a second exercise in gauging wave speed and height.

Olav made it look easy. I held my breath anyway, just in case.

The sea is not the only hazard at Runde. With so many birds soaring overhead, none of which have been adequately toilet trained, a hat is an essential item of clothing. A German photographer, who shared Olav's boat with me, made the mistake of taking off his hat to scratch his head. With impeccable timing a low flying kittiwake took that moment to relieve itself of a surprisingly large volume of grey liquid ballast. Right on target.

With so many birds on the wing at any one time, direct hits from inconsiderate flyers were inevitable. I was bombed on my shoulders, two cameras, and one long lens, during the two hours I spent on the boat. Olav lived a charmed life. He, perhaps because he was a local, was spared the ignominy of black and grey streaks and stains on his person and his clothing.

Guillemots and fulmars, puffins and gannets, gulls and terns, land on the cliff face — when they're not flying off on bombing runs. Every projection, no matter how small, offers potential for a perch. Nests dangle precariously, in constant danger of being blown from the cliff to a watery grave. The birds take off, dive, circle, glide, go fishing, feed their young, and, most of all, they screech. The noise from the base of the cliffs sounds like half the banshees in Hell wailing at once.

Rocky shores, such as Runde, magical though they may be for bird watching, can be fatal for shipping. In 1725 the three-masted sailing ship, *Akerendam*, foundered during a winter storm. She was driven onto the wicked rocks of Kvalneset during her maiden voyage. On board the Dutch East India Company's vessel were two hundred passengers and crew. All perished.

The remains of the wreckage of the *Akerendam* lay untouched for close to two hundred and fifty years. In 1972 three divers, braving the frigid waters, came across a great number of old coins on the seabed near Runde. Since that exciting discovery, over 58,000 coins, both silver and gold, have been found. One of the ship's cannons has been recovered and others sighted. Local lore tells of many more coins scattered on the seabed, waiting for intrepid underwater explorers to find them.

Along Norway's Atlantic seaboard several Coast Culture Museums have been set up to preserve the region's maritime heritage. Mellemvaerftet, or Middle Wharf, sits in a protected end of the harbour at Kristansund. Opened in 1860, the shipyard serviced the vessels employed in the klipfiske (dried, salted cod) trade and the region's fishing boats. Once there were three such shipyards in Kristiansund. Mellemvaerftet being the last built. All were kept busy building and repairing wooden sailing boats such as jekts, jakts, and galeas. By the early 1940's the fleets, which carried woollen goods, timber, dairy products, and fish, the length of Norway, had all but disappeared. The Upper and Lower Wharves at Kristiansund were closed down. Only Mellemvaerftet remained. In 1978 it too was forced to close.

Fortunately for the maritime craftsmen of Kristiansund help was at hand. Across the bay a crew worked on an old jakt. Dating from 1889, *Svanhild* was being repaired and readied for sea. The boat's owner persuaded the yard's custodian to allow he and his crew to use Mellemvaerftet to rebuild the old sailing freighter. It wasn't long before another ancient arrived. *Ella*, a Baltic trader in 1897, was in desperate need of repair.

With both vessels being restored in full view of the local population, interest in the shipyard naturally increased. Supported by a grant from the national culture fund and loans from the town of Kristiansund, Mellemvaerftet became a working shipyard museum. Douglas Wilmot, an American from Oregon and a former member of *Svanhild's* restoration crew, had been running the yard for over four years when I arrived. He'd been in Norway since 1977, working on boats and learning Norwegian.

"My job is to keep the yard running while maintaining its historical integrity," he explained. "It's not an easy combination."

Doug introduced me to Øle Tønder, one of *Ella's*

former owners. Øle's latest restoration project is *Kvernes*, a 23 metre passenger steamer built towards the end of the 20th century. Øle said his goal was to have the ship back in working order by the year 2000.

I went to Grip with Øle in a modern fibreglass motorboat. Fourteen kilometres to the north-west of Kristiansund a group of eighty or so islets and skerries form the first line of defence against ocean storms. Grip, the largest island, has been battered regularly.

"Almighty God, spare us further destruction and misery."

That fervent prayer is recorded in the early annals of the lovely old fifteenth century red stave church. On February 24, 1804, the North Atlantic launched another violent attack on the Norwegian coastline near Kristiansund. Grip and its neighbouring uninhabited skerries took the brunt of the storm. The howling wind and angrily excited sea raged at the cowering fishing village. Houses were severely damaged, boats wrecked, fishermen drowned. Only seven years before, during a similar tempest, close to one hundred houses were smashed into the sea by mountainous waves. Three lives were lost. No wonder the residents prayed for salvation.

No one can remember how Grip got its name: only that it has served seamen as a rocky haven for at least one thousand years. In its heyday the tiny island boasted a population of around four hundred souls. Sailors all, the hardy descendants of Vikings worked the nearby fishing banks, in open rowing boats, year round.

Grip was the property of the Norwegian Crown until 1728, when it was sold to a businessman in Kristiansund. At one time it was even owned by a Scottish merchant who regularly traded along the rugged coast. Eventually it was purchased by the islanders. Life was hard. Violent storms were not the only drawback to island living.

In the late 1700's the schools of cod inexplicably disappeared. The fishermen went out each day, as they had always done. More often than not they came home with empty nets. For a number of years the catch was disastrous and the hungry, poverty stricken residents were forced to move on. By 1818 only twelve fishermen and a few widows remained to defy the terrible winter storms.

Today Grip's rocky shores, still ravaged by seasonal gales, are barren in winter. There are no permanent dwellers now, only summer visitors. One elderly lady, who was born on Grip, crosses from Kristiansund each year on May 1. She stays on the island until the end of summer.

"Because I get seasick so badly," she told us.

In summer the island awakes. A few fishermen re-appear, repairing their nets where winter waves violently scrubbed sea walls. Their harvest is coalfish, pollock, and cod. It is juicy crab and succulent lobsters, which crawl unsuspectingly into pots and traps with no exit, only to be served later at fine restaurants in Oslo and Bergen. Colourful eider ducks bob for delicacies while, up above, noisy gulls aggressively scavenge for anything remotely edible. Day visitors sun themselves on the rocks, while waiting for the evening ferry to take them home. Fair weather residents mend damaged buildings, tend tidy garden plots and savour the peace and quiet.

Øle and I wandered back along the sea wall to the protected harbour. In places the concrete wall was broken, as if it had been hit repeatedly with a sledgehammer.

"Last winter's storms did that," Øle answered my unspoken question. "Every year things get broken."

We left, trailing a white wake around Grip light-house on nearby Brattharskøllen. Dating from 1888, the forty metre high beacon has withstood countless storms and guided thousands of vessels to a safe haven. The throb of the motorboat's powerful engine was comforting be-neath us. Astern, Grip settled into a hazy August afternoon. The hell that can blow in on a January gale was far from our thoughts. Øle had a passenger ship to restore. I had a date with a different version of Hell. Norwegian, certainly, but Hell — in name only.

"If you don't behave you'll go to Hell."

"Sinners will burn in Hell for eternity."

We've all heard the warnings, thundering from the

lips of irate mothers and fathers or booming from the lectern in church as Christian ministers admonished their flocks to follow the ways of righteousness. Hell, according to my encyclopaedia is 'the eternal home and place of torment of those damned to descend to the Devil's lair.'

I'd never been to Hell. It wasn't far from Kristiansund, not by 'plane. I was in the area so, I thought, why not? A short flight, listed as going to Trondheim but actually landing close to Stjørdal — about thirty kilometres further east, deposited me as close to my destination as it could. Outside a lone taxi waited.

"Take me to Hell!" I ordered, excitement rippling through my veins.

The driver's face registered no surprise. Perhaps he had known I was coming. Perhaps all those doomed to be consumed by the fires of Hell, were met by the same taxi. Perhaps there was a fleet of similar cars shuttling between the airport and reception. Perhaps it was lunchtime.

We drove into a light rain. Trondheim fjord stretched into the distance. The windshield and passenger's windows misted up. The driver turned on the defogger to give himself a little vision. After five minutes, you see — Hell is not really far away — we pulled into a station yard.

"Hell," my driver announced.

I paid him the required number of Kronor and got out. The rain was falling heavier. It was cold. "This can't be right," I said. "Maybe this is just the earthly reception."

I walked toward a large wooden building and around the front. A sign on a wall clearly stated: 'Hell – Expedition.' Now that caught my interest. It had to be the starting point for the ultimate descent. An expedition to Hell might even offer the possibility of a return fare and a chance to write another story about the adventure. I looked up the word in my pocket dictionary to make sure my thinking was correct.

'Expedition' the book stated: as in 'expediting or sending. Shipping.' Perfect!

The front door was locked. The building was deserted. Behind me railway tracks gleamed appreciatively as the rain washed them clean for the next train. On the wall a poster, faded by weather, gave the arrival and departure times for the trains. The next scheduled arrival was a couple of hours away. I couldn't wait that long. If I couldn't go to Hell when I wanted to, I sure wasn't prepared to stand around in the rain for an hour or two and wait. I went back to the airport.

About the time the next train rumbled into Hell I was ten thousand metres closer to Heaven.

LOW TIDE: LANGUAGE SLIDES

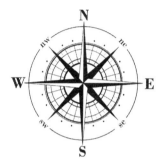

Europe's a funny old continent. The languages, a mind-blowing array of them, seem to change by the hour as one travels from north to south, or east to west. English, spoken perfectly in a few places, sounding dreadfully wounded in others, is almost understandable everywhere: almost, but not quite.

   Apart from the linguistic challenges, Europe is full of cobblestone streets and alleys, gabled roofs with gilded ornaments on the apexes. It's got castles and monuments, battlefields, religious shrines, regal palaces and majestic places of worship. Think of Europe. Think of history. It's been there, cultivated and cultured, for so many centuries. Many of the grand buildings of Europe have lasted longer than some so-called civilizations in other parts of the world.

   Civilized and cultured it may be, but Europe's

not the sort of place one thinks of in terms of adventure. And adventure is my business. Europe's been tame for a long time now. Centuries have elapsed since really wild beasts roamed the lands we know as Germany, France, Switzerland, or the three Benelux nations. There are still a few wooded pockets in some small countries, where wild boars do their best to avoid mankind. Most have been killed off because they didn't. The odd snake turns up here and there; none are really dangerous. So where's the adventure? Where's the element of risk?

Somehow wilderness travel and Europe don't really go together. Mountainous areas, such as the Alps, or the Pyrenees, for example, attract a certain type of adventurer, but nowhere on the old continent is much more than a yodel from a pub or a restaurant. Not many people go to Belgium, or Holland, in search of adventure. They go for culture, for history, or for the beer. There's no uncharted land, no new streams to follow to their source, no woodlands where footprints cannot be found. No, people don't go to the Low Countries for adventure.

They might go to tilt at windmills, or to look sadly at the war graves of Flanders' fields. They certainly go to see the magnificent cathedrals. Anyone who has stood reverently inside the massive 14th century Cathedral of Our Lady in Antwerp knows how awe-inspiring that can be. The adventure though was in the construction itself: a daunting operation spanning a few centuries in the middle ages. All we see is the end result. Impressive though it definitely is, the adventure is over. There may be other adventures waiting beneath the city's old streets. There are enough underground wine bars and beer cellars to suggest a potential warren of catacombs, but no one knows for sure. Or if they do they're not telling.

Fields and fields of tulips and carnations have thrilled visitors to Holland for generations, and they still do. In spring, when Belgium brightens up after the long grey winter, the beautiful wild orange and red poppies of Flanders adorn meadows and decorate country roads. And flower shows are ten a penny in both countries. But, somehow, visiting a flower show is not exactly my idea of exploring the great outdoors.

For a few wonderful years I lived in Antwerp. One morning I got invited to a flower show. It was a weekend and I was alone. I thought about it for a second or two, just to be polite, but I declined with thanks. I had nothing better to do. I just didn't feel like driving to Ghent to see a few dozen flowers.

"What about a nature walk along the river?"

That got my attention. A nature walk beside the Schelde? Hmm. Why not? The River Schelde flows through Belgium meekly, following a slow meandering path across low-lying ground. It looks as if it's trying to visit as many towns and villages as it can, until it gets close to Antwerp. Then it turns into a real river; a big one, anxious to meet the sea, although it has to course through Holland to get there. Ships from all over the world navigate their way far inland to Antwerp, to the second largest dockland in Europe. Some of them tie up to mooring bollards on the quay right across the street from outdoor restaurants. Even those in the heart of the docks are almost in sight of the cathedral's great tower.

The river is the main artery to the economic heart of Belgium. It has been said that "Antwerp has God to thank for the Schelde and the Schelde to thank for everything else." Napoleon Bonaparte, the stocky little French warrior, called Antwerp and its river, "A pistol aimed at the heart of England." He was so impressed by the strategic location that he built a naval dockyard in Antwerp. It's still in use today as the Napoleon Dock and the Willem Dock, part of Antwerp's sprawling dockland area. Some summers the river and those two original docks are crowded with masts and yards of great sailing ships from many nations. In scenes more fitting to the mid 19th century than late in the 20th, tall-ships come to show their matchless grace to the people of Flanders. My dog and I could sit and watch the Schelde all day. There's always something interesting going on by the river.

A nature walk by the river was an appealing idea. I

assumed we would be three for the educational afternoon stroll: myself, Herman, and his wife, Ria.

"No, no," said Herman with a smile and a certain vehemence, "I'm not going. I'm playing tennis later."

It sounded like a bit of a cop out to me, perhaps an instant allergy to the inevitable proximity of thick viscous river mud. Tavi, my dog, would have enjoyed it, but dogs and birds tend to disagree on nature walks.

So it was that Ria and I set off, just the two of us, clad in rubber boots, jeans, sweaters, and windbreakers. We started by car, crossing into Holland a few minutes later. On the south bank of the river, where Holland still keeps a foothold in what I think should be Belgian territory, we parked in a narrow lane beside a towering dyke. Off to my right Antwerp's skyline was clearly visible. We were on the south bank of Belgium's river, even if the local residents did think they were Dutch.

About a dozen similarly clad hardy souls awaited us. They were all Dutch, including the designated leader of the walk. For a few minutes we listened as she explained a little about the tidal wetlands we were about to explore. Speaking in rapid Dutch she emphasized that we only had limited time. In a few hours the incoming tide would send the river flooding along the deep muddy channels between the soggy islands of sedge. She soon lost me. My fractured Flemish was not equal to understanding a rapid-fire lecture. I wandered off alone to study the possible routes from the advantage of a dyke. Ria soon caught up with me.

"Do you understand what she says?" She asked, eager to be of help.

"No, only a few words, but I'm a sailor. I know all that stuff about tides anyway."

Politely we waited while the nature-lovers passed us and tramped down to the first muddy encounter. Everybody greeted me warmly, in English. Ria had thoughtfully told them I was Canadian. To the Dutch, a Canadian is just about as perfect a visitor as one can have. The Canadians performed a sterling task of liberating Holland from the Nazi war machine in WWII and the Dutch continue to show their gratitude. I was only a boy, not yet five when all that happened — and I was still English in those days. Still, it's nice to be appreciated. My father was attached to the Canadian force and spent time in Holland, fighting for his beliefs and their land. The Dutch appreciated that too.

Walking on wet mud is not easy. Feet tend to wander in opposite directions, without considering what their partners might be doing. It's tough to stay vertical when one foot is stuck in a glutinous hole and the other begins an impromptu slide. Within the first hundred metres a couple of unsuspecting waders found themselves leaving imprints of their bums to mark their passing.

For a while we helped each other scramble up slippery banks to take the higher ground from one channel to another. The vertically challenged among us had to be assisted regularly. Ria, being one of the smaller types, was dragged at arm's length and face to the mud up one incline by a well-meaning Dutchman. She wasn't amused. She's the independent type.

"I can get dirty by myself. I don't need no one else's help," she announced as she scraped half a semi-liquid hummock off her jeans.

"You mean — you don't need anyone's help," I corrected her.

"No! Next time I do it."

There was no arguing with that. I went up the next one with only the barest hesitation, leaving the independent Ria to her fate. If she stretched her arms high above her head and stood on tiptoe, her fingers would have been close to the grass at the top. She didn't need help. She had said so. I continued in search of winged marsh dwellers.

A Mallard took off at my approach. As the terrain was ideal for a nest, I thought there might be also be eggs. Behind me I heard muffled curses and breathless grunts as someone tried to scale the mud wall. It sounded like independence day to me. I kept moving. A handsome clutch of half a dozen chicken-sized eggs were hidden in a tidy nest a few metres away. I backed off to show the duck, wherever it was, that I was no threat.

A grubby hand came over the rim of a bank and tangled its fingers into the grass. Tenaciously it gripped. Another grunt. The other hand reached over and found its own purchase. Slowly a head of short blonde hair worked its way into view.

"Do you want some help?" I knew better than to put my hand down. It might have been bitten.

"No, I can do it."

With enough panting to make the others suspicious of her heavy breathing, Ria slithered over the edge to the relative dryness of the thick grass. Without stopping to rest she got to her feet. She was wearing more mud than she had earlier.

"You're dirtier now than you were before," I told her helpfully.

Ria didn't seem to hear, or didn't care. "I like this," she puffed as she smeared the mud around a bit more. Her smile said the rest.

"There's a nest over there with eggs in it. Don't go too close." I showed her the duck's incubating area. "We'd better get moving so she can come back and keep these warm."

There were many such nests, as we were to discover, with and without eggs. Gulls and ducks and assorted wading birds had made good use of the highest ground and densest vegetation. Ria switched the subject I was thinking about without warning.

"There used to be a lot of *zeehonden* here," she told me, pointing to the river.

I mentally translated the Dutch word into English, came up with sea dogs and thought of pirates. The image didn't work somehow. I couldn't imagine pirates, such as that old sea dog — Henry Morgan, sheltering among those muddy channels out of choice. The Caribbean was a much more exotic locale for buccaneering. The weather is considerably better year round and the girls all wear bikinis. I know. I've seen them.

"What's a *zeehond*?" I asked, wishing I'd carried my Dutch-Engels dictionary with me: it's always useful when

Ria's nearby. I thought in terms of sea lions, but I knew the Dutch for lion was *leeuw*, so sea lion would be *zee-leeuw*. I didn't realize I was getting close to the answer at that point, so I strayed off at a slight tangent. "Do you mean an otter?"

That didn't work. Neither of us knew the Dutch word for otter, so the question was left hanging.

"What happened to the *Zeehonden*?" If I asked more questions, I reasoned, I might eventually work it out.

"The fishermen shoot them. Now they are all gone."

"Why did they shoot them?" As I asked the light went on in my brain. I could see the marine mammal in question. "I know. They shot them because they ate all the fish. You're talking about seals."

"Yes," Ria agreed knowledgeably, as if we had both known the answer all the time. "Seals."

Having finally worked out which creature had become extinct in the River Schelde, I promptly commenced looking for signs that my informant was incorrect. Flipper marks, and the smooth gouges of a slithering belly in the drying mud would be a sure indication that the fishermen had missed at least one old sea dog. Harbour seals do look like dogs. My dog, a Labrador terrier cross, used to get confused on a daily basis when we lived in western Canada. Anytime we were out in the boat and a seal's head popped up, Tavi jumped in for a swim and general frolic. Just because the seals had grey coats with spots on them didn't mean they weren't dogs. They had dark brown eyes like hers; that suggested a relationship of some kind. And they barked. They had to be dogs. Sea dogs. *Zeehonden*.

The North Sea, which sends its tides boring up the Westerschelde as the moon dictates, is a known breeding ground for herring, flounder, cod and pollock. A few of those fish must wriggle up stream too. A seal could live quite comfortably off such a marine harvest. I looked, but there were no signs, because there were no seals. The fishermen, as I had been told, had obviously 'shoot' them all.

There are times when Ria's version of English, much

of which in the years since she left school has been gleaned from modern novels, is guaranteed to make one think about the mess English-speaking people have made of their own language. I lend Ria English and American books. She reads them, then comes to me with a list of words or expressions she can't find in her Engels-Dutch dictionary.

"What means, 'Hellooova'?"

"The question should be: what does hellooova mean?" I corrected in my usual pedantic style. Ria hasn't learned 'pedantic' yet. When she does I'll be in trouble.

She thrust a square of white paper into my hand. On it was written, HELLUVA!

It's not easy keeping that smile off my face when we are exchanging snippets of information about each other's languages. I try, but usually fail.

"That's, 'hell of a', not hellooova," I explained, trying not to laugh and failing miserably. "English speaking people run all three words together until it sounds like 'helluva.' The writer simply spelled it phonetically."

I explained that, occasionally, it's worth separating the English syllables to find a collection of words. Just the way I work out the meanings of long incomprehensible Dutch words. Of course, I'm not immune to error either. Some of my efforts in Dutch have resulted in major miscommunication. Ria was always far too polite to laugh, either that or linguistic mistakes in Dutch just aren't as funny as they sound in English.

One day Ria asked me to explain: 'hoisted by his own petard.' I had to stop and think about that one. When I finally explained that the expression meant self-inflicted damage, or harmed by one's own actions, she was ready with another square of white paper.

"The dictionary says petard is like a firecracker. Look!" She held the piece of paper up to my nose. "How can you hoist by petard? Does it mean blow up by explosion?"

She was right, of course. A firecracker is close enough to one meaning of petard. It doesn't help to understand the expression though. I suggested, with barely concealed amusement, that she look up petard and its derivatives in a

French dictionary.

Close to the river we dropped off an embankment to find firm sand. A marine navigation chart of the Schelde, between the sea and Antwerp's docks, would show the presence of multiple sand bars and mud flats. Ships can't sail in a straight line from the river mouth to the wharves. Wide though the river is, the ships all have to carve lazy S-shaped patterns from one side to the other as they follow the deepest channel.

Standing on the sand, with a flock of aerobatic Arctic terns practising their manoeuvres overhead, we were about a kilometre from the southern shore. Passing ships were closer to us than to either bank. It was time to turn back. Already the tide had ceased its ebb. The river was still, gathering strength for its return to infiltrate the wetlands we had recently crossed.

"I saw a wooden hut off to our right, it's about halfway back to the dyke," I said as we angled away from the hard packed sand. "We'll aim straight for that."

The other Sunday adventurers were nowhere to be seen. They had not ventured as far from dry land as we, the intrepid pair.

"What means 'to hit the hay'?" Ria's search for knowledge was inexhaustible.

"It just means to go to bed."

"There's no hay in a bed."

"I think pillows might have been stuffed with hay way back in the past," I explained. Then I had a better thought, "Mattresses used to be stuffed with straw, which is the same as hay. I expect it stems from that. I'll bet that was uncomfortable. Especially to the one underneath."

Ria chuckled and punched me on the arm. "Oh yeah," she drawled.

Determined to trek the shortest possible distance to the hut, and from there to the car, meant lowering ourselves into innumerable muddy channels. Then we had to climb out again on the other side. Some were wide, almost riverbeds in themselves, others no more than creeks. It was time consuming and slippery work. I jumped the narrowest ones, standing on the flimsy edge afterwards to catch Ria as she launched herself across. Once or twice we heard voices and I saw a hat or two bobbing above the grass, otherwise we were alone. Even the birds had abandoned us.

The hut, sadly in need of repair, was a bird blind, placed there by ardent ornithologists. Wind, seawater and generally wet conditions had not treated it kindly. Large gaps between the vertical planks were open invitations to chilly winds and teeming rain. Mould, green and grey, grew on the walls. One would have to be an exceptionally dedicated bird watcher to spend more than a few minutes in such damp confines. We pressed on.

My socks, which had started the walk correctly positioned over my feet and ankles and stopped just south of my knees, had progressed deep into the recesses of my boots. Scorning the comfort of my feet they curled in irregular shapes where my toes were supposed to be. My toes, all ten of them, complained about the lack of space. A blister built up a sore point between a bare heel and boot. Ria was suffering from a similar problem.

"My socks have come down," she laughed as she danced around on one foot while trying to remove a boot and replace a sock without falling over.

"Lean on my shoulder," I suggested gallantly, as I attempted a similar gymnastic movement.

"I can do it!" Independence, still in charge.

"How do storks and flamingos do this?" I asked Ria, as I staggered backwards on one shod foot before placing the other — bare — foot into cold mud.

She was too busy trying to stay upright to think and speak as well. She shook her head. We got our socks up, our boots back on and our toes began to appreciate the feeling of spaciousness again. It didn't last long. By the time we'd crossed two more gullies my socks had retreated to sulk in full view of my aching toes once more. I left them there until we finally dragged ourselves back up the dyke.

Without being aware of it, in our energetic haste to beat the tide, we had passed the other walkers. From the top of the dyke we could see them clearly, still making their way along a deep brown trench. By the time they hauled up on to dry land the first insistent trickles of the returning Schelde were probing their footprints.

Sliding my feet into clean dry socks and warm running shoes ranked high on my list of pleasures that day. We sat on either side of the car, treating our feet with a reverence only adventure walkers could understand. The blister on my heel was weeping in pain.

"Oh well," I reasoned to myself, "it's your own fault. You're the one who said there's no adventure to be found in the Low Countries. You could have gone to a flower show instead."

I considered suggesting to Ria that we had each been hoisted by our own adventurous petard. I actually looked at her and started to say it. Then commonsense took over: the drive home was short and I was looking forward to a hot shower. There was no time for a difficult long-winded discussion in a mixture of Dutch and Engels.

WITH EYES AT HALF MAST

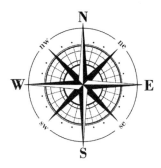

When we're awake we dream of sleep. When we sleep we dream the boat is falling apart. When we wake up, seemingly only seconds after our eyes have slammed shut, *Warpath* is still afloat, pounding her way across Pacific Ocean waves. It's been like this for weeks, on the Pacific and, before, on the western Caribbean.

"Tony. It's twelve fifteen!" It was a quiet voice, well modulated, very much under control. Still it boomed into my slumber.

"What?" My mind struggled to catch up to the present. I forced my eyes open, peering in the direction of the disembodied voice. It was gone. Message delivered. From outside came the sound of rushing water. From somewhere behind my head there was the rumble of powerful engines. I came properly awake fast.

"Shit. I'm late!"

I scrambled off my bunk and hauled on my jeans. One hand grabbed a sweater the other tried to get my zip done up. One was more successful than the other. Still swearing at myself, I ran through the galley and the saloon. As I opened the door to the open deck, a blast of hot moist air wrapped protectively around me. Clinging. Suffocating. I shrugged it off and took the steps to the bridge two at a time. I got the door open and my sweater on at the same time. The zip could wait. On the bridge the air was icy. As usual the air conditioner was on full. In the blackness, lit by a soft green glow from the instrument panel, Captain David Scherer stood motionless watching the radar. Kenny G's soprano saxophone trilled in the background.

"Sorry, Dave. I can't believe I did that."

"Don't worry about it." He had other things on his mind. "I'm going to the engine room. You take over up here."

I extricated the end of my tee-shirt from the lower teeth of my zip and did my pants up properly. The radar beam scanned through 360 degrees every few seconds. There was nothing within twenty nautical miles of us, except South Negril Point, the western corner of Jamaica — and that was rapidly dropping behind. I sat on the captain's chair in front of the console and softly chided myself for sleeping in. I had been due on watch at midnight. The fact that I had only been on my bunk for less than two hours was no excuse. David hadn't been anywhere near his since early the previous morning.

It all started as a joke really. A group of friends sat in a seafood restaurant in Steveston, a few kilometres south of Vancouver, talking about Denny's new toy.

"I'm gonna call her *Warpath*," he told us. "We're gonna take that sucker through the Panama Canal and bring her up the coast to Vancouver."

Without hesitation I jumped in with both feet and no lifebelt. "If you need an extra crew member I'm available."

Denny laughed but made no comment. He continued his monologue on his boat and the cruising he was planning in Bahamian waters after the current refit in Florida.

"She's a sixty foot Hatteras Sport Fisher with two big Detroit diesels. Once she's ready we're goin' fishing."

Dinner ended and only rarely after that did I think of the possible voyage. Until one day, a couple of months later, Denny 'phoned from Florida.

"Tony, can you get to Montego Bay by April 20th?"

Of course, I went. How could I say no to the opportunity of a month or so at sea, not to mention a transit of the Panama Canal. I signed on for the duration of the voyage from Montego Bay to Los Cabos, on Mexico's Baja Peninsula.

That first night at sea, en route from Jamaica to Panama, was my introduction to the business of delivering an expensive motor yacht. Denny, his partner, and a friend, had flown home from Montego Bay. I was on board as the owner's representative: a difficult position to be in as I was also the least experienced at expensive yacht deliveries.

David and Cindy Scherer had been delivering motor yachts between various Caribbean ports for some years. They had sailed to and from South American countries and David had made a previous delivery through Panama. Jim Goettel, also a licensed captain and David's long time friend, made up the fourth member of the crew. I was the unknown entity. My experience at sea was limited to sailing vessels — the craft David rather rudely referred to as 'blow boats' — and fishing boats. After finding me on my hands and knees in the engine room, looking for a dropped bolt, Jim nicknamed me 'the bilge rat.' And that was in the marina. In the first few hours of my maiden delivery voyage I had another strike against me already.

Montego Bay had been a serious test of our patience in dealing with the inevitable setbacks to be encountered in offshore voyaging. Jim flew in a couple of days after me, with a replacement satellite navigation system. The Jamaican customs officers insisted it was a radio and refused to clear it until *Warpath* sailed. Jim and David wasted valuable hours arguing the point with a variety of officialdom.

"It's not a radio. It's a navigation system, so we know where we are. We can't sail without it."

"You can't have it 'til you leave, Mon." Stalemate.

It took two days of frustration and immense control on David's part before the red tape was unravelled and the SatNav finally released.

On board, of course, the work of preparing for the voyage went on. There was a long 'To Do' list. Each of us had a copy and not enough hours in which to work through it. Somehow we did it anyway. A blown converter had to be replaced. Turbo socks, made of thin sponge rubber, needed to be washed and cleansed of oil: my job. Fresh-water filters had to be changed: my job again. The forward bilge pump system insisted on reverse syphoning. It had to be attended to. A fuel bladder, to enable us to carry more diesel oil, had to be rigged in the cockpit and a transfer pump wired to effect the flow when required: Jim's job. Cindy made a last minute shopping expedition.

"We need lots of TV dinners," David announced, "so the crew can have a hot meal they need it. That's the advantage of having a microwave on board."

Once the SatNav was finally installed and everything was ready for departure, David sent Jim and me ashore.

"Take a few hours off. Go see the sights."

We didn't need any additional prompting. Jim commandeered a taxi and told the driver to take us to the hills. We spent an amusing afternoon visiting a substantial marijuana plantation owned by the 'Zephman,' who smoked an enormous joint as he showed us his produce. We declined his kind offer of sampling his wares, pleading the need for sanity that coming evening. His furrowed brow and quizzical look eloquently expressed his failure to understand our refusal to partake. Still, he smiled happily as his own smoke burned closer and closer to his lips. Watching wood carvers in another village was not as interesting somehow.

As the day wore on we stopped for a beer at a village where, we were told, "Tourists don' come here, Mon."

We had a couple of beers each anyway, explaining we were sailors, not tourists. Somehow the distinction didn't quite get through. The dark interior of the bar, which had

signalled a certain joie de vivre from outside, was virtually
silent for the duration of our stay. No one acknowledged
us, apart from the bartender's grunt. Nobody wanted to
talk with us. I felt like a spy. Perhaps we should have gone
in on one of Zephman's highs after all. The bartender was
happy enough to take our money anyway. I suspect he was
even happier when we left.

At 21:30, after Immigration and customs formalities
were completed, *Warpath* slipped her mooring and eased
away from the yacht club in Montego Bay.

Once clear of the harbour David set the watches:
four hours on and four hours off. I shared two hours of
David's watch, followed by two hours with Jim. Cindy
took the remaining hours with the two more experienced
skippers. David and Cindy stood the first watch.

Gradually we left all land references behind and
put our complete confidence in the SatNav. Ahead, and a
little to port, Pedro Bank, a large rise in the sea bed, showed
clearly on the marine chart. The sea, which quickly built up
to challenge us with waves varying from one to two metres
in height, crashed into the port beam. *Warpath* was equipped
with a hard-top flying bridge, a substantial weight standing
well above the water level. With the waves kicking us
square in the side, she began to roll. The rolling increased
to become a constant, often violent, annoyance. For sixty-
three hours, *Warpath* creaked and groaned her way south
across the Caribbean. We all showed signs of nervousness,
wondering whether the luxury motor yacht was equal to
the strain. We wondered — one or two of us anyway, if we
were equal to the stress.

Sleep became a memory as I spent my few off-watch
hours in the forward cabin bouncing between the top bunk
and the head-lining. The thought occurred to me that, if
we hit a floating tree trunk, or some similar deadly marine
missile, I would be the first to know about it: and the first to
get wet. It wasn't a comforting thought. I kept it to myself
and tried to bury it beneath my fatigue.

On watch or off, while on deck or on the bridge,
all hands kept a lookout for other vessels. The Caribbean is

notorious for its drug smugglers, most of whom have little or no respect for other people's property. An expensive-looking Hatteras like *Warpath* might prove too much of a temptation for modern day pirates. Captain Morgan and his ilk may have been long dead, but piracy was not. Before we left Jamaica Jim positioned a wickedly sharp machete over the exit door from the engine room.

"If some sucker comes over the transom uninvited, I wanna be ready for him," he explained.

The precaution made sense to me. If the deck had not been so expensive, I would have been all in favour of famed solo sailor Joshua Slocum's simple protection against unwelcome boarders. Based on the theory that anyone boarding a boat illegally would do it stealthily, in other words — in bare feet — he reportedly sprinkled sharp tacks all over the deck. Somehow I didn't think Denny would appreciate a few thousand tacks buried in his clean white gelcoat.

Approaching Panama, David made the initial contact with Cristobal signal on VHF Channel 16 from eleven nautical miles out. The operator came back asking for the boat's registration, gross and net tonnage, overall dimensions and number of crew on board. He then asked that we call again when closer in. At three miles out from the breakwall David requested permission to proceed directly to the Panama Canal Yacht Club. Permission denied. We were instructed to anchor in the small boat anchorage known as the Flats and proceed to the club by dinghy.

General Manuel Noriega, then the driving force behind Panamanian politics, had been flexing his anti-American muscles. This was during his drug running days, before the military might of the U.S.A. sent in an invasion force of 13,000 to persuade him to change his habits. Just before leaving Jamaica we had been warned that we might find Americans were no longer popular in Panama. They might even need visas. Three out of four of us carried U.S. passports. With some trepidation David and I set off to pay a visit to the immigration authorities.

Leaving Jim and Cindy on anchor watch, we lowered

Papoose (*Warpath*'s dinghy) over the side. At the yacht club dock David ordered me to chain it securely.

"I'd like it to be here when we get back," he said, showing a complete lack of confidence in the honesty of other yachties and visitors to the club.

Our fears of a conflict with immigration were groundless. While I watched, listened and occasionally helped him out with a useful Spanish word or two, David worked his way efficiently through Immigration, the Panama Port Captain's office, Ad-measurement, and Insect Control. He was a master of patience and diplomacy when necessary, although his tension was obvious to me. Two and a half hours after we left we were back on *Warpath* with visas and our cruising permit for Panamanian waters. David later observed that the exercise had been a bit like walking on hot coals.

With all our permits in hand we moved *Warpath* to the yacht club. An air-conditioned bar, open twenty-four hours a day, and cold beer at $1.00 per bottle, was within easy reach, as were the crews of other yachts. Moored next to us, a sleek cruiser, half as long again as *Warpath*, had a crew of good looking and intelligent young Brits. In the employ of a Mexican media baron they were en route from Acapulco to Florida. Jim, our token bachelor, spent many of his leisure hours trading 'play your cards right and I'm yours' looks with a particularly beautiful golden legged stewardess from the Mexican mini liner.

Cristobal was depressing. The city was squalid, the people grim-faced. Presidential elections were only a few days away. Anti-American feeling was running high. 'Yankee Go Home!' was the most popular form of artistic expression on walls of houses and businesses. Jim did not enjoy the city. His patriotic blood bubbled to near boiling point at the constant insulting graffiti. With every step, passing every slogan, Jim's face whitened a little more, his lips became more tightly clenched.

There was a look of neglect about the place, as if no one really cared whether Cristobal lived or died. The tropics are never kind to buildings. The dank humid air plays havoc with bricks and mortar. That said, an occasional coat of whitewash or paint, even a scrub down with soapy water, can do wonders for appearances. Nothing in Cristobal had been cleaned for a long time. We purchased a few mechanical parts and retraced our steps to the yacht club. The first cold beer soothed Jim's mood.

Sitting in the bar late that night, when good sailors should be in their own bunks, I got into a discussion on U.S. — Panama relations and politics. It surprised me to learn from one of my drinking companions that most Americans believed the canal, and indeed the Canal Zone, were American owned.

"Not so," I argued, prepared to live dangerously. "Panama was civilized hundreds of years before America became a nation. The U.S. has never owned the area."

"Ronny Reagan said America has as much right to the Panama Canal as she has to Texas," he interrupted. "He should know. He's the President."

Any possibility that the conversation might eventually reach a reasonable intellectual level disintegrated right there.

"Reagan," I countered, probably a little pompously, "was not president at the time. And what he said was more like, 'North American claims to the Canal and to Texas are equally valid.' In my opinion he was wrong on both points."

Now that was living dangerously. Rejecting America's ownership of Panama was one thing. Denying their right to the Lone Star State was tantamount to heresy. There was a great opportunity begging for debate. Tentatively, to ease any additional discord, I raised the suggestion that North America and the United States of America were not the same thing. Eyebrows wrinkled in distaste at the thought. The beer was working, but not all the brains were in gear.

"Canada is part of North America. That doesn't make it part of the States," I reminded them. "As far as I know, Canada has never laid claim to either Texas or the Panama Canal."

I was really tempted to bring in Mexico's age-old claims on Texas. Just to be difficult. Being outnumbered two to one brought me to my senses: that and the knowledge that I couldn't see any way to win such an argument. I left my erstwhile drinking companions with one parting shot.

"If America owns the Panama Canal, how come a U.S. registered boat has to get permission from a Panamanian to go through it?" Confused black looks followed me into the tropical night.

Two members of the Panamanian narcotics squad came to visit *Warpath* in the morning. "Just routine," they told David in Spanish.

David had stressed that, in the event two or more officials came on board to inspect the boat, none were to be left alone for a second. I sat in the saloon with them while they chatted with the skipper. It didn't take long for us to hear the important parts of their lives. It was, apparently, imperative that we understand that times were tough in Panama. Putting kids through school took a lot of money. Feeding and clothing a family was a terrible burden for a poor man. Etc.

David was prepared for the encounter. Two ten-dollar bills, which had somehow been left in one of our passports, experienced a classic sleight of hand. They were in the passport, then they were not. At least there was no possibility remaining that a future immigration officer might consider the presence of the bills as a bribe.

While David and one of the Narcs took a tour of the boat, I stayed with the one who was, he said, content to sit alone in the saloon. Being a responsible host, even though I was, in effect, little more than a bilge rat, good manners demanded that I remain with him. Commonsense had some bearing on the decision as well. They left, an hour or so later, as politely as they had arrived.

To take a small boat through the locks of the Panama Canal strict regulations must be followed. Four line handlers are required for each vessel, in addition to a captain and a Panamanian pilot or advisor. We took on two, as partners for Jim and myself. Apart from the obligatory line handlers, it is also strongly advisable to have a substantial supply of ice-cold soft drinks on board. They are most definitely needed.

Leading a flotilla of motor yachts and sailing boats we cast off from the yacht club and made way for the Gatun Locks, the first of three on the Caribbean side of Panama. David insisted on positioning *Warpath* in centre lock, with a scruffy fishing boat against the wall and another motorboat between the fishing boat and us.

"No quantity of fenders will keep the hull from some major scrapes as the boat is buffeted against the wall," he explained. "Centre lock is the only way to go."

Less experienced skippers took the least desirable sidewall slot. Astern, crews on the smaller sailboats were busy rafting together, three abreast. They, due to their obvious fragility, had to be held in centre lock by line handlers above them on the lock walls.

In Gatun Locks we learned the importance of the cold soft drinks. Panamanian line handlers, standing high above us, hurled monkey fists attached to thin lines at each vessel. The monkey fists, made of lead wrapped in leather, could make a hell of a mess of anything they hit. With unerring aim the monkey fists flew over our heads, dropping their lines into waiting hands. We tied on our thick mooring lines and a bag of drinks, to be hauled to the lock's rim.

"Without the reward of those Cokes, monkey fists have been known to miss their targets and shatter a few windows," David observed dryly.

Behind the flotilla the massive black gates silently closed, trapping us all in a deep canyon of sheer walls. It was hot and humid. The dirty water churned and swirled as billions of additional litres were pumped in. Slowly, inexorably, *Warpath* lifted up to the second level, to increased daylight, to cooler air.

The Panama Canal, which effectively links the Atlantic and Pacific Oceans, was built by the U.S. Corps of Engineers between 1904 and 1914. Crossing the Isthmus of Panama, the canal stretches eighty-two kilometres from

Cristobal to Balboa. Ferdinand de Lesseps, a Frenchman, who engineered the Suez Canal, originally started to dig his way across Panama. He planned a straightforward canal without benefit of locks. His was not a successful effort. Mudslides filled in his work behind him, thwarting his endeavours. Perhaps he should have retired after his triumph at Suez.

The credit for the engineering marvel we travelled through should go to President Theodore Roosevelt. He charted the course by creating the Isthmian Canal Commission in 1904. Ten years later President Woodrow Wilson, seated at his desk in the White House, pressed a button to detonate forty tons of dynamite nearly 7,000 kilometres away. The resultant explosion removed the final obstacles between the Atlantic and Pacific Oceans.

There were no ships in the first locks with us, only smaller boats. As the water rose and *Warpath* came level with the rim of the lock, we could see the railway lines running on either side. At one end, large engines waited. Similar in appearance and design to the diesel shunters used in railway yards to move rolling stock from place to place, the Panama Canal versions are known as mules. Their function is to pull large ships into the locks without the use of water-borne tugboats. Unnecessary for our use, they stayed idle while we exited the first lock under our own power.

The process was repeated at the next two locks. As soon as the final gates swung ponderously open, we were under way. Our pilot wanted to get us through to Balboa in one day. Waiting for the much slower miniature armada to catch us would only cause a delay of twenty-four hours. We left them behind.

David opened *Warpath*'s throttle and she responded immediately. With her knife-edged bow slicing through the water, we raced across Gatun Lake at twenty knots. Before Gamboa we passed the *Pegasus Diamond*, a car transporter out of Tokyo, and a large container ship with an indistinguishable name. Motoring in the opposite direction, a couple of Canadian yachts with sails furled, chugged towards the Caribbean. In the narrow Gaillard Cut we slowed to thirteen knots and pulled in to the Pedro Miguel Locks well ahead of schedule. A supertanker, which we passed a few minutes before, joined us in the lock. As the mules eased *Tian Shan Hai* into position the massive bow towered over *Warpath*, leaving us with a distinct sense of inferiority.

In the Miraflores Lock the deep blue hull of *Anangel Progress* loomed ominously over us. Her dark colours made the gloomy depths of the lock even less inviting, more oppressive. Then we were down the watery staircase and running free at full speed for Balboa. The huge suspension bridge linking Central and South America carried cars and trucks over our heads as we prepared for refuelling and the Pacific Ocean.

The pilot and line handlers went ashore at Balboa. David had arranged official clearance of ship and crew's papers in Cristobal, so there was no delay in departure. Once our tanks were full we motored out into Panama Bay.

Now that was a trifle confusing. Our voyage was from the Atlantic to the Pacific: in other words, from east to west. Our canal transit, however, had actually been from northwest to southeast. The ship channel into Panama Bay also points southeast. We departed Balboa at sunset. The sun, therefore, was setting on our starboard side, right at the stern. It is said that it is possible to stand on a couple of locations on the Balboa side of the Panama Canal and watch the sun come up over the Pacific. It is probably equally possible to watch the sun set over the Atlantic from the Caribbean side.

Jim took charge as *Warpath* navigated the mass of sea traffic heading into and out of the Canal Zone. I remained with him on the bridge. In the darkness the radar lit up like a firework display, there were so many ships in our way. Jim held us as close to the right edge of the channel as possible to avoid any possibility of a collision. Once clear of the main channel, and past Taboga Island, we set course south southwest to pass Punta Mala and greet the Pacific.

We had a reasonably easy run for our first two

nights and one full day on the Pacific. Although *Warpath* bitched and moaned at the rockin' and rollin' she developed a rhythm we eventually learned to tolerate, if not actually enjoy. David called a halt in mid afternoon of the second day.

"We'll stop here for a while and do a little fishing. Our sushi supplies are running low."

All four of us were great fans of sushi, with fresh sliced ginger and hot green Wasabi sauce. No one suggested we press on. Within minutes we had the fishing outriggers extended and hooks baited. Although we were close to shore, the water was deep. David had chosen well.

A hammerhead shark coasted slowly by, looking up at us with its two eyes set on opposite ends of its transversely elongated head. It looked as if it was trying to grow wings out of its nose.

It didn't take long before one outrigger took a hit. Jim planted himself in the fighting chair and braced his feet on the transom. The fishing rod arced as something long and strong raced away with the line.

"Hang on to him," David shouted. "He'll come up in a minute."

No sooner were the words out than a blue marlin hurtled out of the ocean pointing straight at the sky. Before Jim could react the powerful fish danced a rhumba on the surface, shook its head once, somersaulted and dived for the safety of the deep. The line went slack. Minutes later another line screamed and Jim got there first again. This time, after having to do some serious work with his arms, Jim kept the fish. With a bit of help from David, a sparkling green dorado, weighing around ten kilos, slid onto the deck. Fresh sushi was guaranteed. We were snacking within the hour. Life at sea was good again.

The next morning we anchored off Golfito, Costa Rica, at 05:00 local time. We worked all day refuelling and re-provisioning. The fuel, having to be transferred by gravity feed from a tank truck, took hours. While the diesel oil trickled into the tanks we amused ourselves by tormenting a pair of teenage girls. Unfazed by our attentions they giggled, listened and watched. Young boys came to show off, partly for our benefit, more for the girls. They were ignored by all of us. The girls had eyes only for Jim. Being a man of strong willpower, he resisted all temptation. We had work to do. In the evening, while David stayed aboard on anchor watch, Cindy and Jim and I went ashore for dinner.

Golfito is a small town, once no more than a port for shipping bananas to Europe. Since the maritime trade has dried up, it has declined into a smaller port. As far as we could see there was a main street running parallel to the harbour and not much else. Behind the town a deep green jungle sweated in its natural fecundity. Much to our surprise, and to my delight, we discovered the best restaurant in town was owned by a Frenchman. My companions, expecting to have to struggle through the menu in Spanish, gave perfect impressions of surprise — their lower jaws dropped visibly — as I chatted happily away in French to Le Patron. I could have stayed talking and drinking wine with him all night. Jim and Cindy failed to share my enthusiasm. They enjoyed their meals and prepared to leave.

Le Patron invited us to visit his new disco, opened, I assumed, more for the benefit of visiting yacht crews than for the locals. We expressed our apologies and bade him goodbye. I thought about staying on for, as I said, a night of good cheer. Unfortunately that meant swimming back to *Warpath* the worse for wear. For once commonsense took charge. I let Jim drive me home in *Papoose*.

Underway at 06:30, wind from the west at 10 - 15 knots, seas running up to one metre in height. Wind and seas constant throughout the day. *Warpath* still rocking and rolling, bitching and complaining. The non-stop creaking and groaning was getting us down. Tired as we were, we could not sleep. *Warpath* just did not like beam seas. At night a series of thunderstorms made life a little more miserable. We did our best to avoid them but it wasn't always possible. Off Cabo Blanco we had to cut right through one gigantic storm. High winds slammed into us while torrential rain made visibility impossible without the radar. As the lightning lit up the skies and the thunder crashed, I asked David what he would do if we got hit. He was quick to point out that, as long as the electrical system was properly installed and bonded, there was no problem. I had to ask another obvious question.

"What happens if the electrics get burned out?"

David's answer was a terse, "We'll turn for shore and run her up on the beach, then phone Denny and tell him where she is." He was joking, yet there was an element of potential truth in what he said.

The ship's log for that day states, "We arrived in Porto Potrero at 06:00. Crew tired as usual!" We were. Porto Potrero, also known as Flamingo Bay, was our jumping off point from Costa Rica for Mexico. Between lay the political instabilities of Nicaragua, Honduras, El Salvador, and Guatemala. David had every intention of steering well clear of all four.

From Porto Potrero to Puerto Madero, first port of call in Mexico, was a planned 470 nautical miles. A two-day and two-night leg. Our course was set to take us around sixty nautical miles off shore. We saw little other traffic. The Pacific Ocean still hit us beam on. We still rolled. A hot wind blew steadily. Late in the day the wind veered from north to northeast, to east and then to southeast: a typical hot wind cycle.

That night the thunderstorms returned. One cell stretched forty kilometres by eighteen kilometres across the radar. It's incredible strength was reflected in its size. The crew and *Warpath* were puny intruders on a vast ocean. The storm played with us unmercifully. *Warpath* complained more bitterly than usual. We held on to any handy projection and hoped the purgatory would soon end.

In the early morning hours Jim listened in to a conversation between three other motor yachts. On a southbound course, they were audibly nervous at our approach. We were the only other vessel on the radar at the time. Rumours of pirates off the Central American coast obviously unsettled them. Jim maintained radio silence, letting them chatter back and forth for a while, before he identified us and put their fears to rest.

On the long watches conversation kept us alert even when the storms didn't. David was our guide, our stabilizer, and captain. Jim, forever quoting his grandmother, "Idle hands are the tools of the Devil!" was our slave driver and resident comedian. Cindy looked after our health and morale with excellent meals and regular attention. I helped everyone. I worked. I watched. I listened. I had a story to write.

Jim was late for his 02:00 to 06:00 watch. David greeted him with a cheery, "Good morning, Jim."

"What's so fucking good about it if you're waking me up?" Jim grumbled as he staggered into the engine room for a thorough check before joining me on the bridge.

The strain of non-stop work with little sleep began to take its toll. Jim decided he was beginning to look as old as me, a difference of only six years. He said we both had our eyes at half-mast. Later, off watch, I checked. He was right. My eyes did need a facelift.

I finished my watch at 04:00 as we closed the land again, the Guatemalan coast clearly visible to starboard. The sun would soon come up over the mountains. I decided to stay on deck. Our Mexican landfall was only two hours away.

Puerto Madero was almost a welcome sight. It spelled relief from the rolling and the suffering, otherwise it offered nothing. Great Pacific rollers broke on the beaches and surged through the narrow channel into the port. Fishing boats scurried back and forth past a huge dredger. David expertly piloted us in through the entrance to the Club de Yates, a misnomer if ever I heard one.

I stared in amazement at the rectangular pond, ringed by muddy banks. There was no resemblance to any yacht club I had ever seen. Grubby shrimp boats crowded a jetty and three sailboats were at anchor in the filthy water. The bottom was loose, nothing for our anchor to grip on, so we tied up at a deserted oil-streaked pier nearby. Welcome to Mexico!

A short taxi ride inland lay Tapachula. Once the day's work was over Jim and I headed into town for an outdoor cantina and a few glasses of cold cerveza. Content to feel solid ground under our feet for a few hours, we sat and watched the world of southern Mexico drift by. It felt good to relax. Our trials at sea were far from over. We knew the next leg would be another rough one. For one evening we were sailors on shore leave.

The Isthmus of Tehuantepec is a two hundred kilometre wide strip of Mexican land separating the Pacific Ocean from the Gulf of Mexico. It is notorious for the winds it generates. David had suffered through a storm the previous year off that coast and had no desire to repeat the experience.

"We'll take it easy," he said. "We'll keep one foot on the beach and one foot on the boat."

There was no running far offshore across the Golfo de Tehuantepec. We ran close in and still got hit by a Tehauntepecer wind. For five hours we battled what David calmly referred to in his log as, "...Just a lot of wind and an enormous electrical storm."

I thought the boat was trying to tear itself apart!

Once across the gulf the rest of our two-day run to Acapulco, still hugging the coast, was a treat. We saw two marlins jitterbugging on their tails, a lone killer whale minding its own business, a few hundred porpoises acting like marine ballet dancers, and two thoroughly unpleasant semi-submerged tree trunks.

Acapulco heralded a change of crew. Jim left us and flew back to Miami. Three new members came aboard: Penny, and another couple. Together we enjoyed the delights of the Mexican Riviera, from Acapulco to Cabo San Lucas. And there it came to an end.

David and Cindy took *Warpath* north to California alone. Denny was due to take over in Long Beach. As *Warpath* headed out to sea in the early dawn, with the Pacific Ocean pounding on her port side, I sat high on a rocky crag. It was light, though the sun had yet to put in an appearance. As *Warpath* battered her way north I stood up and waved. Suddenly, even though she was rolling like a drunk and, probably, making deafening noises inside, I wanted to be back on board. Instead I had to go home.

ALL HANDS ON DECK

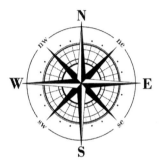

"Paruznj avral! Paruznj avral!" The metallic voice echoed through the tannoy. "All hands on deck! All hands on deck!"

Somewhere between two and three in the morning tired bodies followed sleepy minds off rows of narrow bunks to the cold floor.

"Is it raining?" It's hard to ask a question in German while trying to wake up and think in English at the same time. Somebody understood me anyway.

"Ja. Of course it is raining. Why else would they call us?" Sharp, to the point and, more important, spoken in English. The sarcastic Teutonic rasp added emphasis to the answer.

"What a way to spend our last fookin' night on board," a Lancashire voice grumbled. We struggled into yesterday's damp clothes, pulled wet weather gear over the top and stumbled out of our quarters. With eyes out of focus and brains half asleep we felt our way along a corridor, which was leaning at a strange angle, and up a companionway to the deck. It was raining as expected. Horizontally. The deck was heeled over far more than necessary, as if trying to dip the masts and rigging into the sea.

"Why is it," I asked myself, as I made my way from one hand hold to another, "that gravity has only a marginal effect on same rains?"

We assembled at the second main mast, leaning with backs to the wind. At the fore and the main, similar groups of sailors mustered. We listened carefully as Anatole, our bos'un, shouted orders. He'd had plenty of practice. His stentorian Russian voice cut through the storm. The members of the former Soviet Union understood him perfectly. He repeated some of his words in fractured German. A few Germans understood. I picked up one word in twenty. Wasting no time he assigned men to their tasks. The cadets were already racing up the rigging like a troop of half-drowned monkeys.

"Anthony. Wolfgang. Dieter. Up!" He pointed to the lower yard for emphasis.

We buckled on our safety belts and followed the cadets as Anatole bellowed again, "Brassen! Brassen!"

Below us, the deckhands leapt to obey the order, which meant, "Hands to braces." Struggling on slippery decks to swing the yards, they tried not to trip over coils. Even as we reached our loftier station the heavy yards were coming round. My deck shoes were tightly laced, with loose ends tucked in for safety. I stepped gingerly to the right, my shoe feeling its way along the foot-rope. Snapping my safety harness onto the jackstay, I continued my side step until I was nearly three metres from the mast. Behind me a safety line cut across my rear end. The bright yellow steel yard offered strong support as I leaned over, bending almost double, to help secure the wildly flapping sail. Far below me, in spite of the howling wind, I fancied I could hear the sea slapping angrily at the white hull of the majestic old windjammer.

To gather up a loose sail in a storm requires strength and balance. The wind is there to test both resources. I don't know about the others, but my heart was thumping like a tom tom. Leaning over the yard together, we collected the canvas in our arms, tucked some of it under our stomachs, and thrashed the wind out of the ballooning sections by beating it with our fists. Once under reasonable control we only had to hold it together, and keep the wind out, with one hand. The other had more serious work to do.

To tie a sail in place, gaskets or thin rope ties, must pulled around the sail and knotted. Standing on a thin rope, suspended high above a deck at night, in the pouring rain, with a malignant north wind screaming abuse, we massaged the sail into a reasonable semblance or order, while trying to maintain our positions. The wind punched us, pulled us, deafened us, threatened us. My fingers ached with the cold and the strain as I fought to furl my part of the sail. One mistake, or a faulty safety belt, and death was a certainty. Once we had the canvas tied, looking like an elongated white sausage, we then had to lash it to the yard. We completed the job together.

Straightening my back, but with my head bowed into the vicious wind, my left hand gripped the yard. Carefully I unhooked my safety strap and clipped it on my belt. As the cadets finished their tasks they filed swiftly to the mast for a rapid descent to the deck. Eager to be out of the wind, I shuffled with them. As soon as our feet found the shrouds we scampered down to more substantial footing.

With feet firmly planted on the deck we laughed at each other, brushing aside recent fears. The deck hardly seemed to move though the storm showered spray over the side every few seconds. Far above, the yards still swung in unison with the masts: a continuous motion across the black sky.

I'm a bit of a glutton when it comes to punishment. That's how I came to be on a tall-ship in the first place.

"Sail With Us," the advertisement invited. A black and white photograph of two square-rigged sailing ships, under full canvas, added impact to the message.

Kruzenshtern and *Sedov* stated the caption. I looked at the
two Russian vessels. *Sedov*, the largest fully operational
sailing ship in the world, raced *Kruzenshtern*, the second
largest windjammer. It was a scene to stir any red-blooded
writer to action. I signed on for two weeks before the mast.

Sedov was due to sail from Malta to the French
port of Brest. I went along to learn the ropes, so to speak.
From La Valletta harbour she looked huge. Close up, seen
from sea level, she was gigantic. Her four bare masts and
eighteen yards, all made of steel, loomed overhead like
a forest waiting for springtime. A vast network of lines,
sheets, halyards and braces, dressed her from royal yards
to mahogany pin rails in geometric spider webs.

Built of steel in the Krupp shipyards of
northern Germany in 1920, she is a fraction over 117 metres
long and has a beam of 14.6 metres. The tip of her main
mast stands 58 metres above the sea on a calm day. She has
18 square sails and 14 fore and aft. When all sails are set the
total area exposed to the wind is an impressive 4,192 square
metres. That's an immense weight of canvas.

When she was launched in 1921, she was named
Magdalena Vinnen, after the owner's daughter. Designed
as a bulk carrier with four cavernous holds, the *Magdalena
Vinnen* and her crew of forty men roamed the globe with
diverse cargoes. She loaded wool and wheat in Australia
and raced competitors to Europe. She carried saltpetre and
guano from South America. From the idyllic South Pacific
Islands she hauled anything she was offered.

Working under sail for most of the time, she
managed some exceptional voyages. In 1931 she made
Port Victoria, Australia, eighty-seven days after leaving the
Thames. In 1932 she made the return journey in ninety-six
days. Later that same year she reached Melbourne eighty-
one days out of Gibraltar.

1936 saw the graceful ship sold to North-German
Lloyd. Under a new name, *Kommodore Johnsen*, an increased
workload ensued as the four-masted barque took on the
additional role of training ship. Seventy trainees were
added to the crew. They lived aboard and did the same

work as the regular seamen, but without the benefit of pay.

Following World War II a sorry looking wind-jammer, with yards and stays piled on deck and her screw missing, was handed over to the Soviets under the war reparation scheme. For the next five years she languished in sight of the Baltic Sea at Liepaya, until a deep sea captain took command of her.

Since 1952 the grand old ship has carried the name *Sedov*, in honour of Georgy Sedov, the Russian sailor and Arctic explorer who died in 1914. *Sedov* is owned by the Murmansk State Marine Academy and is employed by the Ministry of Fisheries. She's a sail training ship with a busy schedule.

Today the permanent crew of sixty-five is augmented by one hundred and fourteen cadets. They share their voyages with up to fifty foreign trainees. Through the well meaning auspices of Germany based Tall-Ship Friends, trainees pay for the privilege of working in partnership with crew and cadets on regular ocean passages. All revenue generated is intended for the ship's upkeep. And that's where I came in. I shipped out as a trainee, for the experience, and to write a story or two.

Thirty six trainees assembled under a blazing hot sun in Valletta. We were a cosmopolitan group ranging in age from the early twenties to the late sixties. We came from six different countries and between us we spoke a Babel of tongues. On board, orders were given in Russian, broken English, and mutilated German. Most conversations took place in German and English, with German predominant because there were more Germans in the group. We were embarking on a linguistic adventure, as well as a nautical voyage.

I stowed my sea bag on a top bunk in one of the sleeping alcoves in Kubrick 5, the living quarters I was to share with seventeen strangers for fifteen days. Kubrick 5 was only just big enough to swing the proverbial cat without hitting the walls. We, one Canadian, one English, one Swiss, and fifteen Germans, had to live together in harmony. It was a necessity which, for the most part, proved to be a reality. United by a common interest, for a short while we shared our lives and our languages.

Much of the daily work on board ship is mundane. We polished brass, painted over rust spots, scrubbed the teak decks with a mixture of soap, sand and hot water, cleaned and oiled blocks. Each morning two volunteers were required to peel potatoes: names to be printed in pairs on the notice board. An unknown humorist added 'Hansel und Gretel' to the roster.

The Mediterranean Sea was relatively kind to us, although the rolling swells sent many a cadet running from the mess hall with hands clamped firmly over mouths. Thankfully I have never suffered from sea-sickness. Two days from the Pillars of Hercules a sudden squall whacked us hard while we were at lunch. Two topgallant sails blew out and *Sedov* heeled over violently.

Meals were only eaten on *Sedov* under protest. We worked hard, burning calories, our stomachs got hungry and protested. The food was atrocious, although the daily cabbage soup did have some flavour. Hard crusty bread was a necessity to assist the other unidentified morsels to their destination. When a meal was put before us we had a choice of inspecting it, never a good idea, or downing it quickly while thinking of something pleasant. Under extreme conditions, such as a storm, the mess room, or dining hall, was not a good place to be.

The mess lived up to its name as the squall hit. The room turned into chaos as food, plates, cutlery, cadets and trainees mingled on the floor. I sat in a pool of soup, with one hand on a large moist piece of lukewarm gristly meat, and the other in an accumulation of fresh vomit. My appetite faded. My stomach began to explore the possibility of succumbing to mal de mer for the first time. Wiping my yellow-stained hand on a cadet's discarded jacket, I forced my insides to behave.

"Paruznj avral!"

The welcome order sent everyone slipping and sliding to their stations, adorned with interesting patterns of lunch — uneaten and regurgitated. Cadets and crew raced to the yards to shorten sail and lash the ripped topgallants. We ran out new sails in preparation for hoisting aloft when they were ready. It was all good practice and much more interesting than lunch. Ahead lay the Atlantic Ocean and the notorious Bay of Biscay. Out there anything could happen.

By the time we motored through the Straits of Gibraltar, the sun rising in our wake on a windless day, we were ready for the Atlantic Ocean. Most of us fitted in well on board and took readily to any given task. Inevitably a few shirked at every available opportunity. Some of those suffering from mal de mer steadily improved, others continued to decorate the ship without notice. At meal times we of the lead-lined stomachs learned to protect our plates from airborne surprises by hunching over the table and shielding our food with our arms. It wasn't the best of table manners. But then, it wasn't the most elegant of tables.

The Atlantic proved rather gentle, with sunny days and long easy ocean swells. Porpoises came to play on the bow wave for our amusement. A minke whale surfaced and took a quick look at us before sinking to obscurity again.

Under a scorching sun we stripped the torn sails of all re-usable equipment. Head ropes, foot ropes, cringles, bullseyes, and stitching we retained. The canvas, ripped beyond repair, was consigned to the afterburner, my name for the old oil drum clamped to *Sedov*'s taffrail.

The afterburner was used to burn most waste. The plumbing on *Sedov* was, sadly, not what it could have been. In the heads, used toilet paper was deposited in buckets, not in the toilet bowl. Twice each day a cadet collected the contents of all buckets and cremated them in *Sedov*'s fiery tail — hence the name. Contrary winds were known to play with the acrid smoke and distribute it among the deck hands. On those occasions, in view of the lack of face-masks on board, sensible sailors took to the rigging.

Off watch there was much visiting between kubricks. The Russian cadets and sailors were always eager for hard currency. Any item having sales potential was hawked around the ship. One enterprising cadet sold his complete uniform well before the voyage's conclusion. When asked how he would explain the deficiency back in Murmansk, he simply shrugged his shoulders and smiled.

As the final storm subsided the rain bucketed down. Outside Brest the wind died completely, the rain turned to drizzle. Off the harbour wall we made ready to drop anchor as a French naval submarine slid by under our stern. The huge white windjammer, graceful relic of a byegone era, responded in kind as the slim black vessel dipped its colours in salute.

I should have stayed at home after that. Two weeks at sea eating Russian meals could seriously endanger the health of a stomach used to better things. I wrote a couple of stories. They were duly published. Then a new invitation arrived.

The Ukrainian barque *Tovarishch* needed positive exposure. Would I like to join the crew for a week and tell the world her story? Without a second thought I boarded a train from Antwerp for the old Hanseatic port of Wismar on Germany's Baltic coast.

From the rail terminus I had no doubt as to the direction of the ship. Towering over the red tiled roofs was a forest of masts. I could see five, then six, then seven. Two ships in, I decided. *Tovarishch* was there docked outside a pub. I couldn't argue with that location at all. Across the water, about a windjammer length away, stood *Kruzenshtern*. After years of neglect at sea she was finally in port for some sprucing up. She looked a sorry mess. Her normal shiny black hull was streaked with rust, her brass was tarnished, her rigging in disarray. In comparison *Tovarishch*, only twelve years younger, looked like new.

I showed my pass at the gangway and went aboard. A smaller ship, fewer crew and fewer trainees. With only seven of us in one living quarter I had my choice of bunks. I selected the one closest to the door. The air, I had learned on *Sedov*, tended to be a little fresher there.

Unlike *Sedov*, *Tovarishch* was a segregated ship. Male crew shared one dormitory, females another. There were five girls on board I was told. Also there was more discipline, the food was a great improvement and, of paramount importance, the plumbing worked. The only real drawback was a tiresome young German lady who was, we were told, in charge of the trainees.

"I vill now teach all off you to climb rigging properly," she announced in heavily accented English our first day at sea. She managed three or four steps up the ratlines, then one foot slipped. Before she could save herself she was tangled with one leg on one side of the ratlines and one on the other. On the *Sedov* such a manoeuvre was known as a crotch scraper. Somebody laughed. It sounded like me.

"It iss important to be careful alvays," she warned as she dragged the errant leg back into position. "This is not a choke," she added, looking directly at me.

"Ve must remember to move arms and legs at the same time." She raised her right arm and reached for the next rung as her right leg took a step up. It was an ungainly movement. On the opposite side of the ship a cadet ran up the ratlines. In total disregard for her teachings, he scuttled upwards like a crab on an important mission. I wasn't the only one to notice.

"He climbs better than you do," Tania spoke up, "and he does it differently.

"That is not correct, this is the safest way," with that assurance she took a few more steps, keeping both legs on the same side of the ratlines. I couldn't help noticing she looked uncomfortable, as if her jeans were too tight.

We humoured her for a while until Andrei, the bo'sun, asked for three volunteers to help change the flying jib. Tania, Magda, and I had our safety belts on before any of the others figured out what a flying jib might be. We left the climbing teacher with a depleted class.

The flying jib is one of four fore and aft sails which stretch from the bowsprit up towards the square sails on the foremast. To change it necessitates placing oneself as close to the end of the bowsprit as possible. All that separates the bowsprit from the sea is fresh air and a large net. The position is ideal for watching the ship and the sea. It was my favourite place, as it had been on *Sedov*. Perched on the end of the bowsprit, with feet dangling on either side, I felt as though the ship was a separate entity. It appeared to be about to sail right between my legs. I wondered what Freud might have had to say about that image.

Facing me, Tania sat astride the bowsprit wearing denim shorts. Freud would have had a field day. Tania had long well-formed legs, and a healthy looking body which had seen no more than twenty-one years. Under a cap of short dark hair she flashed lively brown eyes and a quick smile. As we worked she told me she was in medical school, training to be a doctor.

"Lean back a bit," I coached her into position for a photograph with *Tovarishch*, under almost full sail, looming in the background. "Your boy friend will like that one," I told her.

"I don't have a boy friend," she put the emphasis on boy. I looked at Magda, who stood on the safety net beside Tania. She smiled back and said, "Neither do I."

I had the distinct impression that I was not being offered an invitation of any kind.

"That's a waste," I said ruefully, wishing I was at least two decades younger.

"Two lovely ladies like you. Don't tell me the young bucks in Berlin haven't noticed you."

They both laughed. A look passed between them. Tania explained it for me.

"We have girl friends. Not boy friends."

She raised her eyebrows, looking at me thoughtfully. Andrei stood up on the bowsprit behind her. His eyes met mine. He thought he followed the conversation correctly, but he wasn't sure.

"Ah, yes," I nodded. "I understand."

"Are you shocked?"

"No, not shocked. Disappointed perhaps, but not shocked," I smiled with them. Not sure what else to say I made a feeble attempt to change the subject. "Which branch of medicine will you specialize in?"

I think I knew the answer before I'd finished the question. It was written in her eyes. Tania answered me with a perfectly straight face, "Gynaecology."

Andrei interrupted to show us a rainbow off to starboard: a colourful compliment to the stately old sailing ship. Suddenly the sailing alarm sounded — all hands required on deck. Andrei sent the girls who didn't want boy friends back and told me to stay.

"You finish here first." He hesitated, then, "Are they...?"

"Yes," I replied regretfully. "No men, just girls."

Andrei turned to watch the lithe figures climb over the bow to the deck. His expression, when he looked back at me, was one of great sadness. It mirrored my own.

While I completed the job of bending on a new sail, the yards swung through another ten degrees. I finished my job and returned to the foredeck. All hands were told to stand down. I went to the engine room for a chat about mechanics with the engineer. As I reached the lower deck the engine rumbled into life. The noise was LOUD! The engineer's knowledge of English was roughly equivalent to my Ukrainian vocabulary. I had a lot of questions to ask, difficult enough under normal conditions. In the bowels of a ship with an ancient diesel engine trying to shake itself to death, it was impossible. We resorted to sign language.

Our eyes and hand gestures talked for us. I wrote Skoda on my notepad and pointed to the engine. He nodded, took my pen and wrote the technical details for me. We both persevered. I managed to ascertain that the engine was in dire need of replacement. I never did discover its true age, only that it had been installed as a re-build in 1965. A slight bowing effect on the propeller shaft prompted another question. That too was in need of replacement. Much hard cash was needed to keep *Tovarishch* at sea. After half an hour my notepad was covered in scribbles and a sketch of the engine room. It was also smeared with oil. While we 'talked' the order came down the pipe for, "All hands on deck." I shook the engineer's hand, transferring a significant amount of diesel oil to mine in the process.

"Dosvedanja," I shouted as I left.

The wind had changed drastically. Instead of coming from the northeast, which was ideal for our course down the North Sea, it had veered through one hundred degrees. Cadets, crew, and trainees climbed the ratlines to furl all sails. No one followed correct procedure during the climb. On deck the fairy godmother of the trainees fumed.

"Why doesn't she just admit she's wrong?" Tania asked as she tied off a gasket beside me.

"It's beneath her dignity," I replied. "She told me she has officer status on board. I don't think officers are allowed to be wrong."

Once the sails were secure we lingered on the yard. The swaying of the ship was greatly emphasized from on high. It was a peaceful motion though the wind was blustery. Far below on the surface of the sea white caps formed and scattered. The bow wave flowed creamy and bubbly under the bowsprit. In our wake the disturbance of our passage reached back to the horizon.

The wind was stubborn. It refused to blow from the desired direction. Sailing manoeuvres in square-riggers like *Tovarishch* take time, effort and experience. The best a square-rigged ship can point towards the eye of the wind is about sixty degrees. To sail to windward she must be worked. In days long gone sailing masters kept moving forward, into the wind, by following a zig zag course, called tacking, to keep the sails full.

Tacking can take twenty minutes or more with all hands. In light winds, less than ten knots, a large sailing ship may not have enough momentum to complete the exercise. Conversely, in strong winds the foremast carries a vast frontal wind load when the sails are aback. Because the masts are braced from behind, that load has the potential to snap a mast. In strong winds and heavy seas, when tacking could be dangerous, a square-rigger can be put on the opposite tack by turning away from the wind through two hundred and forty degrees. This is known as wearing ship, an exercise which requires plenty of sea room and loses ground.

With a deadline to meet, Captain Oleg Pavlovich Vandenko was in no mood to tack all over the North Sea to reach Bremerhaven. The sails stayed furled, the motor kept running. We settled down to enjoy the last day as if it were a pleasure cruise.

WHERE DEATH RIDES A CAMEL

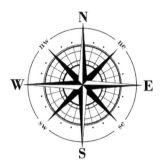

The bespectacled Malien student, clutching a ballpoint pen in one hand and a writing pad in the other, stood looking at our two four-wheel-drive vehicles outside the little hotel in Timbuktu. Others watched also, out of idle curiosity, because we were different from them. The student watched because he wanted to learn. Hesitantly he approached.

"May I speak English with you?" He asked politely, with an accent any Etonian would have been proud to possess. "For my education, of course."

I looked down from the Land Rover's roof rack at the intelligent face posing the question.

"Sure," I answered, "just give me a minute to tie this lot down."

He stepped back a few paces, still watching the activity.

"You speak good English," Lawrie told him in

Hassania, a dialect of Arabic.

"Thank you," came the answer, again in English.

I tied the last knot, jumped to the ground and dusted myself off. "What can I do for you," I asked.

The young man consulted his notepad. "Taoudenit is for slaves," he announced without preamble. "Why do you wish to go there?"

I glanced at Lawrie. His expression was as bemused as mine had to be.

"How do you know there are slaves at Taoudenit?" I countered. "Isn't it just a big open salt mine?"

"There are slaves at Taoudenit. Everyone knows that."

We had heard rumours of slaves at the salt mines of Taoudenit each time we mentioned the place. In Bamako, in Mopti, and in Timbuktu, the comment was invariably the same. "There are slaves at Taoudenit."

We were going to the mines, some seven hundred kilometres north of Timbuktu, to make a documentary film for Canadian television. A film about the mines and the camel caravans which carry the salt across the Sahara to Timbuktu. Our journey was no secret. Everyone in town, from street urchins to the Governor and the Military Commandant, knew of our plans. We were known to all and sundry as 'Le Mission Canadien á Taoudenit.'

The student did not fully understand why people in other parts of the world would be interested in, as he put it, "…Such a terrible place." He did admit, after a little prompting, that he would like to see the film and added that he thought many people in Mali would find it extremely educational.

We assured him that his government would receive a copy of the film to broadcast on national television. It was part of our contract. He acted pleased with the knowledge. When he learned I had been to Timbuktu many times before, and that I knew its history well, he was somewhat surprised and, perhaps, a little piqued because he hadn't met me on an earlier occasion. Another youth reminded me that I had given him a ride in my Land Rover when he was younger.

Timbuktu has long been a synonym for remoteness. Most people in the western world have heard mention of Timbuktu. Few know where it is, or anything about it, yet it has a fascinating history. The city, which dates back to about 1315 A.D., was a renowned centre of learning and a busy slave-trading town long before its name reached European ears.

In the eighteenth and early part of the nineteenth centuries, amazing stories of the incredible wealth to be found in Timbuktu finally began to echo through the great trading houses of Europe. The quest for Timbuktu was about to begin. There was certainly gold there once. Slaves were bought and sold; salt, cloth, jewellery, and food products were traded. The preferred medium of exchange was gold. In dust or in nuggets, it didn't matter much which, as long as it was gold.

By the time the earliest European explorers arrived, in 1828 and 1830, Timbuktu had long been in decline. The gold and the affluence were gone. Only the mud-brick buildings, the sand and the dust remained. And the desert was doing its best to reclaim them.

"Okay," I called to the crew, "let's roll. Bob, Guy, and Paul, ride with Daouda in the Toyota. Lawrie, Moulay, and Tyfor, ride with me in the Rover."

With excited children running alongside we made our way quickly through the dusty streets to the open desert on the north side of town: to the place where I had first seen a salt caravan a decade before. Rolling dunes and camel tracks disappeared through the acacia trees to the distant nothing. We were on our way, at last.

Days later I watched a long line of camels padding silently northwards, threading their way through the dunes. They were obviously bound for the salt mines of Taoudenit. They had to be: there was precious little else in that or any other direction.

"We'll meet them at Foum el'Alba," advised Moulay.

For centuries great caravans, laden with trade goods

for the miners and fodder for the camels, have trekked the ancient trail from Timbuktu to Taoudenit. Those same caravans returned along the same route groaning under the weight of large slabs of coarse salt. I had travelled the traditional trade routes of the Sahara for many years. Regularly I heard stories of the salt mines of Taoudenit, in northern Mali, and of Bilma, far to the east in Niger. My dream was to one day join a camel caravan, or azalai and travel to the Taoudenit salt plains, 700 kilometres to the north of Timbuktu. Occasionally I had seen half a dozen or so camels arriving on the northern outskirts of Timbuktu, two slabs of salt on each side of their bodies. I was always busy, with a group of my own, unable to join them when they made the next trek. Until...

...My early romantic dreams of riding with the azalai had, through circumstance, changed somewhat. Instead of sitting proudly astride a tamzak, a Tuareg saddle with a dangerously pointed cross immediately in front of my virtually unprotected groin, or settled in the winged rahala of the Reguibat, I rode in a reasonably upholstered car seat as the leader of an expedition. It wasn't that much more comfortable.

Behind us our tire marks stretched back over four hundred kilometres to Timbuktu. Ahead lay Foum el'Alba, the 'pass between the dunes,' the only route through the sand dunes of the Erg Atouila, gateway to the Krenachich Plateau and the salt mines beyond.

Off to my right a little and half a kilometre to the rear, our second vehicle chased my tail of dust. I swung the wheel occasionally to veer round small outcrops of rock, otherwise there was little to break the monotony.

Serif Moulay el Moktar of Araouane, Moulay to us — the expedition's guide, knew all the nomads on the route. We later learned he also owned many of the camels, and most of the chameliers worked for him. As Moulay had predicted, we met the caravan at the pass. It was no great surprise to learn that the leader was Moulay's brother. Following a brief stop to enquire after their welfare we had to move on. Salt was our priority and Moulay wanted to get to Bir Ounane, where we planned to stay a few days as all caravans stop there for water on both north and south journeys.

Moulay's presence was our advantage. The nomads, trusting Moulay, trusted us. Lawrie, our interpreter, added to the trust through his linguistic skills, and through the magic of his Polaroid camera. The simple gift of an 'instant' photograph made the difference between being tolerated — and being accepted, to an extent.

Although clearly marked on maps of northern Mali, Bir Ounane is nothing more than a deep well, with a low concrete surround, in the middle of a vast dry windswept plain. There is a second well close by, but no one used it while we were there.

A few large sand dunes partially blocked the wind but, like us, they too were transients and would not be there forever. It was a peaceful place, but dangerous. The nomads have a saying about this region of the Sahara: "It is so dangerous that here even Death rides a camel."

Tragedy has long been part of this inhospitable land. At night under the incredible brightness of millions of stars, we could almost hear the cries of the spirits of long dead caravaners who left their bones here after being massacred by marauding Tuareg. Legend tells that, in a caravan of ten thousand camels and many hundreds of men, all were murdered during an unexpected and unprovoked attack.

We heard the camels before the caravans arrived. A faint gurgling, the gentle rasp of salt against salt, the creaking of dry leather; the soft shuffle of the camel's pads: all the sounds carried on the wind. First came a line of ten camels and two men, heading south. A short time later a larger caravan arrived, also southbound. The two groups settled down together on the other side of a dune from the well, and from us. After unloading the salt and hobbling the camels to prevent them wandering too far, the men walked to the well. Seeing Moulay they squatted beside our fire and joined us for strong sweet tea. The talk was of the route they had followed, conditions at the mine, the salt and, of course, us — the foreigners.

"What will they do at Bir Ounane?" They wanted to know.

Moulay explained about the film. The nomads nodded wisely and looked at us curiously. When they drew water and filled their goatskin water bags, called guerbas, to bursting, they ignored us as we filmed and shot still photos. They left the guerbas on the sand and walked away. Later they returned with a camel and took the water to their chosen site. The camels were not watered at all, which we found surprising as they had already travelled a considerable distance. Perhaps they were offered a drink beyond our sight.

It's a hard life for these steadfast men. Rarely do they ride during their long journey. They walk ahead, or beside the caravan. One, usually a boy — or an old man, walks behind the camels to pick up dung for the fire. The daily routine never varies. The camels are rounded up and loaded in the morning, a laborious business which takes place accompanied by screams, gurgles, roars and grunts from the camels. Not the most tolerant of beasts, they object to being forced to do anything they are not already doing. Loading is anguish for them. So is unloading. Everything, to a camel, is a nuisance. As each item, no matter how insignificant, is placed on a camel's back, its bellow of despair can be heard echoing across the desert. Once loaded and tied nose to tail, they will happily follow the leader wherever he goes. Such scenes are enacted each morning and at midday, when the camels are all completely unloaded for a rest. Then they have to be reloaded. Before nightfall they have to be released from their burdens again.

Half way between Bir Ounane and the mines we saw a caravan in the distance walking on a huge lake. We stopped and watched as the camels and the lake got closer and closer. Eventually we heard the chameliers talking, probably about us, and the camels groaning. There was no splashing. The camels, somehow, were able to walk on the water without breaking through it.

"Great mirage," I commented to no one in particular.

The lake shimmered and gradually faded as the caravan took its rightful place on extremely dry land. Behind us a northbound caravan, one we had passed a short time before, caught up with us. There was much running back and forth by the chameliers, and by Moulay, between caravans, as important desert gossip was relayed from one to another, but the camels passed each other without comment and without offering recognition. No long eyelashes flickered, no snorts of amusement, no sideways glances. They simply kept nose to tail and savoured their own thoughts and a little juicy cud.

Leaving the caravans behind we followed the obvious camel trails north. As we drove down the long sloping dunes and through Foum el'Alous, we could see Taoudenit shimmering in the mid-afternoon heat across the wide salty plain. A haphazard collection of hovels, made from salty rubble cast out of the open pit mines, Taoudenit is not a destination for the faint of heart.

Our time of arrival was nearly perfect. While Moulay went off to pay our respects to the local garrison commander (a sergeant), we were treated to the spectacle of a camel about to be butchered.

The doomed beast was couched and hobbled. Unable to rise, it trembled and bellowed with fear and rage. From the slack appearance of the lower half of its face, it looked as though it had fallen and broken its jaw. Unable to eat, its usefulness was almost at an end. As the butcher approached with knife in hand the luckless camel struggled to rise. Instinctively I turned away: I had no wish to watch another creature's life end in blood-stained violence. The camel spat and raged to no avail, its desire to be somewhere else even stronger than mine. Against my more sensitive wishes, my mind ordered our eyes to watch the final seconds. Lawrie moved in close, camera at the ready, his photographic professionalism taking charge.

One man took the agitated camel's halter and stretched its head to one side, until it was parallel to the body and facing the tail. The rope-thick jugular vein stood out invitingly on the elegant curved neck. One quick slash with a freshly sharpened blade sent the camel's lifeblood spouting in gouts of crimson over the golden sand. I watched, my stomach rotating in warning. With a tragic moan, and a deep sigh accepting the inevitable, the camel's head sagged to the ground. Its eyes glazed over, the long dark lashes flickered and closed over the now sightless orbs. The camel's life ended.

Watching the camel die was one thing. Standing by while it was gutted and its secret entrails dragged into daylight for all to see was another. Already flies circled thirstily, hungrily, waiting for a chance to settle on the warm raw feast. My stomach did another revolution. I acknowledged the warning and left the butchers to their bloody task. I had other work to attend to.

As a child I really was squeamish, liable to faint at the sight of a drop of blood, particularly my own. In later life, travelling the world, much of that weakness was knocked out of me. I had caught and gutted fish for food. I had, on occasion, slaughtered and roasted junior members of the goat family to feed former expedition members. Somehow that injured camel was different. I realized, with sadness, that I felt sorry for it. Its only crime was a misplaced foot, a trip, a stumble, a broken jaw. A butcher. Death.

Within less than an hour there was little left to show that murder had been committed. All the meat was gone. Cut into family sized roasts, it had been carted off to a dozen or more homes. Camel steaks and stew were on most menus that night. The miners had fresh meat. We ate reconstituted freeze-dried goulash. The camel's empty skin was rolled up and taken away. Someone would find a use for that too. The butcher scattered fresh sand thickly over the remaining blood: most had already soaked in to find its own way to the salt layer below. Ashes to ashes, dust to dust, blood to sand.

Moulay found us an uninhabited dwelling with a small courtyard, well away from the other residents of that slice of purgatory. Whether our isolation was for our protection or for the miners' benefit we never discovered. In short order we unloaded the vehicles, stuck a Canadian maple leaf flag on the salty lintel over the door, and declared Canada House fit for habitation.

Our house was, in fact, just about the only habitable dwelling in our part of the tiny migrant town. All around us the houses were crumbling into ruins. Eventually they will disappear into the sands from whence they came. We discovered that, as the mining area progresses gradually eastwards, as it has been doing for a thousand years or more from beyond Terhaza, so the miners build new huts. Once the pits have been worked and emptied of salt, the houses and pits are abandoned to the fickle whims of desert weather. Building another house a few hundred metres away doesn't take long.

Life at Taoudenit is hard and lonely, with few distractions. There were no women there to demand attention. No enticing walks, no rhythmic buttocks or firm bouncing breasts. No flashing eyes so men might glance up from their labours and smile or whistle in chauvinistic approval. No distractions of the sensual variety, just backbreaking work from dawn 'til dusk. Most miners only stay for three months at a time; then they return to their families in the south. Only a few stay permanently and they, we decided, must have had little reason to visit civilization.

Most miners work in pairs, or in groups. A few work alone. At each arbitrarily selected area the miners mark out a patch of sand as large, or as small, as they require. They dig the pit with shovels and primitive pick-axes. The salt layer is usually found about one and a half metres down. The upper layers of sand, clay and impure salt are discarded around the rim of the pit, or taken away to build another house.

Once the pit has been emptied of unwanted material the bottom is levelled and marked with a rectangular grid. Each rectangle represents one bar of salt to be carefully pried from the bed. At this juncture the bars are about twelve centimetres thick, one and a half metres long and sixty-five centimetres wide. Using a sharp adze, the miners trim each bar to age-old specifications. By the time the delicate task is completed the bar resembles a slab of off-white marble, roughly three and a half centimetres in thickness. The finished slab is stacked on the desert above to await shipment to Timbuktu.

The precision, we were told, is of the utmost importance. Taoudenit salt is believed to have almost magical properties; consequently it is highly valued throughout West Africa and must be easily identifiable. West Africans consider Taoudenit salt to be a cure for most ailments from eye infections to syphilis.

Once the salt has been removed the empty pits are left for the constantly moving sand. The wind blows it through the air and whisks it along the ground, to infiltrate, settle and fill.

Bob, our film producer and a great believer in progress, refused to understand why the Malien Government had not attempted to improve conditions in Taoudenit, and for the miners.

"This is labour intensive," he announced, repeating one of his favourite expressions. "A couple of back-hoes and a fleet of trucks would soon turn this into a profitable venture."

Moulay, following Lawrie's translation, rose to the bait. "Many of us work as chameliers and miners. Modernization would destroy a way of life and the chance of employment."

He thought for a while, no doubt thinking of our long bumpy ride from Timbuktu.

"Trucks carry much more salt than camels can, it is true, but breakages would be high and Taoudenit salt is only valuable when delivered intact. If a bar is broken it doesn't earn as much."

The conversation swayed back and forth, with Moulay weaving a spell of nomadic commonsense.

"For me," he continued, "a camel is more than transportation. It serves as a protection against sand storms and the cold of the long nights. When it gets too old to work I can eat it. But," he added philosophically, "if I have a truck it would be expensive to buy and to operate. It would be smelly, noisy and uncomfortable and, if it died in the desert, I couldn't eat it, so I would die too."

For a long time we sat in silence, savouring Moulay's logic. We decided, although Bob still wasn't convinced, that the Government of Mali, which even depicts the industry on bank notes, had, in this instance, been wise in leaving well enough alone.

To reach Taoudenit we had crossed the Tanezrouft, which roughly translates as 'barren as the palm of your hand.' The fact that we had reached Taoudenit safely could not be allowed to lull us into a false sense of security. While the film crew wrapped up this stage of the story, my team prepared the vehicles and prayed for a trouble-free journey back to the Niger River. Once again we planned to spend a few days at Bir Ounane and again at Araouane. In between were long hauls over desolate terrain.

Unlike on the northbound journey, our southern crossing was plagued by mechanical problems and flat tires. We had no sooner crossed the plain from Taoudenit and begun our climb up through the dunes, when the Land Rover decided to quit. It wasn't a good place to stop, the sand was loose and we were in danger of sinking up to our axles. A quick check showed the carburettor was malfunctioning. I explained the problem to Lawrie.

"Can you hold that open while I drive up the rest of this hill to hard ground?"

"If you can drive with the hood open," he answered.

Lawrie stretched himself along one wheel fender, his right arm inside the engine compartment and his left holding on to an extremely hot metal hood.

"Daouda," I ordered, "you take the Toyota up and wait on top in case I need you. The rest of you guys walk beside us, we might need a push."

Our Africans watched with smiles of amazement and, I believe, appreciation as the Land Rover ground its way to the top. Lawrie didn't have anything to say, he just raised his eyebrows at me, wiped the perspiration from his face and grinned.

"Well done," I told him. "This won't take long."

I stripped the carb and cleaned it. As I was re-assembling it I told Lawrie a story about another desert driver, a former employee of mine, who assembled a carburettor incorrectly while repairing it. When he tried to drive he found the only way to speed up was to raise the gas pedal, instead of depressing it. To slow down, or reduce revs, it was necessary to put his foot hard down on the pedal. Needless to say he didn't drive the vehicle far in that condition.

After weeks in the desert the vehicles were tired and so were we. Tempers began to fray. Fuel was running low. We began to ignore each other in the evenings. Lawrie and I were used to being in the Sahara for long periods and used to the privation. The film crew were not. They were unhappy. We were due to meet an army truck at Bir Ounane in a few days; there would be fuel on board for our return journey. No one looked forward to hanging around waiting.

We picked up a chamelier from a caravan and took him to Bir Ounane with us to get water. His delight at the opportunity of riding in a vehicle suggested that it might have been his first such experience. His beaming face brightened my day immeasurably. On arrival at the well he immediately tossed his leather bucket into the depths. The water level in that well was about thirty metres down. The bucket, attached to a long rope, was allowed to sink, then pulled up, hand over hand, once full. He poured the water into a circular concrete trough and dropped the bucket back into the well. On the second toss, the bucket and rope parted company, much to his dismay. He stared at the rope's end unhappily, sighed, and made as if to step into the well. It was obvious he had every intention of sliding down the vertical shaft to the bucket, tying on the rope and, somehow, hoping to climb back out again. None of us thought it a particularly inspired idea. I intervened.

"Wait," I called, before his head disappeared from view. "We can do this for him."

While the young man watched in wonder, I

unbolted the towing hook from the Land Rover's front bumper. I passed the end of a rope easily through a bolt-hole and tied it off with a bowline.

"This should work," I said, hopefully.

Carefully I lowered the hook into the well, hearing a satisfying splash when it reached the water. After a bit of fishing, and rude comments from my companions, I managed to hook the bucket. Strong helping arms from others did the rest. Seconds later a full bucket of water rose over the well's rim, to the delight of the bucket's owner. Eagerly he untied the knot, poured the water into the trough, tied his rope back on the bucket and dropped it once again into the well. He was really happy that we had helped him retrieve his bucket, but it never occurred to him to expect us to haul his water. He could do that himself, and he did: by hand.

Filling the guerbas was simple. He took a small bowl, filled it from the trough and poured the contents into the neck of the skins until they were all full. They stayed there on the ground like bloated brown slugs with stubby legs stuck up into the air until the caravan arrived much later.

Caravans came and caravans went. We waited, albeit impatiently, for our fuel. The days dragged. There was nothing to do that we hadn't done the day before, or the day before that. The film crew became increasingly restless. Late one night Moulay's keen hearing picked up an unnatural sound. He stood up and looked into the southern darkness. A flash of light bounced off the top of a dune. Moulay looked at me with a big smile on his face, "Le camion, Tony!"

The army truck pulled up to the well about an hour later. The soldiers, on their way to Taoudenit to replace the garrison, had fuel for our vehicles, and dinner for all. Earlier that day one of them had shot a young gazelle. We barbecued it over an open fire. The soldiers, Moulay, Lawrie, and I carved off tender pieces of succulent well-done meat and ate them with relish. Our film crew declined the offer of a good meal, having some doubts as to the cleanliness of the meat. They missed a fine feast.

Once our tanks were full again we retraced our route to Timbuktu. The locals greeted us on the outskirts with great enthusiasm. They waved and shouted to us. We waved back, but we didn't slow down. I followed the shortest route to the town's only large shop, where reasonably cold beer was sometimes on sale. The shortest line between our position and the beer led through the garbage dump. I wasn't in the mood for detours, only minutes remained before the shop was due to close. I ploughed through.

Our two vehicles emptied themselves of five men (Moulay was far too dignified to join us) in a second. We left doors open and engines running as we swept into the shop, just in time. As it turned out we could probably have purchased beer at midnight if we wanted to, the manager was so thrilled to see 'Le Mission Canadien' back in town again.

Laden with precious throat-soothing sparkling fluid we strolled out to the vehicles. A small boy tugged at my sleeve as I deposited my treasures on the front seat.

"What?" I asked.

He tugged again and pointed to the front of the Rover. I peered round the door, letting my dusty eyes find the source of his interest. My right front tire was flat. The garbage dump had not been such a good idea after all. But, I did have half a dozen bottles of beer and I was rather dry.

I drove the final two or three hundred metres to the Hotel Buktu at a limp, with a smile on my face. There was gold in Timbuktu after all: a golden liquid in a long-necked bottle.

OF DUNES AND DENIZENS

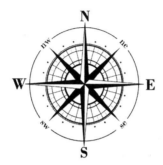

"Just follow the road to the end, you can't miss it."

I looked ahead to where the unpaved road aimed at the Atlantic Ocean. Before it got there it curved to the south. I went with it, turning the steering wheel lazily in sight of the sea. In a huge gravel parking lot, with my windows open, I caught the first of two indelible clues as to my whereabouts. The second assaulted me a fraction later.

First — the smell. Some smells — aromas, odours, scents, call them what you will — some smells waft delicately from source to sensor. Some drift competently, albeit with a certain urgency. A few rough tough hardy olfactory vandals invade with all the subtlety of a sledgehammer. This was one of those hardy types. It attacked from all sides at once. I sat, semi-paralyzed for a moment or two, trying not to breathe.

The second clue was the noise. Some noises are

soft. Some are sweet. Others are loud, though musically appealing. Then there are those that penetrate with the sort of raucous din usually associated with full-scale riots. The hubbub assaulting my ears that day was of the latter nature.

I quickly wound up the windows and got out of the car. The sound was even louder, the smell stronger. Casting fate to the onshore wind, I strode defiantly towards the thigh-high wall. There were supposed to be one hundred thousand of them waiting for me. I was a few minutes late. I hoped they were exercising patience. From the urgency and stridency of the voices I determined they were all there and getting unruly.

The scene before me resembled an open-air banquet hall filled with ill-mannered drunks. A burp here, a burp there. Here a burp, there a burp, everywhere a burp burp. Some were loud, uninhibited — the sort of stentorian rasps schoolboys dream of creating. Others were softer, a little more discreet. Not exactly lady-like, but discreet nonetheless. Clumsily the burpers staggered into each other and over each other. Impotently they glared, gurgled, burped again and fell over. After each burp, and there were so many of them, the air thickened with the overpowering stench of rotting fish.

There were big ones and little ones. Black ones, brown ones and some with a golden tint to their coats. There were males and there were females. Thousands lay on the beach sleeping, sun-bathing, arguing; loving. Thousands more frolicked in the surf, riding the ocean waves from far out to the point where the curl crashed to earth and disintegrated in a shower of foamy flecks.

I wasn't the first European to set foot on the coastline of south-western Africa. In fact generations of visitors have suffered, more or less willingly, for the privilege of viewing one of nature's great spectacles. The first known European to arrive was Diego Cao from Portugal. He landed in 1486 and had a cross erected in honour of his king, John I. The Cape fur seals, or eared seals, would have been there in the fifteenth century. Not the same ones, of course. But their ancestors surely made use of that crowded beach. I don't imagine it took Diego's crew long to put up that cross. It's not the sort of place a normal person hangs around for too long: unless they're like me.

Just offshore the cold Benguela Current drifts north from the Southern Ocean. As it passes Namibia it arcs west, out into the South Atlantic. The Benguela is rich in small schooling fish, pilchards among them, which play an important role in the diet of the rude, rowdy, repeaters. Scientists call them *Arctocephalus pusilus pusilus*. The fur seals don't care what they're called: they just hang out on the beach at Cape Cross, on Namibia's Atlantic coast, and belch whenever they feel like it.

Most visitors to the colony tend to cover their noses with any available material. They take a look, snap a photograph or two and make their escape. Even so it's a popular spot. The seals like it so much they don't bother to travel with the seasons: they just stay put year round. Visitors don't stay quite that long. Usually a few minutes, about as long as the average human lungs can last without taking a breath, will suffice. Only the exceptionally hardy, with no one important to meet for the next few days, linger and really observe the action.

I stayed for about three hours. I had a job to do. Gradually my nose became immune to the airborne onslaught, or perhaps it simply went numb after a while. I watched. I listened. I made notes. I took hundreds of photographs. My clothes took on a reasonable facsimile of the air around me.

The air, like the seals, has been there a long time. It has had time to ripen. The aquatic mammals make sure of that. Onshore breezes and offshore breezes come and go. They have little cleansing effect on the beach, the rocks, and their environs. The seals and the air they continually enrich keep each other company. Unlike true seals, which have no external ears, Cape fur seals do not migrate. Cape Cross, 115 kilometres north of Swakopmund, is their home and they tend to stick close to the place they know best. Occasionally odd individuals will take it in their heads to go exploring, but not many of them. An adventurous few however, tagged at another colony, were discovered at Cape Cross having made a sea journey of 1,600 kilometres. I guess they'd heard about the scenic delights of the cape and couldn't resist the urge to migrate.

Males, called bulls, don't spend a lot of time at the colony. They're happier foraging in the ocean. Around mid-October however, after months of supposed celibacy, the desire for female company overrules everything. Then, in the breeding season, they strut clumsily ashore — puffed up with their own importance and sensuality — and mark out their territories. For the next six weeks they are kept busy protecting their harems, of up to twenty-five cows, and defending their established domains. And, as if that's not enough for hard working males, there are all those females to service.

The often already pregnant cows come ashore after the bulls have negotiated their land. They give birth to just one pup. There's not a great deal of recuperation time allocated to the portly marine ladies though: no more than a week after the birth of his pups the bull mates with each member of his harem again. Perhaps it's the bull's chauvinistic way of expressing 'pregnant, barefoot, and on the… beach?'

In late November the pups are born. Weighing up to seven kilograms, they start to suckle almost immediately. They need to get to know their parents really quickly, just as the mothers have to be able to readily identify their offspring. Before long the cows must return to sea for days at a time to catch food. The pups stay on shore, wandering dejectedly through the herds crying bleakly for their mums, or playing with other temporary orphans. When the cows get back they find their pups by calling to them. The babies respond in shrill voices and the pairs waddle carelessly over any obstacle in their paths to reach each other. Inevitably the pups endure risky lives for their first year. With their mothers at sea so much the little ones are constantly at risk from predators.

At my feet the tracks of a black-backed jackal

wandered along the perimeter, mixed up with the much larger imprints of Homo sapiens. The four-footed predator had obviously taken an early morning stroll across the sand hoping to snare a tasty pup for breakfast. I felt a certain admiration for the hungry jackal. It would take great courage to dart into the heavyweight blubbery mob and snatch a meal. Some of the bulls weighed up to three hundred kilos. When a mass like that started moving and barged through the crowds, roaring with indignation, it was a truly awe-inspiring sight: like an out-of-control bulldozer.

The cows weren't so gentle either. They were all right when they stretched out on the rocks in the bright sunshine to catch a few warming rays. Once they started moving, and they were quick off the mark, anything in their path had a choice of getting out of the way, starting a fight, or being summarily squashed: another danger for an inexperienced pup.

I watched one young seal, flopping along on unwieldy flippers which were obviously much too big for him, trying to catch up with a couple of cousins. He bumped into everything between himself and his pals and yelled belligerently each time. He fell over near one of the grey-whiskered ancients and earned a smack from a wrinkled flipper, which helped bowl him along his way. At the sea, where the others were already happily hot dogging, he didn't hesitate: he plunged right in head first. The first wave picked him up and held him for a second, then it tossed him contemptuously into a maelstrom of white on the shoreline. The determined little pup didn't quit. He shook himself and went right back at that wave. Last time I saw him he was surfing with the supreme elegance of his kind.

Smelling like an overripe kipper I packed up my cameras and tripod, loaded it all in the car, and took off in search of new adventures. First on my list was a bank: money was running low. As I turned on to the Swakopmund road the lights of an approaching car flashed on and off. I stopped and leaned out the window.

"Can I help you?"

"Is this the way to...?" the voice tailed off while the

driver closed his eyes and sneezed. He stared at me. For some reason his eyes were watering. He looked like he was trying to hold his breath as he gasped, "Is this the way to Cape Cross?"

"Sure is," I answered leaning out and pointing back the way I had come. "Turn left and follow the road. You'll find it."

He shuddered in my direction and took off without a word of thanks. Instinctively my nose aimed itself at the front of my safari shirt. It didn't smell quite as clean as it had first thing that morning. Must be left over from Cape Cross, I decided and left the window open wide. That driver was in for a shock in a few minutes. If he didn't like my perfume he certainly wasn't about to enjoy the pungency of the seal colony.

You'd think bank tellers would be used to surprises, wouldn't you? So many different people pop in and out of banks. Even in a small town like Swakopmund the banks must have been visited by more than one walking anomaly. I strolled in as if I owned the place. It was large, clean, modern, and it wasn't crowded. Only three customers and four staff that I could see. Plenty of space for everyone there without encroaching on each other's business. Still, I couldn't help noticing a subtle change in the atmosphere as I entered. There was nothing too obvious. A wrinkle of a nose here, a handkerchief pulled hurriedly from a purse and held to the face over there. A shuffling side-step away from me by a prosperous-looking gentleman.

"Good afternoon," I greeted all politely. A few nods and furrowed brows acknowledged my pleasantry.

"May I help you over here?" A sweet voice called. I smiled and approached with my credit card in hand.

"I'd like to take out three hundred dollars please."

The young lady teller, no more than mid-twenties I guessed, flinched and turned her head to one side. Tears glistened in her eyes. She was the second person to get emotional at my approach in as many hours. Perhaps, I thought, something about me reminded her of her beloved father.

"I won't be a moment," she choked and hurried away, apparently overcome with emotion.

I waited patiently, tapping my fingers lightly on the counter top. Without being too obvious I strained my ears to catch conversations spoken in hushed voices. No luck. I went back to perfecting my bongo-playing skills.

You know that feeling you have sometimes? That little voice inside you which says, "Someone's watching you?" I had the feeling right there in the bank.

I looked round, half expecting to see someone I knew, forgetting I didn't know anyone in Namibia. I was being watched though. And not just by anyone. Everyone was doing it. I smiled at them. Hey, I was a visitor, a dual nationality representative of Britain and Canada. It pays to be polite wherever you are. No one wants to let their own country or, in my case, countries, down. As I said, I smiled at them. Straight faces stared back, as if in shock.

"Oh, right," I thought, remembering my sense of smell was temporarily paralyzed.

"Cape Cross," I said in explanation, pointing vaguely to the north. "I've been at the fur seal colony."

A few heads nodded in horrified comprehension.

"Sure smells up there," I added unnecessarily. The heads nodded again in vehement agreement.

"Here's your money, sir. If you'll just sign this." Sweet voice was back and standing as far from the counter as she could. I reached forward the full extent of my arms and signed the slip of paper. A thin wad of bills was dropped in front of me by fingers determined not to touch mine.

"Thanks, Miss." Still polite and businesslike, I stuffed the money in my wallet and turned for the exit.

"You can leave the door open if like," a strangulated voice suggested.

Namibia seems to alternate between being an empty wilderness, where the sun has scorched everything, and an open-air zoo. Some days I drove for hours without seeing a living creature. I'd had a shower or two, and changed my clothes, so the scarcity of people and animals had nothing to do with me, or the seals at Cape Cross. Then, just when I least expected it, there was proof the world was populated after all.

Cruising down the corrugated gravel, with a peacock's tail of dust billowing out behind me, I followed the road through a short canyon. On each side red and black rocks stretched up to stroke a cloudless blue sky. A break in the granite ahead showed a grove of trees packed into a fertile green triangle. It was occupied. A troop of baboons, like spectators at an important sporting event, sat on rocks facing the road. As one they turned to watch my car approach. I slowed down, planning to stop a few metres before them and capture their images on film.

Unfortunately I'd forgotten about the following wind — and my open windows. Within seconds I was enveloped in my own dust cloud. I coughed and spluttered as I peered through the gloom. The baboons glared at me in annoyance, rubbed their eyes, and slid off among the trees. One, probably the leader, stayed put. I raised my camera and pointed the long lens at him, hoping he would keep still until the dust settled. He coughed and spluttered in near perfect mimicry of my own outburst as he too presented his rear and fled.

"Ah shut up," I called after him.

I'd had a previous encounter with baboons. That was before the fur seal episode. I went looking for a troop deliberately. Baboons tend to keep to high ground. Rocky escarpments and cliffs are favourite stomping grounds. I saw a likely looking ridge one day and cut across country to inspect it.

Growling along in four-wheel-drive through soft sand I worked my way into a box canyon. Beside me a small yellow dune showed a trail of miniature footprints: baby baboon's prints. With steep cliffs on three sides I stopped and settled down on the hood of the car for a picnic lunch. It was quiet, peaceful and hot.

A sudden movement on the skyline broke the

stillness. A dark grey shape scampered along the ridge followed by a line of similar forms of varying sizes. The leader barked at me. I barked back as I reached for my camera. The big male baboon stood up and stared at me, a puzzled expression on his face. The troop gathered around him. Mothers, with babies hanging tightly from their chests, wrapped protective arms around their infants. Frisky young stopped playing to study the intruder from a safe distance. The rest of the adults watched warily.

The leader barked again. I stood up and barked harshly at him in reply. The troop fled chattering excitedly. The big male stayed right where he was. He scratched himself thoughtfully on his bottom, though no pleasure showed on his ageless pink face. He flicked a glance at his charges, now out of my sight, and back to me. He barked again. I answered, still standing tall on the Toyota's engine cover.

Disdain is not a word I would normally use to describe the expression on a baboon's face. Puzzled? Maybe. Bored even? Perhaps — complacent? That one, the big male, richly deserved my first adjective. He looked disdainfully at me for a long moment then turned on all fours. A bright red rear winked at me and, with studied insolence, he deliberately broke wind as he ambled nonchalantly after his companions.

Off to the west, far from the baboons, row upon row of great sand dunes form an imposing barrier between the land and the sea. Some are shaped like stars. Others resemble the crescent moon. All are spectacular. Experts say the dunes of the Namib-Naukluft region are the highest in the world. I couldn't argue with that.

Well before day break one morning I parked the Toyota in the shade of a large acacia tree. Alone I set off to climb a steep knife-edged ridge of cold sand. At each step my feet sunk in up to my ankles. Sand trickled into my desert boots. I leaned into the chilly wind and forced myself higher. My chest heaved with the exertion, my breathing noisy and uneven. My legs ached and persuaded me to stop a few times, while I wondered what the hell I was doing

out there before breakfast. Stubbornly I goaded my legs
into taking me to the summit. They did so slowly, less than
willingly. On top I sat down with my legs stretched out in
front of me, my back to the wind, and waited for the sun.

In the half light the dunes were grey, some darker
than others. They stretched in all directions, ridge after ridge
of centuries old wind-blown sand. Dunes like mountains
where no man had ever set foot. I wondered how many
there were and how long it would take to climb them all. I
wondered why I was the only person out there waiting for
the sun.

The dawn sky paled as Africa prepared to meet
the daily arrival. The dunes shimmered in anticipation. Far
below me, studiously feeding its face on a selection of barely
visible green shoots, a complacent gazelle took no notice
of the impending change. The sun's upper rim splashed an
erratic golden line across the east to announce its presence.
Without delay it climbed sensuously over a mountain of
sand shadowing the sky and beamed at the scene before
it. Streaks of pastel light raced across the dunes turning the
grey to pink and soft red. Gradually the sharp edges of the
dunes became clearer, the shadows more defined. At my feet
millions of grains of sand sparkled joyously like miniature
diamonds. The valley, where the car stood patiently like a
little red toy, looked far away as the light spread over it
turning night into day.

The wind stopped playing. Swirling into the lea of the
dune it hid from the sun's countenance, as if it should never
have been there in the first place. The sun climbed rapidly,
eliminating shadows and flattening the colours. Namibia
quickly warmed up. The show was over for another day.
I took off my windbreaker and ran back down the way I
had come. Slipping and sliding and sending clouds of sand
flying in all directions, I churned the formerly pristine ridge
into an untidy mess of footprints as I descended. The wind,
I knew, would clean up after me when it was ready to come
out again.

In the heat of the day, when sensible creatures
are hidden from the blistering heat, I walked — perhaps

struggled is closer to the truth — over a couple of well-rounded dunes to the stark white salt-flat of a small dried lake. Around the shores, like long-dead sentinels, a few bare brittle trees waited for eternity. Nothing moved, except the haze trying to obliterate the scene and erase my foreshortened shadow from the earth. There was a stark beauty about the tableau, conflicting a little with the thought that I was actually looking at Hell.

The bleached bones of an ostrich reminded me of the potential danger of being where only mad dogs and certain irrational nationalities go in the mid-day sun. My mouth went dry and my lips threatened to crack. I tilted the brim of my cap over my eyes, squinted against the painful light and headed for the safety of my car. I needed a drink.

Warm water from a plastic bottle, tasteless and unappealing, soothed my throat like honey as it trickled luxuriously down. Ahead of me lay a vast, mostly barren land of heat-shattered rock and scorching dust. I checked the rest of my water supplies before turning north for a date with one of the most expansive natural zoos in the world.

There's an enormous wildlife preserve called Etosha Pan National Park in northern Namibia. Covering thousands of square kilometres, it is home to 114 species of mammals, 340 different types of birds and over 50 reptile types — mostly snakes. Etosha means 'huge white area.' Nearly one third of the park is covered by Etosha Pan, a dry white salt lake. It is forbidden to drive on the pan, only native creatures are allowed out there and few of those bother to go. The stately oryx, impervious to the heat, goes anyway.

In one long day, exploring from sunrise to sunset without a break, the only well-known creatures I didn't see were cheetah and the nocturnal leopard. Known by my loved ones for an amazing ability to be in the wrong place at any time, I got mixed up in a brawl between two rival zebras. Showing a total disregard for me and my rented vehicle, those two stallions carried their dispute from the scrub to the track around my car. Hooves flailed the air wildly as the two stood on hind legs to fight. Wicked teeth bit into each other's necks and faces. Dust clouds pulsated around the conflict.

"Hey, watch it you two," I yelled out the window. "I have to pay for any damage to this car."

The combatants ignored me and continued brawling. Over in the bushes another black and white striped face watched. Coal black eyes, framed in exotic long lashes, took in every movement.

"This is your fault isn't it?" I called to her. "You started this, why don't you stop them?"

She shook her head once, lazily. Her long eyelashes fluttered appealingly at me for a second, then returned to her heroes.

Gradually the battle moved away from me and out of sight among the trees. The mare wandered off in the same direction; probably hoping the rivals wouldn't tire each other out too much before they remembered why they were fighting.

I should have been tired too after a full day of excitement, but the lights around the water hole at Okaukuejo kept me awake. Designed and positioned in such a way as to convince nocturnal drinkers they are natural, the soft yellow lights bathe the water and its visitors in an eerie glow. I sat under them and waited.

A noise like a far off avalanche echoed round the night. I opened both eyes, which insisted they had not been asleep. One closed again and had to be prised open by two fingers. The dull sound of pebbles being knocked together reached me. Intrigued I leaned forward searching the blackness beyond the lights. A huffing and a puffing and a stumbling and, I'm sure, muffled curses, came to me on the breeze. A rhinoceros staggered myopically into view, tripping over stones in the dark. It made its way to the water's edge without falling in, bent its head for a drink and stopped. With its mouth open and tongue ready for action it hesitated. The hefty elongated head, protected by a formidable looking horn, turned while rheumy eyes tried to pierce the gloom. There was a snort of annoyance, nothing more; then the rhino, still without taking a drink, crashed off into the darkness.

For two minutes nothing happened. No creature stirred. None came to drink. Like a great grey ghost, a huge elephant materialized out of nowhere on the other side of the pool. Without a sound it walked on tree-trunk legs to my side of the pool. She — it was definitely a female — flopped her trunk in the water and inhaled. Opening her cavernous mouth she turned the hose on herself and drank noisily. She wriggled suggestively, the folds of skin on her rear rippling like un-pressed corduroy in a strong wind. I should have known what was coming. In my youth I would have reacted immediately. Perhaps I was too weary. I stayed where I was and paid for it.

The elephant raised her tail and treated us late night watchers to a thunderous display of flatulence. I should have moved. I've seen people caught like that before. I didn't. The shock waves of warm foetid air, which had been fermenting deep inside the animal's being, hit me like a stack of manure being pushed by a hurricane. My nose tried to close: a bit like locking the barn after the horse, etc. My eyes stung and involuntarily I gasped, inhaling as I did so. I've done some really stupid things in my life, but nothing to equal that faux pas. I tried to breathe out in the same reflex and damn near choked myself.

While I coughed up all vestiges of her warm offering, the elephant continued drinking. Occasionally she turned her nether regions towards another part of the circle beyond the lights and treated someone else to a blast. As a change of pace she inconsiderately peed, then crapped, in the pool — and continued drinking. She was there for close to an hour, all by herself. Drinking. Farting. Peeing. Crapping.

Eventually, for no reason I could discern, she stopped slaking her thirst and looked back up the trail from whence she had come. I looked too. There was nothing there. Or was there? I heard no call. I recognized no sign. Yet, somehow, she had signalled the herd to join her. Nineteen elephants of varying sizes and stages of growth silently took up their positions. With trunks immersed they rudely aimed wrinkled grey bottoms at the human watchers. I wasn't getting caught again. I ducked behind the low retaining wall as a potent 'whoosh' scorched the earth.

A warthog came to drink, sensibly staying on the far side of the pool. Strutting self-importantly, with his tail stuck strait up in the air like an advertisement for the perfect penis, he ignored the guzzling pachyderms. A young bull objected to the interloper and splashed across swinging his trunk to chase him away. The warthog was smart; he went. Then I realized there were more animals out there in the night, all waiting their turn to drink. None dared, after the warthog's chastisement, until the elephants left.

The warthog and a couple of zebras drank together. A hyena, giggling hysterically over some private joke, followed. The rhino came back, still tripping over everything, still sounding out of breath. As the night wore on a constant procession of Noah's survivors stopped by. Then, for a while, there was silence. All thirsts, it seemed, had been satisfied. I dozed.

A rough cough woke me. I sat up straight and tried to get my eyes back in focus. A pride of lions crouched low, lapping at the water with long pink tongues. It was that time of night when morning is not far away and the dew lies heavy. The air had chilled. I pulled my sleeping bag around my shoulders and snuggled inside, still on my folding camp chair.

"This wall used to be lower," a voice near me said quietly. "Over at the other end it was really low. Until someone got killed."

I nodded to myself. I had heard the story earlier in the evening. Two Germans spent a night as I had done, wrapped up in sleeping bags and stretched out – in their case – on deck chairs. They slept right through the lions' drinking session and one only woke up when he heard his partner being eaten beside him. Apocryphal? Perhaps. However, the gruesome story helped people stay awake.

Once the lions had gone I left too. A short walk took me to my safari cabin. Seconds later I was asleep on the bed fully clothed.

There was tension on the plains later that morning. Delicate springboks, arrogant ostriches and nervous zebras, backed up by a brace of concerned giraffes, stood in a group watching death approach. Padding silently towards them in arrowhead formation came three lionesses. Well behind, resting under the shade of a tree, a long-maned male feigned complete indifference.

Relentlessly the three predators moved forward. The watchers stayed immobile. A few tails flicked at flies. All eyes were on the lions. All minds were wondering the same thing. Which one would it be that day? Which one would not live to see the sun set? As if on a signal the potential meals scattered.

One pretty springbok, less fleet of foot than the others, was quickly run down. As the prey fell under the three lionesses the male stood up and stretched. Without further ado he made his way to the kill and shouldered his ladies aside. No 'thanks for a good job' from him. He calmly took his rightful place at the head of the table and got on with lunch.

There was a collective sigh of relief from the ostriches, the other springboks, the zebras and the giraffes. With the danger over for a while they turned their attention to foraging for their own lunches. The giraffes stuck their necks out and nibbled on the top-most twigs of a tall camel-thorn tree. The zebras and springboks put their muzzles to the ground and sniffed out the juiciest blades of grass, while the ostriches loaded up with a few more stones to aid their digestion.

All that activity made me aware I was hungry too. I pulled the gear handle back, slipped the clutch, and went back to Okaukuejo for lunch.

SLOWLY DOWN THE OKAVANGO

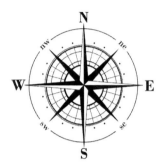

"How long have these boats been in use on the Okavango?" I asked of a well-dressed young African waiting for a ride across the river. He shrugged and laughed at my question.

"Forever," he replied.

We stood on the south bank of the Okavango River, in front of Kaisosi Safari Lodge, on the Namibian side, just east of the town of Rundu. One hundred metres away was Angola. The boats we discussed were at our feet: long slim dugout canoes, called watu in the local dialect.

The Okavango River begins its journey in the highlands of Angola, on the Plateau Bela Vista. As she flows south she is called the Cubango. Only when she reaches Namibia does she become the Okavango, and then only on one side of the river. For roughly 320 kilometres she forms the boundary between the two countries. At Dirica the Cuito River joins her and, united, they cross Namibia's

Caprivi strip to enter Botswana. Unlike its neighbour, the Zambesi River — which flows into the Indian Ocean, the Okavango will never reach the sea.

Flowing steadily south into the vast Kalahari Desert, the Okavango fans out into the largest inland delta in the world. Further downstream, as the flow weakens, the river exhausts itself in large salt pans on the thirsty sands.

Throughout most of its journey the river is home and work place to fishermen in dugout canoes. The only variation in the canoes, from one country to another, is the name. In Namibia and Angola they are called watu. In Botswana the name changes to makoro. Under either name, dugout canoes are probably one of the oldest forms of water transport in the world. I wanted to know more about them.

A long, almost straight finger of road stretches far to the northeast from Tsumeb to Rundu. In late April this road, which is normally quiet and traffic free, becomes heavily congested. Four-wheel-drive vehicles of all makes and sizes take up their positions nose to tail, following each other to Namibia's northern boundary. Behind each vehicle is a trailer carrying some form of floatable device. Many in the convoy started their journey as far south as Windhoek.

I found myself in the middle of the procession soon after leaving Tsumeb. Wondering what I had unwittingly got myself into I stayed where I was, knowing we all had to be going to the same place. There was nowhere else to go, not with a boat.

Helmut explained it all to me later, over a beer in the bar of Kaisosi Safari Lodge.

"It's the annual Rundu Float Carnival. This is the social event of the year up here."

I soon discovered it was little more than an excuse for a major drinking party with loads of harmless fun in the great outdoors. For over a decade the Canoe Club of Rundu has organized the event to raise money for charity. Each float and crew is subject to an entrance fee and additional funds are raised from a huge braai, or barbecue, and bar set up on the grounds of Kaisosi Safari Lodge.

Technically the carnival is a race. The rules are quite simple: be ready for the start at 08:00. Participation is at one's own risk. Organizers accept no responsibility for children, no speedboats among the floats, immediate disqualification for littering on the river.

Helmut invited me to join his crew on board the Kaisosi Safari Lodge float. I accepted gladly, for the race next day and a pre-race party that night. In the meantime there were those dugout canoes to find.

Three watu were pulled up on shore in front of the lodge, chained to a stake to prevent theft. On the river I could see a few more. On the opposite bank at least another four. In mid- stream a man was fishing, holding the line in his teeth as he paddled his watu to maintain position against the current. Coming towards me, just visible through the reeds, another watu was so well laden with passengers it looked in danger of sinking.

The local tribespeople, the Shambyu, cross the Okavango as and when they wish, without consideration for the imaginary border line snaking its way down the middle of the river. Seeing no obvious sign of officialdom on either side I decided to take a ride as well. After a short bargaining session which consisted of, "How much?" from me and two fingers from the boatman, I passed over two coins of little value. My watu boatman placed dried grass in the boat for me to sit on. I stepped aboard and made myself comfortable. Smoothly, with no sensation of a potential upset, he speedily paddled me across to Angola. His balance and dexterity with the paddle was impressive. I knew I would have to try it for myself.

Watu are carved from a single tree. The carvers favour a hardwood tree they call mukwe. Scientists know it as Rhodesian kiat (*Ptereocarpas ambolensis*). Usually one man can hack and carve a tree trunk into a serviceable canoe in about three to four weeks. For a quick build the sausage tree (*Kigelia africana*) is employed but, as it is a very soft wood, the boats do not last long. Silver-leafed terminalia and copal wood are both used as alternatives to mukwe, although they are only of medium hardness.

Most of the dugout canoes seem to be between three and four metres long and just about wide enough for the average hips. Some, I was told, are over half a metre in beam. Looking around at the slender trees on both sides of the river, I wondered where the carvers found such giants.

In some parts of the world, dugout canoes are fashioned by simply burning out the interior wood. Watu builders carve out the unwanted wood with a locally crafted tool called an okajimbo. Rather like an adze, with a rounded blade at right angles to the handle, the tool's head forms a large knob to add weight to each cutting blow.

The carver, having selected and felled his tree, quickly cuts the rough exterior shape of the watu with his okajimbo. The dimensions, of course, are limited only by the size of the tree. The exterior shape is the easy part. Carving out the interior, without cutting through the hull, takes a lot of practice. The okajimbo is an ugly tool but, in the hands of a master — it would appear — it can be as delicate a tool as a fine wood chisel. A glance at the finished interior of any watu would soon convince most sceptics of the wood carver's skill.

"Where can I see watu being made?" I asked my ferryman.

"Maybe along the river in some places," came the vague answer.

While we talked I watched other watu. Simple in design and effective in operation, they require considerable skill to paddle safely and efficiently. Over on the Namibian side of the river a pale-skinned visitor made a valiant attempt at propelling a watu across the Okavango by himself. He lasted exactly three paddle strokes before he capsized. With a narrow beam and a flat bottom, the canoe requires paddlers to keep a low profile until they become really proficient.

I tried my hand. The boat's owner sensibly declined the invitation to join me. Having many years experience with canoes in Canada, albeit of a more modern design, I managed to keep dry: just! The watu seemed to have a mind of its own and rocked alarmingly from side to side until I found my balance. On shore the expert laughed until his eyes shone with unshed tears as he viewed my efforts to stay upright.

Back in Namibia I went for a drive along a riverside track, in search of a watu under construction. I walked where the trail ran out. Nowhere did I see watu being carved. Perhaps it is not a profitable occupation now. There are many watu available, most in good condition, and not many trees of sufficient girth.

The watu (I was assured the name is both singular and plural) of Namibia's Okavango River are used as taxis and water buses. They carry freight and they carry passengers. Hospital patients have been, and still are occasionally, transported quietly and comfortably to their destinations. Men and boys fish from them. Children and dogs play in them.

Watu have been an important part of life on this great inland African river "forever," as I was told. I couldn't help wondering how much longer there will be dugout canoes in the region. There are not so many trees now, too many have been cut down for fencing villages; even more have fueled the cooking fires. One day, it is inevitable, the trees along the Okavango will be gone. As the existing watu age, the aromatic sandy coloured wood will turn grey. Cracks will appear. The watu will be abandoned to rot among the reeds. And the Okavango River will never be the same again.

With Helmut, I went to the rowdy pre-carnival party on the riverbank at the starting point for the race. It was noisy and crowded. The steaks were excellent. Wine and beer flowed freely, courtesy of the breweries and wineries sponsoring the event. Many of the crews, we noticed, were bent on going overboard before they even got afloat.

At daylight the early morning mist drifted smokily along the river. On the banks a scene of tolerant bedlam spread over the area, ignoring the dawning beauty. Hangovers held many heads in vices and bodies in painful, stomach-churning grips. My head was broadcasting a battle between rival drummers. Somehow, in spite of the agony, we managed to launch the floats safely. Right on time the participants pushed the cavalcade of multi-coloured craft out into the stream.

There's not much current flowing down that portion of the Okavango — only about two kilometres per hour. The sixteen kilometre course, consequently, takes all day to navigate. Soon after departure, crew from many floats dived overboard to swim alongside their charges. Some even got behind to give a helping push.

"Aren't there crocodiles in this river?" I asked

"Yeah, little ones about one and a half metres long, but they'll stay hidden today 'cause there so many boats," Helmut replied.

I wondered when the crocs were last measured: they could have grown since then. Some could be well on their way to reaching full size. No one seemed concerned, so I let the thought simmer in my mind, taking care not to fall over board.

It was hot on the river. Soon iceboxes were opened and cold drinks passed around. None of the crews had anything much to do, apart from keeping their craft away from the banks. The current did all the work. Even so, it was thirsty work just watching the swimmers in action; especially those trying to push. Thirsty work requires a thirst quenching drink, Helmut insisted on it.

To our left was Angola, to our right, Namibia. We switched from side to side as the river flowed python-like across the land. A breeze came up, catching some floats unprepared, forcing them ashore. It looked like tough going to get them back into the stream again, with wind and current conspiring to hold them among the reeds. Passing the mouth of a lagoon Helmut stopped sipping his beer long enough to tell me, "Last year the wind pushed us up there and we couldn't get out for over two hours."

Out in the middle of the river a kitchen table floated by. Around it the upper halves of four men played a noisy game of dice. A Volkswagen car, an old Beetle decorated in an eye-catching assortment of pastel shades, balanced precariously on a float jammed against the Namibian shore. A solo swimmer, wearing a safari hat and little else, splashed by. Whether he was trying to catch up with his team-mates, acting as bait for the crocs, or merely leading the way, we could only guess.

Two white canoes, joined amidships like a catamaran, moved up and down the river. On board the five judges made notes. Prizes, we knew, would be awarded for sportsmanship, originality and the best Crocodile Dundee interpretation. I didn't envy the judges the task of making the choices, particularly for the sportsmanship award.

Not being above bribery, like all the other entrants, we offered the judges a libation or two. Being men, and one woman, of high moral character they smilingly declined. I tried the sophisticated approach.

"You're gorgeous!" I shouted across the river to the lone female judge. She acknowledged my compliment with a laugh, a wave and an inverted thumb.

"Nice try, Tony," Helmut said. "Let's have another drink."

Standing shyly on the banks, or sitting among the reeds in their watu, Shambyu men, women and children, watched the activities with wide open eyes and mouths.

At midday and nearly halfway through the tournament, Rundu came in sight. On board barbecues began sending up smoke signals. The breeze carried wonderful aromas down river. Helmut did us proud. Restricted though he was within the confines of the float, he had prepared a fine goulash, liberally laced with his favourite tipple. Helmut believed in recipes with pizzazz: one splash of schnapps for each person on board, then the same amount into the pot. We followed that recipe religiously, long after the goulash was gone, until our eyes began to lose focus.

The afternoon sun beat down turning the river into a shimmering haze, further to confuse our optical apparatus. The temperature climbed higher. On the floats, the meals over, there was silence, broken only by the occasional burp and less sociable noises. Everyone rested from their labours.

The riot of colour, which had started the day so long before, stretched from one end of the course to the other. A reasonably wide awake, but rather drunk canoeist told us there were a few floats still caught by the wind on the first bend. We later learned the lead float had reached Kaisosi while we had lunch cruising past the halfway mark.

The sun was aiming for the horizon when we steered for harbour at Kaisosi. An impressive looking floating mine derrick, festooned with flags and bearing a crocodile figurehead, was already moored to the bank. On either side other floats, obviously faster than ours, were tied securely to stakes driven into the ground.

"We won!" the derrick's owner told us gleefully.

Far down the river, in the direction of the start, the stragglers could be seen and heard as they drifted lazily with the old Okavango. It was after seven in the evening when the final float crossed the finish line. No one, least of all the crew, could have anticipated the tumult their arrival would create.

Preparing to go out and greet the latecomer, a motorboat owner turned on his ignition. The engine exploded into flames. With great presence of mind the occupant threw himself overboard carrying his fire extinguisher with him. Up to his waist in water, he calmly fought the fire until it was under control. Seated on the bank, because standing had become a battle with gravity, we raised cold beer bottles to our lips in salute to a fine boatman.

The float race was not the only activity of the carnival weekend. The braai, ably supervised by Helmut, had its own highs and lows. High point was the steer Helmut cooked to perfection on a spit. Low point was the fist fight between two men. One, closer to thirty than to twenty, had been caught *in flagrante delicto* in the back seat of a car with a thirteen-year-old girl. Her mother's boyfriend dealt out immediate punishment with his knuckles. A few others intervened and, for a while, the scene resembled a good old western bar room brawl.

The final day of the carnival saw another series of

river events. The watu races were designed to sort out the men from the boys, or the drunk from the merely partly drunk. As I had learned, the dugouts are difficult to control when in full command of one's faculties. Nursing a monumental hangover or, worse still, completely intoxicated, did not enhance the paddlers' skills. Races between locals and visitors proved that a mix of enthusiasm and cocktails were no match for sober experience. The Shambyu, masters of their craft and the Okavango, won every race.

BY GHAZNI'S PILLAR

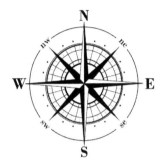

There's a sandstone tower looming up out of the desert beside a rutted gravel track. From a distance it resembles a giant grooved phallus. A short distance away is a second similar structure. Beyond, rounded blackish-brown foothills of the Hindu Kush are brightened by a line of white Arabic lettering carved into the flanks. It reads, 'Allah el Akbar.' God is great! Nearby a mud-brick wall encloses a small domed mosque, also of mud-brick. There's nothing else around.

   Two men walk slowly past. They wear the traditional loose fitting wide-sleeved shirt over baggy cotton pants, with the crotch hanging to their knees. One has on a pinstriped double-breasted jacket, with a long tear in one sleeve. On their heads and around the lower part of their faces they sport dirty white turbans. Their dark Afghan eyes roam over my dusty Land Rover and settle on me. I'm sitting cross-legged on the hood with my back against the windshield. My camera is on my lap, a notepad and pen in my hands. Their eyes meet mine.

"Salaam Aleikum," one greets me, with a perfunctory wave of his right hand.

"Aleikum asalaam," I answer politely, returning the salute.

They pass without further comment. Three dromedaries, one almost black — the other two the same colour as the desert, are tied nose to tail behind the men. The camels pad softly, breathing lightly and sighing gently. All three are heavily laden with what looks like carpets. A pushtin, a highly embroidered fleece-lined overcoat, is slung carelessly over one load. Tomorrow the cargo will be sold in the bazaar at Ghazni, before the men and the camels go back to wherever they came from.

The pillar of Ghazni, an ancient minaret, which I'm sitting beside, is an eight-pointed star in cross section. I tried to describe the pillar to an old man in a chai khana, or tea shop, in Ghazni yesterday. He had never seen it. Like me, he was a traveller. I came from far to the west, following the trail of Alexander the Great. He came from the north — from Mazar I Sharif. We both stopped for a few days to rest and to explore what is left of the glory that was Ghazni, a powerful kingdom which once stretched from India to Persia. But that regime was over more than a thousand years ago.

The old man, people just called him Baba (Father), spoke a little English, a little French, a little Russian. Mostly he spoke in Pushtu, the language of the Pathans. With the help of a young man, a student he said, Baba and I traded stories of the history of his land.

Baba claimed he was descended from Iskander: Alexander the Great. As evidence he touched his reddish hair and nodded knowingly. The roots were grey, almost white. The red was from henna, almost certainly as a mark of his having made the holy pilgrimage to Mecca: the Haj. His place on Iskander's illustrious family tree looked precarious to me.

"You are Haji?" I asked.

"Acha," he replied nodding his head vigorously. "Haji Baba."

He slurped his tea noisily. "Mecca," he said, pointing unerringly in the direction of the Holy site in distant Saudi Arabia.

The chai khana had seen better days. The wooden walls were cracked and faded with age and the combined efforts of external sun and internal fire. Two hard benches, made from the same nondescript material, lined two walls. A corrugated metal roof absorbed the sun's rays and heated the interior to furnace-like temperatures. Only a threadbare carpet covering half the floor offered a semblance of comfort.

The proprietor squatted on the bare wooden floor beside his stove, washing cups and glasses in dirty water. Occasionally he grunted at something one of us said. Across his face he wore a band of dirty cloth. Once it might have been white, before time, constant dust and dribbling mucus changed its hue. I realized the cloth was there to cover the cavity where his nose used to be. Last time I had been in that chai khana, about five years before, he had sported a normal nasal organ. Somewhere in my files at home there was a photograph of the man, smiling happily, as he made tea for me. I nudged the student and cast a silent question to him with my eyes. He shrugged, opening his hands eloquently to show his lack of knowledge.

"Syphilis, leprosy, I don't know," he answered quietly.

I looked down at my less than clean glass. Instinctively I threw the contents out the open door to soak into hard-baked soil. Without a word the proprietor took the glass from me and refilled it. With an attempted smile I accepted my fate. The tea tasted good anyway.

"Tell me about Iskander," I asked Baba. "I have crossed his path many times from Pella, in Greece, to the Punjab."

"Where in Afghanistan have you been?" the student broke in. "Iskander went everywhere."

"I have followed Iskander's march throughout Afghanistan," I told them, "from Herat to Kandahar to Ghazni, and all the way to Balkh."

"Iskander came to Ghazni?" The student seemed surprised.

"Yes, he rested his army here before taking them over the Khawak Pass of the Hindu Kush."

"Merde. Where is this pass?" Baba sounded sceptical. He seemed to resent the extent of my travels, as if they might overshadow his own.

"It is hard to reach. Over eighty kilometres northeast of the Salang Tunnel." I drew a rough sketch map of Afghanistan in my notebook, adding the Hindu Kush and well-known places such as Kabul, Herat, and Mazar I Sharif, to clarify the direction. "There is a turning to the right from the main road at Gulbahar. A rough track follows the Panjshir River to the pass."

"Merde. I came through the Salang Tunnel," Baba interrupted. "I came by bus from Kunduz to Kabul. It is easier."

I laughed at a fleeting image of Alexander's massive army travelling by a convoy of ramshackle Afghan buses through the modern tunnel. My audience looked at me in wonder, thinking, perhaps, that I was a madman. I explained the humour to the student. He told a Pushtu version without success. Frustrated he tried again, explaining in more detail. It worked. I don't know what he said, but it sent Baba into loud cackles which progressed into a paroxysm of coughing. When he'd finally finished wheezing and spluttering, Baba patted me on the knee and started laughing again. I called for more tea, "Chai, ishedeli ubuh," reminding the owner to use boiled water.

"You have been to Balkh?" Baba asked, once he'd regained his composure.

"Ten days ago," I confirmed. "In Iskander's time it was called Zariaspa. I think that's where he married Roxanne."

"Rushanak," Baba corrected. "Rushanak."

"Yes, her name could also be, Rushanak," I agreed.

"She came from the mountains to the north, from Soghdiana: that's in the Soviet Union now I think. She was the daughter of Oxyartes, a local warlord. Perhaps she was a Russian."

The effect of my last sentence was a bit like throwing gasoline onto an open fire. Although I expected a strong reaction, I certainly didn't anticipate the depth of their feeling against the Russians. Expressions of horror blazed across each face. Baba hawked and spat thick green phlegm on the worn carpet. Absentmindedly he rubbed it in with the sole of his bare foot. He shook a calloused index finger at me. His fingernail was long, chipped, and dirty.

"Rushanak," he coughed in exasperation. "Rushanak was not a Roossian. She was the most beautiful woman in the world. She was Afghan."

Apparently, in Baba's mind, Roxanne could not have been a Russian because she was beautiful: an interesting observation. I assumed he had more experience of that subject than I did and let it pass. All heads except mine bobbed in agreement with Baba.

"Afghani. Afghani," he began to shout in broken English. "No Roossian. No Roossian. Rushanak Afghani."

He swung one skinny hand as if to hit me, possibly only to emphasize his point. I lurched away and spilled tea on my pants.

"Shit, that's hot," I cried.

"Merde," agreed Baba, continuing to exercise his favourite French word. His eyes twinkled in amusement as he tapped the warm stain on my leg with his dirty fingernail again.

"Rushanak Afghani," he repeated. "No Roossian."

"You have seen Buz Kashi in Balkh?" My young interpreter decided to change the subject.

"No, I've only seen it played once. That was in 1973, at the big sports stadium in Kabul. President Mohammed Daoud Khan was there."

Baba hawked and spat again. "Mohammed Daoud Khan. Merde," he grunted, followed by a string of what sounded like Pushtu flavoured oaths. A general murmuring of similar sounds echoed round the chai khana. Obviously their current leader enjoyed a similar standard of popularity as their northern neighbours.

Buz Kashi is the national sport of Afghanistan. It is rough and it can be extremely dangerous to players and spectators alike. Legend says it was the inspiration for the more modern, more civilized game of polo. The contest I witnessed, in front of a massive crowd, was reasonably organized. Contrary to what I had heard about the rough and tumble tournaments, there was a vague sportsmanlike air about the event. In other words, no one was deliberately injured or killed.

Two teams entered the arena on horseback flanked by other riders carrying colourful flags. Behind them, towering above the stands, was an enormous colour photograph of Mohammed Daoud Khan. A stockily built man, with a completely bald head, and eyes framed by thick horn-rimmed tinted glasses, he looked rather too well fed to be a true Afghani. He reminded me of the actor, Telly Savalas.

One team wore bright red thigh length jackets. The other wore brown. Each player carried a short whip. At each end of the field there were two circles: one with a red flag in the center, the other with a blue one. An official dropped a stuffed goatskin, or perhaps it was a beheaded goat with the innards intact, on the centreline. The object of the game, as far as I could tell, was to pick up the goat and ride with it to the far end of the field, circle the flags, then race to the opposite end and deposit the goat in one of the circles. The rider brave, or foolhardy, enough to pick up the goat had to ride like the wind while fending off the advances of the opposing team. The whips, I noticed, were kept clenched between the teeth until needed, not to spur on the horse, but to slash at the competition. The rival teams had one thing in common: they were, to a man, the finest horsemen I had ever seen.

Many riders clamped the goat part way across their saddle and held it in place by tightening one leg over it. Opponents risked life and limb to tear it away. Even with a mob of thousands screaming for their favourites, the thuds of horse colliding with horse, of man colliding with man, and of man and horse slamming together, could be heard. It wasn't long before the goat was reduced to an untidy scrap of skin wrapped around a collection of mangled bones. The game went on.

The spectators, all men and boys, protected from the riders by a chest-high concrete wall, were not beyond danger. Three riders, two from the red team, one from the brown, struggled with each other for possession of the scruffy remains of the goat while riding at full speed a hair's breadth from the white-washed wall. Behind them, at the gallop, came the rest of the field. The brown, who dangled most of the goat from his right hand, was forced to make a decision: crash into the wall or jump it. His horse decided for him. With a spectacular leap it cleared the barrier pursued by one of the reds who was still hanging on to one of the goat's legs.

Suddenly there were half a dozen wild riders on the spectator's side of the wall and the remainder on the other — all travelling at full speed. Pandemonium ensued. Those watching in the front row threw themselves as far backwards as possible. Those behind leaned forward to catch the action. Hooves pounded where sandaled feet had been seconds before. The spectators clung to each other to avoid falling under the stampede.

Two teenage boys, dislodged into the path of certain death, with no chance of being rescued by the crowd, jumped the wall with the intention of reaching the temporary sanctuary of the field. One was knocked aside by a horse and bowled like a ragged ball under the flashing hooves. As one the following horses bunched their muscles and cleared the prone figure. The second boy, realizing he couldn't get to safety, jumped back onto the wall and hurled himself into the arms of men about three rows back. Just in time. The two teams thundered past, still fighting for the goat.

Out on the edge of the field in a cloud of thick dust, rising like a phoenix from the ashes, a boy got to his feet. Discovering that Allah had not called him: that he was still alive and relatively unhurt, he waved both arms at the crowd to acknowledge their applause. He took a quick look to see where the horses were, found he had time on his side, and sauntered casually back to the stands. His arrogance, considering his recent escape, was comical — and impressive.

Less structured Buz Kashi tournaments are held on open fields in the north. There are no restrictions on the number of team members. Anyone who can ride, and who believes in his own immortality, is welcome to join in. Injuries are common and death is not unknown. The standard of horsemanship, I suspect, would be among the highest in the world.

Baba and two other tea drinkers talked animatedly about Buz Kashi events they had witnessed, after hearing my story. The wildest versions, Baba insisted were held on the plains outside Mazar I Sharif, where the sand-laden winds blow unceasingly from the Hindu Kush to the Amu Darya River — the Oxus of old. The student, however, was more interested in me than in Baba's reminiscences.

"Where you will go from here?"

"To Kandahar, then to the Dasht I Margo and the Helmand River."

"Why do you go so far?"

"Because I'm interested. I want to visit Qilai Bost, the great arch. It's the only thing left of what was once a fine city, second only to Ghazni."

"Do they have minarets there, like the two here in Ghazni?"

"I don't think they're minarets...," I started, about to discuss the differences between minarets, towers, and pillars. I recognized the effort would not be worthwhile. "No," I changed my tack, "there are no towers, or minarets, left — not like Ghazni anyway."

Baba asked how he could get to the towers of Ghazni. The student told him he could walk there in less than half a day.

"No, it's not far. Just outside the town. I'll take you there tomorrow, in the morning," I heard my voice offer.

I collected Baba from the chai khana in mid morning, as we had agreed. He wasn't alone. The student was there, as was one of the inmates of the previous day. Each was ready for a ride in the country. I think they were all disappointed when they found out the drive was only of a short duration.

Baba studied the circular pile of broken rocks supporting the first handsome pillar: the minaret of Sultan Masud III. His eyes lifted up to examine the intricate detail carved on the six separate layers comprising the whole unit. He stepped back a dozen paces, the better to see the top. The cap appeared to be made from small sheets of galvanized tin. Baba grunted in approval. The fact that at least two of them were loose and flapping in the wind made no impression on him. He walked right round the pillar, his lips moving constantly. I wondered if he was praying, or whether he was simply counting the number of missing bricks, as I had once done.

"Who built this?" He asked, indicating the monolith with one hand. "Iskander?"

"No, not Iskander. This was built more than a thousand years later. I don't know who by," I replied honestly. "It was even here before Genghis Khan came by."

Baba looked thoughtfully at me. He started to ask another question but changed his mind. Perhaps he knew I didn't have the answer. Eventually, satisfied with his visit, Baba stalked back to the Land Rover and took his seat. The three of us followed obediently. I took them on a cross-country sightseeing tour over rough ground to regain Ghazni by a different entrance. Outside the chai khana once more my passengers alighted, greeting the owner affectionately as if they had returned from a long mystical journey.

"Chai, Mister Tony," Baba instructed, pulling me by the sleeve.

Now, in the heat of the afternoon, I'm back at the minaret, or pillar. I've parked the Land Rover in the shade, so I don't get burned to a crisp. I need to scribble my memories of the last two days in my notes before time dulls their edge and my mind changes the sequence of events.

As the sun creeps round the ancient monolith, moving its light over my legs, I finish my entry. One last look up at Ghazni's pillar, before I get in the driving seat, turn the key to make the motor purr, and let in the clutch. Ahead, many kilometres away to the southwest there is another desert. One I have not yet properly seen.

FOUR WHEELS TO IRAN

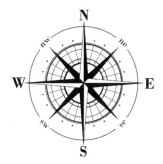

"Did you bring me a present?"

The question came from a scruffily-dressed Afghan kid of about thirteen years old. Standing as tall as he could he still had to lean back to look up at me. An 'employee' at the customs post on the Afghan side of their border with Iran, the midget menace had a far ranging reputation for causing trouble. I had run into similar pests in half a dozen other countries.

"No!" My answer was much shorter than he was and definitely intended to forestall any attempts at corruption.

"You give me a present like everybody else, or I'll have your truck stripped to the ground!"

Now there's a threat one doesn't hear every day. I've received similar warnings, particularly in Algeria, though usually presented with a little more subtlety. My patience was rather thin that late summer day. I replied with a well-worn Anglo-Saxon expression suggesting he should try to have carnal knowledge of himself.

"Help me," he ordered

I howled with laughter. "No thanks Kid, I'm not interested in little boys."

"Help me get in the truck!" He shouted, pulling on the door handle with all his immature might.

"It's locked."

I balled my fist and took hold of the front of his grubby shirt. With a less than gentle movement I swung him unceremoniously aside and reached for my keys. As soon as the door was unlocked he scrambled up into the driving seat. He leaned over and looked in the glove compartment. It was empty. One hand went under the seat and fished around. It came up with nothing.

"Where's my present?"

"Out," I thundered, assisting his exit with one hand. "There are no presents."

I locked the door again. Clutching him by the scruff of the neck, high enough so that he had to walk on tiptoe, I dragged him into the office.

"This little bastard is demanding a bribe, a little baksheesh, or he'll have my truck stripped," I told the uniformed official behind the desk. I still held the offensive little monster by his neck. He struggled, so I shook him.

"That's my son," the seated customs officer advised quietly.

I looked at the kid, then back to the officer. There was a slight resemblance but, as the boy wasn't old enough to grow a moustache, and his father sported a magnificent example, I wouldn't have guessed they were related.

The exclamation, "Oh shit!" went through my mind.

I opened my fingers and let the evil creature drop. He had the gall to smile at me, knowingly. His father's expression, which had been stern when I marched in, had not changed. He lit a cigarette, his eyes watching mine.

It was time to change my approach. As politely as possible I requested the services of a full-time customs officer to inspect my Land Rover and its contents. The officer reached out towards the breast pocket of my shirt and snapped his fingers. Obediently I pulled out a packet of Camel filters and pointed the open pack at him. He took it, turned it one hundred and eighty degrees, offered me one of my cigarettes. I took it, noticing my fingers weren't shaking as much as they should have been under the circumstances. He flicked open his Zippo lighter and held the flame up to my cigarette. I inhaled, managed not to cough, and thanked him. The smokes, my smokes, disappeared into his pocket. He took his eyes off me for a second and glanced at his son. A look passed between them which, as far as I was concerned, could only spell trouble for me. The kid went out.

I wasn't too worried that the teen terror might do something drastic to my property. Not yet anyway. The Land Rover was safe as long as I played along with the game.

"Passport." The officer's hand reached out to strengthen the demand. I placed the requested document on his upturned palm. He motioned me to a chair with a wave of the other hand. For the next ten minutes he studied each page of my passport. I stubbed the remains of my cigarette into his ashtray and waited to learn my fate.

"You have been here before," he said without looking at me. It was a statement, not a question. I guessed he was reading an old visa entry.

"Yes, a few times."

"You like Afghanistan?"

"Yes, I do," I replied honestly, although at that point I would rather have been anywhere else in the world.

"Why do you come here?"

"I like it here. Sometimes I bring tourists from Canada, and other countries."

"Why?"

"It's part of my job, my business. And it makes money for Afghanistan too."

"You know Afghanistan well?"

I had a distinct feeling I was being led, by the nose,

into a trap. I couldn't see any way out of it. Lying about my knowledge of his country was pointless. He could see from the stamps in my passport that I had travelled extensively in Afghanistan.

"Yes, I know it quite well." I stepped neatly into his trap.

"Then you know of our customs?" He smiled for the first time, pleased with his side of the conversation. I nodded my head in agreement, a few times: too many times. Not so excited about my side of the discussion.

"You are familiar with baksheesh?" He slipped the question from oily lips. The trap closed. I opened my mouth to answer but he held up his hand for silence.

"We are a poor country," he began to tell me his favourite sob story. "It is not so much to expect a little something from wealthy Americans."

"Expecting a little something from wealthy Americans is fine with me," I agreed. "I'm not wealthy, and I'm not American."

"It is the same thing," he said, apparently unaware of the non sequitur, as he lit another of my cigarettes.

"I only believe in baksheesh when someone does me a personal service," I decided to go for broke. "If someone asks for baksheesh, without doing anything to justify the demand, my answer is, 'no.'"

"How many people with you?" The abrupt change of subject, no doubt calculated to throw me off, attacked my defenses inexpertly.

"None. I'm travelling alone to Teheran."

"That is a long way. You have business in Iran?"

"Yes, in Teheran."

He scribbled something illegible in my passport. Taking his time he ordained it with purple ink from a rubber stamp to make it official. The smoke from his cigarette curled impatiently towards the blackened wooden ceiling. He snapped my passport shut and held it out to me, looking up as he did so. The smile was gone. I held my breath. His eyes narrowed. "Go," he said, indicating the door, and turned away.

"That was close," I muttered as I walked back into the sunlight.

"Look over there," said a voice with an Australian accent. Its owner pointed to the earthen inspection pit. A four-wheel-drive Bedford truck was slowly being guided into position over it. The driver looked suitably worried. A familiar looking scruffy Afghan kid, aged about thirteen, held up his hand to stop and said something to another Afghan who stood ready with a handful of tools. The driver of that truck was in for a long day. I left him to it. Afghanistan and the Islam Qala border post, as far as I knew, were behind me for another year or so.

For some time the word on the road told that Iran was heading for revolution. The unpopular Shah and his family still clung to power, somehow, but time was running out for them. Riots had broken out that May. I didn't really have much desire to be in the country when the uprising took place. I was on my way back to Europe and, after a final tour of Iran en route, had no concrete plans for a return visit.

The Iranian Customs and Immigration posts were models of efficiency in those days. All officers wore smartly pressed uniforms. They were polite and conscientious. I expected a quick passage through the familiar border at Taybad.

The senior immigration officer, a man I had shared tea with on previous visits, was surly. He checked my visa, stamped my passport and scribbled miserably into it — taking up a complete page. I was not perturbed. It was common practice to stamp an image of a car in a driver's passport and record all relevant details, to prevent he, or she, leaving the country without the vehicle. A full written description of the car, truck or bus, was added in pen.

"You are going where?"

"Teheran, Isfahan, Shiraz, Bandar I Shapur, Ahvaz, Hamadan, Kermanshah, Tabriz, then to Turkey," I rattled off the names.

"You have five days to get to Turkey," he finished his inscription with a flourish and closed my passport.

"That's ridiculous," I argued. "I'm here for three weeks. My permit is valid for three months from date of arrival. I can't get to Turkey in five days. I have work to do."

"Five days," he insisted. "Go!"

His expression told me further argument was useless. I decided I could probably get an extension in Mashad, the first city along the road. I left the office annoyed, yet hopeful. A customs officer followed me to the Land Rover. Ominously he buckled on a belt of tools as he walked.

"Take everything out," he said without preamble. His name tag identified him as Abdullah. I pulled out my kit bag, toolbox, two rolled Tibetan rugs and my camera bag: the only contents. On the roof rack my tarpaulin was tightly rolled and stowed. Without being asked I opened my bag. Abdullah ignored all my possessions. Something else had attracted his attention.

One front tire had developed a bulge where the wall was beginning to give way. I had intended changing it during an overnight stop in Mashad. Abdullah knelt by the bulge and probed it with a finger. Nodding to himself he took out a screwdriver and, before I could stop him, stabbed the bulge. As the air rushed out he sniffed at it, sampling the nuances. The Land Rover settled ungainly to one side.

"Thanks a lot," I said. "That's good Indian air you're letting out."

He was looking for drugs of course. Hiding illegal packages in tires was a well-known way of smuggling in the Middle East. Abdullah was wasting his time on my vehicle. I think he knew it and was disappointed. He showed it by letting all the other tires down as well, on the pretext of inhaling more Indian air. I didn't tell him that one was from Nepal, and two others contained fresh air from northern Afghanistan. He probably wouldn't have appreciated the differences.

On the engine cover a final wheel lay silent, hoping to be ignored. Having reduced me to white-faced anger, and a long job of re-inflation, the officer was still not content. He looked at the spare wheel and made a slight motion with his head. It said, quite effectively, "Take it off."

I unbolted the hub and rolled the wheel, none too carefully, at him. He let the air out of that one too, without even smelling it. Good Himalayan air from Kathmandu, and he ignored it. The man obviously had no class.

"Okay," he told me, "finished. You can go."

It takes a long time to pump up five large tires. I snarled something rude, un-Christian, un-Islamic, at him, in rapid English. He either didn't understand, or chose to play deaf. I had a compression pump with me. All I had to do was remove one spark plug and put the pump in place, the engine did the rest. It was still a slow process.

Considerably later, driving through the Djam Valley, between brooding hills, I was still steaming at the injustice. By the time I reached Mashad night had fallen. I went straight to the campsite. Officialdom could wait until the morning.

By daybreak I was rested and in a better frame of mind. It didn't help. I achieved nothing. As I gradually worked my way up the ladder of hierarchy I was conscious of my five days ticking steadily away. Everybody was sympathetic.

"There is no reason to restrict your stay," I was told at each level.

"Good, then if you'll just make a note to that effect here," I pointed to a blank area in my passport. "I'll be on my way."

Each time I was rewarded with a smile and a look offering little encouragement. "It is impossible to change. The decision was made at Taybad."

Finally, in disgust, I gave up. Another half day wasted.

For more than four decades overlanders have driven the long and exotic route from London to Kathmandu. They've travelled by truck, coach, double-decker bus, minibus, a variety of makes of 4 x 4s, private cars and motorbikes. Most have successfully navigated the potholes, pitfalls, and border formalities. A few, who succumbed to the lure of transporting illicit drugs for profit, have grown considerably older as unwilling guests of less than sympathetic nations.

I've driven the route on paved roads for much of the way. I've also driven all the way from central Turkey to India without ever allowing my wheels to touch a sealed road.

The Middle East is a magical collection of countries where history and strange cultures beg to be explored. Forget politics for a while, if you can. Take a magic carpet ride to yesterday.

The only predictable fact about the Middle East is its unpredictability. There's a surprise around every corner. I've been trapped by monsoon floods in the Indus Valley, caught in a tribal skirmish near the Khyber Pass, been held under virtual house arrest during a little uprising in Kabul, and survived the early days of the war in Lebanon. I've been arrested (I was innocent!) for minor traffic violations in Syria, Iraq, and India. I've lived through earthquakes in Shiraz and Teheran, and suffered from debilitating stomach disorders along the way.

Iran was always a favourite destination for me, before the Shah and his family were hustled out of the country. It wasn't as wild, as untamed, as exciting, as its neighbour — Afghanistan. It had more than its share of history though. And surprises. The surprises tended to spring up while travelling between bouts of soaking up volumes of the past.

Iranian towns were clean and orderly. The approach roads edged in white and bordered by immaculate flowerbeds. Invariably, each was decorated with a concrete plinth — topped by the mangled remains of a car or truck. None of those visually explicit warnings had much effect on Iran's homegrown drivers. Their macho mentality, combined with an immense faith in Allah and a complete disregard for driving etiquette, often proved fatal.

One young lady, who travelled with me by road from Istanbul to Teheran, complained of nightmares for months after she returned home. Each night she dreamed of huge trucks, racing side by side on a two-lane road, hurtling towards us. I understood that. I've had the same nightmare. Taking evasive action and abandoning the road or track in favour of adjoining fields or desert scrub, was a recognized way of avoiding devastating confrontations.

It was not unusual, late at night on a lonely Iranian road, to be suddenly blinded by a pair of blazing headlights only metres away. That illuminating phenomenon was the result of uneducated drivers misunderstanding the functions of their vehicles. They all knew through bitter experience that leaving the lights on drained the car's battery. Many were unaware that the engine had anything to do with the battery's power. So they drove without lights to conserve the battery! The sudden flash, when close to a previously unnoticed approaching vehicle on a dark night, was either to warn of another's presence, or to say, "Turn your lights off, you're wasting your battery!" The effect was not calculated to improve one's nervous disposition.

Night or day, and it should be stated that we avoided driving at night whenever possible, potential hazards kept all overlanders alert. Maniacal drivers competed with monster trucks desperately avoiding camels, sheep, goats, and donkeys rambling unconcernedly across roads. At night, animals settled down on the pavement to sleep. Water buffalo, dark enough in daylight therefore impossible to see after sunset, have been known to stand motionless across the centre of two lanes. In central India I almost ran over an old man sleeping on the road. He felt it was safer than sleeping in a ditch with the snakes.

In retrospect, although it was frightening at times, it probably wasn't as dangerous as driving on a modern multi-lane highway in Europe or America. Back in the 1960's the best that could be said of the route was that, "In some places the gravel was quite stable." There wasn't much traffic back then: the truck convoys were still about ten years away.

Crossing borders took almost as long, without the traffic. But, that had more to do with inexperience, mingled with curiosity, on the part of the officials rather than the long queues of trucks which characterized later years.

In direct contrast to the mundane — the traffic and the noisy bustling cities such as Istanbul, Baghdad and Teheran — there was that magic. The land was old when Alexander the Great marched his vast armies through, three centuries before the birth of Christ.

In the deserts ancient caravanserais lie empty, their walls crumbling to dust. Once the sandy courtyards rang with merchants' voices, the bellowing of camels; the laughter of children. Those fortified wayside inns, standing one day's camel march apart, are rarely visited now. Few are prepared to spend a night with the ghosts of the enormous trading caravans which, in their time, passed the hours of darkness within the safety of the walls.

An hour's drive north of Shiraz stand the great ruins of Persepolis. Built by Darius I around 510 BC and sacked by Alexander and his army a couple of centuries later, Persepolis is one of the most magnificent archaeological sites in the world. Close by at Naqsh I Rustam there are four immense tombs carved into the cliff. They house the mortal remains of Darius I, Xerxes, Artaxerxes, and Darius II. Below are later bas reliefs from the Sassanian era. Across the road, at a spot marked Nagsh I Rajab, I found a beautiful rock carving of a helmeted face and an elegant hand. Further north at Pasargadae the granite tomb of Cyrus the Great stands alone in a valley. Spread out across Iran, there are many such sights. I was looking forward to seeing them again — if I could sort out my visa problems.

I arrived in Teheran determined not to take no for an answer. The routine was the same as in Mashad: start at the lowest official on the totem pole and work up. They were all so polite. They smiled at me, offered me tea. They shook their heads and said, "Sorry, it can't be done."

I demanded, begged, pleaded for an audience with the senior immigration officer. He was busy of course. I waited. I drank so much tea I had to go in search of a toilet. When I returned I discovered the all-important officer had gone out.

"When will he be back?"

"Soon, Insh'Allah." If God willed. It was, and

probably ever will be, the standard answer to any question regarding time in the Middle East.

I waited some more. The man came back, as God had obviously willed. Perhaps God was on my side and had sent him back for me. My silent blasphemy did not go unheeded.

"This is most irregular," he apologized "There was no reason to do this. You are allowed to stay here for three months, if you wish."

"Great," I got quite excited. "Now, if you'll just make a note to that effect here so I won't have any trouble when I try to leave the country."

He looked at me in horror. "I can't do that."

"Why not? You just said I'm allowed to stay here for three months. Insh'Allah." I threw the last bit in hopefully.

"Mister Anthony," he said, reading my name from my passport and only getting part of it as usual, "much as I regret this, I cannot possibly countermand one of my officer's decisions. He must have had a good reason."

As he uttered the last seven words he looked at me speculatively, wondering what heinous crime I might have committed.

"There was no reason. He was just in a bad mood."

The man shrugged in the eloquent way of the east and excused himself. An underling showed me out. As a last ditch attempt I held my passport open.

"I don't suppose you'd like to…?"

He smiled and shook his head.

I drove to Turkey without seeing my favourite archaeological sites again. The Turks invited me to stay as long as I wanted to. I accepted.

On January 16, 1979, a few months after I crossed into Turkey, the Shah and his family fled from Iran. The revolution had begun. Less than a year later Russia invaded Afghanistan. Death and destruction followed.

CAMEL'S MILK FOR BREAKFAST

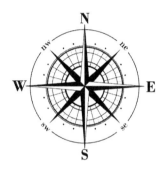

If I could learn to keep my mouth shut long enough to consider all the possibilities, I wouldn't get myself into so much trouble. On the other side of the coin, if I did act a little more cautiously, I wouldn't have so many adventures. What possible harm, do you think, could I come to by discussing my old Sahara expeditions with a mountain Arab from the Musandam Peninsula of Oman?

"No harm at all," you say, expressing just the right amount of naiveté.

"My dream is to cross the Rub'Al Khali," Abdul Khalique told me, as we drove north to Khasab from Dubai. "You know this desert? It is called the Empty Quarter."

"I know of it. That's one of my ambitions too," I replied. "I want to ride a camel across the Empty Quarter from Mughshin to Liwa Oasis."

"Thesiger's route," agreed Abdul Khalique.

In the seat behind me Penny ceased watching the scenery and focused on our conversation. She probably held her breath, reasonably sure of my next line.

"Perhaps we should form an expedition and cross it together."

Penny heard the words and sighed softly. She wasn't surprised.

"I have a friend in Canada," I kept the thoughts rolling. "We've crossed the Sahara together many times. He's a good camel rider. Lawrie will come with us for sure."

That was in April, we were on holiday, Penny's first visit to the Gulf States. Apparently undaunted by the embryonic plans forming a seat away, she added her own ideas.

"If you two are serious then I'll come back to Oman and run your office for you while you're away," she told Abdul K. He looked at me with raised eyebrows.

"She means it," I answered the implied question. "That's one problem out of the way".

Six and a half months of faxes and phone calls went by. Penny and I moved from Belgium to California. Abdul K and I kept talking about the desert. I negotiated a ticket in return for photography with Gulf Air. Back to Oman I went. It was time for some serious face to face discussions about camels and sand dunes and things.

In 1946, British explorer, Wilfrid Thesiger, crossed the Empty Quarter of Saudi Arabia by camel with a small party of Bedu. Thesiger was no stranger to harsh environments. In the 1930's he had explored the Danakil country of Abyssinia. He later served as a Political Officer in the wilds of northern Sudan and then as a District Commissioner. He spent one of his annual leaves roaming Morocco. Another saw him travel west, by camel, from Sudan to the little known Tibesti Mountains in the southern Sahara. During the war he served in Syria and the western desert of Egypt. With such a wealth of desert experience behind him, it was not surprising that his thoughts would turn towards the Rub'Al Khali. Two other British explorers had already

crossed the Empty Quarter on different routes: Bertram
Thomas in 1931 and St. John Philby in 1932. Thesiger chose
to pioneer an, as yet, unknown route where the sands were
highest. Only the Bedu had been there before him.

Typical of a man who was to eventually become
known as the 'Last Great Nomad,' Thesiger chose the
most difficult terrain for his first crossing. A year later he
crossed again, this time on a potentially easier western
route. Thesiger's first crossing runs reasonably close to the
border, undefined in his day, between Saudi Arabia and the
Sultanate of Oman. We chose to plan our crossing, for some
time in the future, on the same or similar route. First we
needed to talk to the Bedu and begin negotiations to buy or
rent enough camels to get us safely across.

"We will go to Wahiba. There are many camels
there," Abdul K said. "Then we will go on to Ramlat
Mughshin."

The drive from Muscat, Oman's capital, to Wahiba
took less than three hours on good paved roads. The Toyota
Land Cruiser did not have to work hard. At Al Shariq, on
the northern fringe of the Wahiba Sands, we sat on a carpet
outside a tidy brick and stucco house. A woman, dressed
in a long black robe edged in gold thread, placed bowls of
oranges and dates before us. She then seated herself some
distance away on the ground. Still within earshot, but not
with us, she constantly added her thoughts and advice to
our discussions.

While we sipped on the bittersweet cardamom
flavoured Omani coffee, Abdul K explained our mission
to his old friend Mohammed. A heavily built young man,
Hamdoun, listened with me and, at times, broke into the
conversation. Although I only caught about ten percent
of the rapid flow Arabic, I knew the topic well enough
to understand far more. Abdul K told the two about my
many Sahara expeditions. They studied me with interest,
nodding their heads thoughtfully.

Mohammed and Hamdoun both insisted Wahiba
camels were the finest in Oman. I wondered aloud if they
were as strong as camels born and raised in, or on the edge

of, the Rub'Al Khali.

"Much better," I was told as if any other possibility was absurd.

"Let's go see some," Abdul K rose as he spoke. We piled into the Toyota and left in a cloud of dust, leaving the woman to clear away the detritus of orange peel and date pits.

On the edge of the dunes, where a wide dry wadi separates the Wahiba from the small town, we saw a line of nine camels approaching. Abdul K slowed the vehicle. Mohammed didn't wait for it to stop. He stepped out while it was moving and went to greet the three riders.

"They aren't very big, are they?" I commented, comparing the slim beasts before me with the large solid Saharan camels.

Mohammed snapped a rapid sentence at Abdul K while looking at me in surprise.

"He said these camels are tough. They go out on forty kilometre walks each day to train them," Abdul K translated.

I was impressed and said so. Privately I still had my doubts. The Wahiba Sands, rugged though the area may be, was not the Empty Quarter. The camels we employed would have to be as tough as possible. Mohammed continued his sales pitch, aided by Hamdoun.

"You must buy camels from Wahiba about two months before the expedition, then they could be properly trained for the crossing," he insisted.

"And how will we get them from Wahiba to Mughshin?" I asked. "It's a heck of a long walk."

"They will go by truck," Mohammed replied, scornfully, in Arabic.

"We still need to look at the stock around Ramlat Mughshin," I reminded Abdul K.

He agreed. Another staccato exchange took place with Mohammed and Hamdoun. We got back in the car. After a quick stop at Mohammed's home for bedding, and a nearby store for water, we headed south into the dunes. The sun had already set. The rolling dunes had turned from pink to rich red to rounded black mounds and I hadn't really noticed.

I'm not a great fan of driving through deserts at night. The risks to life and limb, and of damage to the vehicle, are far too great. I, being a foreigner, wasn't consulted on my wishes. We just went. Abdul K took the wheel. I sat beside him grumbling to myself about driving through the Wahiba Sands for the first time and being unable to see anything. In the back Mohammed and Hamdoun engaged in a shouted conversation with Abdul K. My nervous disposition was not improved when the driver repeatedly turned around to answer a question, while still ploughing through soft sand at over eighty kilometres an hour.

It's about two hundred and twenty-five kilometres, as the camel plods, across Wahiba. I asked how far we were going that night.

"Not far, only to a Bedu camp," Abdul K assured me. The sand got softer. We slowed down considerably. I loosened my grip on the door handle. Off to our left a Nissan four-wheel-drive carved its own track through virgin sand to pass us. We were left with dust in our eyes, noses, and mouths.

Desert mice scurried across the track in front of our headlights. A hare loped out of harm's way before Mohammed could persuade us to give chase. As our lights lit up trees we saw two owls staring back at us, apparently unconcerned by the sudden brightness. Mohammed, who rarely stopped talking, proved he had phenomenal night vision. He suddenly shouted at Abdul K to turn round.

"Why?" He asked.

"Snake back there."

The Bedu do not like to share their desert with snakes, especially the poisonous varieties. Most snakes in the desert are venomous. We went back. With our headlights on full beam I still didn't see the reptile until we were almost on it. Hamdoun did. He jumped out and broke its back with his stick before I had a chance to take a photograph. It was a small sand viper: insignificant but quite deadly.

"Why did he kill it?" I asked Abdul K. "It wasn't

doing us any harm."

"They kill all of them," he replied with a shrug.

We terminated our reckless journey near a Bedu encampment. A little to the south of the camp Abdul K. pulled to a halt. We stepped out into the night and stretched cramped limbs. Mohammed gathered dead wood and built a fire. The camp, I was told, consisted of two families. About a dozen camels wandered aimlessly around. A rusty collection of four-wheel-drive vehicles littered the sand. It was a rather sad, untidy area, far from the romantic traditions of the Bedu of old.

Hamdoun went off to a makeshift dwelling to organize the evening meal. On the way, he later told us, he killed another sand viper. Abdul K began to look distinctly worried.

Old men and young boys came to sit and watch me, the Nasrani — the foreigner. The simple saga of the snake was told over thimble-sized cups of tea and coffee. One teenager was teased unmercifully as the others pretended to throw snakes at him. Mohammed explained that the boy had been bitten on the foot by a viper a few months before. As a consequence he was terrified of snakes. I found it easy to sympathize with him.

The only time the Bedu stopped talking was while we ate from a communal mound of meat and rice. We each stuffed our right hands into the section nearest us. A quick movement of the wrist and fingers wrapped the food into a bite-sized ball. Greasy fingers flipped the balls into waiting mouths. We ate with gravy trickling down our chins and plump grains of rice flying in all directions. As each of us finished we burped loudly to show our satisfaction and moved away from the platter. The locals dived in to finish the remains. No food gets wasted in the desert.

Thesiger complained that the Bedu can't hold normal conversations. For some reason they almost always shout. That night, the Rub'Al Khali expedition was discussed at great volume. I finally gave up trying to understand and busied myself taking photographs of the animated faces round the fire.

It was quite warm and humid, probably because the Indian Ocean was only about twenty-five kilometres away. With the noisy drone of excited Bedu voices ringing in our ears, Abdul K and I moved away from the fire. We lay on our backs on the sand and discussed the stars until we grew too sleepy to recognize the various constellations.

We slept on opposite sides of a low dune close to the fire. I made a hollow for my hip and soon drifted into sonorous oblivion. Abdul K did not sleep well. He told me in the morning he couldn't get comfortable and kept thinking about snakes.

Mohammed and Hamdoun took turns at the wheel on the second day. We got up at five-thirty and left quite soon afterwards. Within seconds we were rattling at bone-jarring speed over the sand. It has been said that the Bedu are excellent desert drivers. That's as may be. The two with us certainly kept the vehicle on an even keel, just. They weren't kind to it otherwise.

It took one hour and twenty minutes to get out of the Wahiba. Add that time to the previous evening's run of two and three quarter hours, and we crossed Wahiba in a fraction over four hours. An average speed of fifty-six kilometres an hour! Once out of the sands and on a corrugated gravel road, Mohammed put his foot down hard. He ignored Abdul K's repeated pleas to slow down. The inevitable happened. One tire burst, unable to stand the sustained abuse. Fortunately we had just passed the village of Ad Duqm and a handy garage. While the tire was being fixed Abdul K gave a short lecture on the need to conserve the vehicle. I think I was the only person listening.

We finally arrived at the small military post of Ramlat Mughshin in the middle of the afternoon. Around us huge dunes rose out of flat gravel plains. Multi-facetted, like dozens of barchan dunes scattered haphazardly over each other, they had created a giant sand pile with ridges, crevasses, and sheer walls. Everywhere north of that point, as far as Liwa, was in the Empty Quarter. I felt the first surge of anticipation.

In the military compound a row of camouflaged

four-wheel-drive vehicles, each with a machine gun mounted on the back, looked business-like. The unmarked border was close. We were politely directed to the headquarters of the Beit Kathiri tribe, half an hour to the west.

There three families lived in considerable comfort in an immaculate yellow and white walled compound. They had brick houses, a beautiful mosque, and paved roads: but only within the walls. Surrounding them on all sides were more huge dunes. The Beit Kathiri Bedu, some of whom had travelled with Thesiger, were clearly not all poor.

We sat on carpets in the sunshine, eating dates, drinking khawa and tea. And talking. Mabrouk, second in line of the Beit Kathiri, offered to take us to their camel herd. En route we stopped at a concrete block topped by a black metal pipe. On one side of the block was a plaque announcing the Sultanate of Oman. On the other, in the direction we were going, another plaque told us we were in the Kingdom of Saudi Arabia. Mabrouk waved his hands, indicating the imaginary line separating the two nations.

"The entire border between Oman and Saudi Arabia is marked by similar concrete blocks every five kilometres," he said. I stored the knowledge for future use.

We followed a defile through the dunes, passing two more border markers. As the sun lowered itself to the horizon we came upon the camp on the west side of a vast dune. The custodian, old Mohammed, greeted us shyly. His companions, a tall Sudanese herder and another from the Beit Kathiri, watched us from a distance. On the plains at the base of the dune seventy camels foraged for grass. Mabrouk told us we could stay overnight. That had been my plan from the start. I didn't see much point in taking a quick look then driving through the desert at night again.

Abdul K called me over to the Toyota. Mohammed and Hamdoun stood with him. "Where do you want to sleep tonight?" He asked.

I looked at him in surprise. Mohammed stared at me, waiting for the answer.

"Right here, this is what we came for," I told them.

"Mohammed and Hamdoun are afraid we will be

murdered in the night," Abdul K told me. Mohammed still stared at me. Hamdoun leaned lazily on the engine cowling, smoking his pipe as if he hadn't a care in the world.

I felt the smile creeping across my face. I couldn't have stopped it if I'd tried. My mouth spoke without warning.

"Tell him," I glanced at Mohammed, "I'll hold his hand while he sleeps."

Abdul K was silent for a moment. Mohammed had understood about half my words. He asked for a complete translation. Abdul K gave him the gist of it, without the bluntness. Mohammed shot me a look of pure venom. Hamdoun shook his head in resignation. Neither expected to see the morning sun.

Old Mohammed started up his ancient Toyota pickup truck and roared off to herd his camels. I've seen sheep dogs herding flocks in Australia. I've seen cowboys riding with their stock in North America. I've seen nomads round up camels on foot in the Sahara. Old Mohammed could have taught them all. He ran rings round any camel, or group, which strayed from the path he wished them to follow. He used his engine noise, his own voice, and the occasional blast from his horn. Most of all he used his wheels. His dexterity was an education to watch. Before long he had them all congregating at the watering trough. From there he led them solemnly to the holding pens. Only one camel was kept aside, and he had been penned up all day. Among a herd of large camels, he was a giant. He was the stud and had to be kept hobbled in an enclosure to keep him away from the mares. One look in his eyes told of his lecherous thoughts. His long eyelashes fluttered longingly as he watched his harem. He drooled expectantly as he waited patiently for his next call to service.

Abdul K and I went for a walk among the dunes after a heavy meal of rice, camel meat and rich gravy, followed up with foaming camel's milk.

"The Wahibis do not trust the Beit Kathiri," he explained. "They are not happy to stay here."

"We'll be all right," I assured him. "I've stayed with

unknown people all over the world. I'm still alive."

Abdul K gave a weak smile in the dark as I reminded him we were four strong men. The Beit Kathiri also numbered four. We were more than evenly matched if any trouble began.

Throughout that night my sleep was punctuated by the gurgling and belching of camels. I suspect I got more sleep than my companions though. When I woke in the dawn Mohammed was lying under his blanket watching me from a few metres away.

"Hey," I called across the intervening sand. "You're still alive!"

His expression, which had been blank, did not change. Hamdoun crawled into the open on hearing the voices. He looked down at himself, as if expecting to find he had been stabbed in the night. The relief on his face was obvious when he discovered everything on his body was in its usual place.

The Bedu find it difficult to use my name. For some reason most could not pronounce Anthony, or Tony, correctly. Abdul K asked if I would mind if they called me Dalton.

"That's fine with me," I agreed.

That didn't really work either. Mohammed and Hamdoun usually addressed me through Abdul K. Mabrouk decided to use the honorific — 'Sheikh' — when talking to me, or about me. He still didn't quite get the name right.

"Sheikh Dilton," he called that morning, "come." He waved a milking bowl in my direction and pointed to the camels.

All the camels, except a handful of youngsters, were big and healthy looking. Darker than the Wahiba variety, they reminded me of mounts I had ridden in the western Sahara. I admired them to be polite, but kept my thoughts to myself. Showing too much interest would only increase the asking price.

Mabrouk balanced his bowl on one raised knee. Talking softly to the camel, he gently stroked her teat to start the flow of milk. I got busy with my camera. Minutes later Mabrouk held a bowl of creamy foam-topped milk. Carefully he carried it back to the open fire and passed the bowl from man to man. The warm milk was delicious.

Seeing my cameras, old Mohammed dressed himself in his finest rich-brown desert robes. Around his waist he buckled a silver belt and an ornate silver khanjar, the traditional curved dagger of Oman. I took the hint and photographed him in front of his tent; with his bull camel, by himself, with Abdul K, and among his herd. Not once did he smile. When I finished he asked me for money. That used to happen in the Sahara too. I had a ready answer.

"It costs me money to take your photograph, so you should pay me, "I told him. "I've used up half a roll of film on you."

He reached into his pocket, pulled out a few coins and offered them to me. I took them and weighed them in my hand.

"Thank you," I said. "Now I can pay you as you asked."

I gave him back his coins. Old Mohammed walked away, shaking his head in wonder at the ways of the crazy Nasrani.

We had to go back to the Beit Kathiri compound to meet with Sheikh Mubarak, their leader. Only he, I learned, could negotiate the sale of camels to us. It sounded like a bit of buck passing to me. Sheikh Mubarak proved to be a well-educated man in his late thirties. I was introduced to him as Sheikh Dilton. The name had stuck.

Our two Wahibis listened intently as Abdul K wandered around the subject of our expedition, occasionally referring to me for a detail. Finally he broached the subject of camels and of price. I flinched as Sheikh Mubarak answered. I thought I'd misheard the outrageous quote.

"What did he say?" I asked Abdul K.

"Later, Tony," came the curt reply.

I resigned myself to being patient. Abdul K spoke soothingly, smoothly, to Mubarak. Mohammed listened to them while watching me. It occurred to me, a bit late, that we had not discussed price with Mohammed for the Wahiba camels. Mohammed, I could see, was already planning his next move.

Abdul K and the Sheikh moved away for a more private conversation. I let them go. My turn was coming. When they returned Abdul K took my hand, in the way of Arab friends, and led me some distance. He spoke softly as we walked.

"They are asking a lot of money for the camels," he began.

"I know. They took one look at me; their brains said, 'rich foreigner' and up went the price."

"Yes, that's part of it," Abdul K agreed, "but a BBC television crew was here maybe two years ago. I think Thesiger was with them. They rented camels for filming in the desert."

"And, I suppose, they paid far too much."

Abdul K nodded, "This makes it difficult for us."

"Well let's go home and work out a budget, we still have plenty of time." A thought struck me, "Tell Sheikh Mubarak we will buy camels elsewhere if he doesn't lower his price, then his community will get nothing."

Abdul K tried but Mohammed messed it up. When the suggestion was put forward he made his calculated move. Mohammed announced we could have his camels.

"How much," we asked.

Mercenary to the last, Mohammed quoted the exact same figure that Sheikh Mubarak had used. It was my turn to offer the look of pure venom.

The expedition starting date was nearly a year away. With months ahead of us for camel-buying and fine-tuning, we drove back to Wahiba. Late at night we sat in the courtyard of Mohammed's house, surrounded by other men, while he and Hamdoun related our adventures with the Beit Kathiri.

"Which part did you like best out of the whole trip," I asked Hamdoun.

"Getting back to Sinaw," he replied to gales of laughter from everyone. Sinaw was a small town on the edge of Wahiba, about sixty kilometres from where we sat.

"And you?"

"Ramlat Mughshin," I answered.

Hamdoun's dark eyes lit up. His face broke into a smile. "Well then," he went on, "you can go and spend your Christmas there."

Everyone roared at the joke. Hamdoun, who loves an audience, had more tales. We had stopped at a mosque a short time before getting back to Wahiba. An underground irrigation system, called a falaj, flowed beneath it. Men use it for their ablutions prior to their prayers. We went because we were filthy. Hamdoun told his delighted audience that, in trying to stop his bar of soap from disappearing into the depths, he had slipped and fallen in fully clothed.

Hamdoun also told the story of my thinly veiled insult to Mohammed at Ramlat Mughshin. Mohammed squirmed uncomfortably as he listened. Watching him I wished I'd kept my mouth shut. Hamdoun spun the tale out, creating as much atmosphere as possible. He finished with, "I was afraid to sleep there too, but this Nasrani, the Inglese, he was not afraid. He will sleep anywhere!"

TIGER TRACKS IN THE MUD

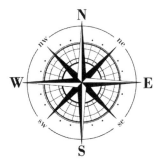

Three triangular black fins arced out of the river ahead of the sharp bow. A deckhand pointed as, for a second or so, the sun glinted on the knife-like intrusions. The Ganges River dolphins broke the surface again, playing in the muddy brown river, crossing and re-crossing in front of our riverboat, riding the pressure wave.

A reddish Brahmini kite soared low, dropping suddenly to snatch a small fish from the surface. Impaled on a sharp claw the fish was eaten in flight — a superb display of aerial dexterity on behalf of the predatory kite. On a bare branch, high on one tree, a lone white-bellied sea eagle watched us as it surveyed its domain. On both sides the monotonous green of the jungle slid by.

Deep within that jungle, the Sundarbans of southwest Bangladesh, a veritable zoological garden of creatures live, breed, hunt and die. At least forty-nine species of mammals, over three hundred different birds, and more than ninety types of reptiles inhabit the forest, and the rivers flowing through it. Emperor of them all, of course, is the Royal Bengal tiger. Once they roamed throughout the Indian sub-continent. Now, a seriously endangered species, there are few left in the world. In India there are occasional pockets where they survive. In Bangladesh they are only to be found in the Sundarbans. One of my boyhood dreams was to see a tiger in the wild, preferably swimming across a jungle river. I went to Bangladesh hoping to live that dream in the wild. I found much more.

The overloaded bus, horn blaring, raced past us on the narrow two-lane road. On the roof passengers clung tightly to their baggage and each other as the vehicle swayed alarmingly. In the open doorway the conductor held on by his right hand and right foot. The rest of him was well out in space. From the opposite direction, side by side, came another bus and a truck. This was the Bangladeshi version of playing chicken, but for high stakes.

At the last possible moment our driver hit the brakes. The passing bus dropped into place in front of us, the conductor waving his thanks. The rapidly approaching truck and bus fell into line astern and we all squeaked through safely once again.

Travelling in Bangladesh is a scenic delight, mixed with a traffic nightmare at times. People seem to be constantly on the move and the risk taking on the roads is monumental. Buses may be a cheap form of transport, but there are safer ways of getting around. I travel by bus when I have the nerve, and only by day. For long overnight journeys I take the train. To get anywhere fast I fly. Biman's domestic air services are cheap and efficient. All major cities are linked by air to Dhaka. Whenever possible I travel peacefully and comfortably by river.

The land is lush, the people are friendly, the rivers are huge. No matter where, or how, one travels in Bangladesh the rivers will never be far away. Those rivers, most of which have their genesis in the high glaciers of the mighty Himalayan Mountains, are important highways for trade and passenger traffic.

On the Sitilakhya River, part of the Old Brahma-putra, I leaned against the mast of *Ruposhi*, an elegant pinish. *Ruposhi* is owned by my friend, Hasan Mansur, an adventure tour operator with a passion for boats and for the rivers of his land. He and his wife, Topu, also have a special feeling for the great poets. Their home has one complete wall of books, most of them poetry. They named their second son Rubaiyat, in honour of the great Omar Khayyam.

Ruposhi is the kind of boat that Bengali poet, songwriter and Nobel Laureate, Rabindranath Tagore, used in verse. He too owned a pinish and sailed the rivers of his beloved Bengal. He wrote: 'The spotless white sail is propelled by a slow gentle wind. I've never seen a boat in such motion.' *Ruposhi* has a bright red sail. It responds in elegant fashion to those same slow gentle winds.

"Do you see that bamboo raft up there?" Hasan broke into my reverie, pointing up stream. "Those men cut the bamboo in the northern forests and float it down river to market. Then they dismantle it, sell the timber and take a bus back to the forest again for another load."

I stared at the five men poling the raft. They looked strong and healthy to me. I thought the venture sounded remarkably cost effective and the exercise had to be beneficial, if a little tiring. Out there on the Sitilakhya it was hard not to believe we were in an Asian maritime museum. There were boats for all purposes on the river: boats carrying mounds of earth, others carrying jute, pottery, oil drums, and people. A floating haystack came into view.

"What the heck's that, Hasan?" I asked. "Is there a boat under all that?"

"You'll see, there is a boat," Hasan smiled back.

As it came closer I saw a man sitting cross-legged on top, shading himself with a black umbrella. As the apparition passed we could just see that there really was a boat underneath. The man on top was simply there to guide the helmsman whose view was completely obscured by the hay.

A swaronga boat, laden to the gunwales with sand,

ghosted past under a well-patched sail. On the bow a man helped the sail keep the craft moving by pushing against the riverbed with a long pole. On the stern another sailor manned the heavy rudder.

The river was alive with boats during the day. Steel-hulled freighters, overloaded barges with miniature tugs in attendance, wooden boats under patchwork sails and the occasional canoe coasted by. Some, powered by wind or muscles, made no sound. Others sent throbbing signals through the water from powerful engines.

Anchored to the east bank of the Old Brahmaputra, as night fell over *Ruposhi*, we dined on deck and listened to the sounds of the Sitilakhya. There was considerable movement back and forth across the river. Workers from our side called to the ferryman at the village across the way. He paddled swiftly over each time he heard the call for a ride. Long after full dark a young man, presumably he had been working late, arrived alone and called for transport. There was no answer. He called again and again, his voice becoming more and more plaintive.

"Why are you treating me this way?" he cried. "I'm hungry and I want to go home."

The ferryman took his time. Perhaps he was having his dinner. Eventually we heard the paddle rippling the water. A dark shape appeared, white teeth flash in greeting, a few words spoken. Thankfully the sad young man jumped aboard and was quickly swallowed by the night.

Hasan and I stayed up talking until well into the early morning hours. We had experienced a few adventures together. It was Hasan who took me into the mangrove jungle the first time. He had been to the forest many times. Never had he seen more than a brief glimpse of the jungle's proudest creature. We went together in search of excitement and those elusive tigers. We got both!

As we cruised through the Sundarbans we saw a few of the rapidly disappearing creatures which once dominated the jungle. The saltwater, or estuarine, crocodile is rapidly becoming extinct. The mugger, a larger version, has probably gone forever. The Royal Bengal tiger, which once roamed all over Bengal, has found its Sundarbans population reduced to, perhaps, as few as three hundred beasts.

On a sloping muddy bank a huge saltwater crocodile soaked up the sun unaware of our approach. Hasan woke it up with a blast from an air horn. The rugged reptile looked up and bared its vicious teeth. It hissed in defiance and slid urgently into the water. It didn't like boats.

In a sheltered estuary, within sight of the Bay of Bengal, is Kotka. A nature reserve, with a large herd of spotted deer in residence, the area is regularly visited by tigers. We arrived late, in the pitch black of a moonless night. Hasan called through a loud hailer to his son.

"Rubaiyat. Rubaiyat."

A flashlight flickered on and moved quickly through the trees in our direction. By the time we tied the boat up at the rickety wooden jetty, Rubaiyat was waiting. He wore jungle green clothing. His long sleek black hair was tied back with an elastic band. When he smiled his white teeth gleamed in the darkness. He looked like a modern living version of Kipling's delightful character in The Jungle Book. So he became Mowgli as well.

Mowgli was only eighteen and not much heavier than my dog when soaking wet. At full stretch he could still stand under my outstretched arm without touching it. His size though had nothing to do with his abilities. Mowgli had been a tracker for some years and has developed into a talented wildlife photographer.

We slept on board that night, eagerly anticipating the sun's return. A government rest house and a garden of colourful shrubs and flowers greeted us in daylight. In the bushes a pair of gold-fronted chloropsis, whistled noisily as they pecked at spiders and insects. A purple sunbird flew in to join them and was chased away without ceremony by the larger birds. Up in a tree, like a great white sentry, a large egret watched and waited for signs of edible movement. Behind the building, between the house and the forest, stands a large freshwater hole. Monkeys had left their tiny footprints at the water's edge. The dainty hooves of spotted deer showed clearly around them. There were no recent tiger's tracks visible.

Not far away, no more than one hundred metres, on the shores of the bay, Mowgli found the first pug marks. In soft mud they told their own story, a tiger had passed only hours before. We searched among the pneumataphores, the aerial roots of the sundari trees. I wondered about the possibility of a tiger, chasing prey, tripping on the vertical wooden spikes. It didn't seem likely somehow. Clumsy humans though, I noted from a few gouges, were not immune to accidents.

Pneumataphores are the breathing mechanisms of trees in the mangrove forest. They have evolved pointed vertical root extensions. When the tide comes in the roots close up to seal themselves against salt water. As the tide ebbs so the roots open again and exchange gases with the outside air. Their height is a good indication of the low tide level.

The more we looked the more tracks we found. In a small clearing Hasan showed me a few old bones.

"This is where the tiger comes to eat," he explained.

Mowgli and an armed guard went deeper into the forest. Hasan and I stayed closer to the water, though still among the trees. Distinctly I heard a deep rumbling 'awoom.'

"Tiger," Hasan warned. "Not far away."

Carefully we made our way back to the rest house, without coming face to face with the striped one. Mowgli also heard the tiger's grumble. A few minutes later he saw the cat as it walked into the sunlight and was silhouetted for a brief moment, then it was gone. He tracked it as far as he could. When he came back to the rest house an hour later he switched on his pocket tape recorder.

"Listen," he ordered; his voice high-pitched with excitement.

"Tiger, tiger, tiger!" The earnest whisper breathed out of the hand-held machine.

"He walked right out in front of us, about fifty

metres ahead," Mowgli told us excitedly. "We followed him until we lost him at a creek."

At a temporary fishing camp on the banks of the Bay of Bengal, we found other tracks. Men and boys dried their catch in the sun on rush mats and on lines strung between trees. Their flimsy huts, elevated on poles to keep them beyond reach of hungry tigers, offered scant protection to my mind.

"Yesterday a tiger chased a deer right through here," an old man told us. He traced an arc with one hand to show the direction. "He came from over there and went into the forest there."

We found the tracks easily. The long distances between each set of the deer's prints told of the panic in the doomed creature's mind. The tiger's spread, we noted, was considerably greater than the deer's. It had covered the ground much faster than its victim.

Across the river from Kotka is a large grassy meadow. On the southern edge stands a watchtower. Twenty metres high, it's there for the sole purpose of watching for wildlife, tigers in particular. A night on the tower, with no protection other than a flimsy piece of wire tied round the gate at the bottom, was a thought provoking experience.

The moon was bright and the jungle played tricks on our eyes. Shadows appeared to creep stealthily towards us, but it was only the trees stretching and yawning in the night. Fireflies began to resemble distant eyes staring menacingly in our direction. A sudden commotion in a nearby tree startled us, yet it was only a troop of monkeys, restless in their sleep.

I heard the deer barking to warn others that the tiger was on the prowl. We woke fully and stared into the blackness. Mowgli listened intently, then aimed the beam of a powerful light in the direction of a faint sound. A large creature crossed the spotlight and disappeared into the long grass. I must have blinked because I saw nothing.

"It's only a deer," said a tired voice.

"It was a tiger!" Mowgli had no such doubts.

I waited all night for a tiger. If it came close I didn't

see it. Towards dawn I saw deer, it's favourite food, caught in our spotlight, nothing more. In the morning, when the early sun had burned away the night's veil of mist, the tracks were revealed. Mowgli was right, of course. The tiger had been there in the night.

Later, while walking through long grass — with an armed forestry guard and Marjo, a young Dutch lady, I found the tracks of a female tiger and her cub. Recent tracks, made that morning — only a few minutes before — my guard advised. He placed his bare hand on the imprints then sniffed his palm. He scooped air from four directions to his nostrils and inhaled deeply. Slowly he turned and pointed to the jungle.

"They are there," he said simply.

"You mean they are watching us?" I asked. He nodded, staring at the jungle foliage.

"If I tell you to lay flat, don't ask why. Just do it," I quietly told Marjo from the Netherlands.

"There is a tiger there?" she asked. "I can feel my hair prickling on my neck."

She wasn't the only one. What hair I have was standing on end like miniature antennae. The guard took the lead, Marjo in the middle, and I in the rear. We walked parallel to the trees for a hundred metres. The tiger watched us every step of the way. The guard signalled that the tiger kept pace with us, padding softly, hidden by the forest. With adrenaline coursing through our bodies, we made our way to the base of the tower, keeping to a well-worn path. Once she realized we were no threat to her or to her young, the tiger returned as silently to her infant. Without fuss we left the area, seeking the safety of the boat.

Heading for home, we cruised back up river to Mongla Port. It took all day against the current. The estimated three hundred or so resident tigers were hidden, as they usually are. All except one. Rounding a bend, a voice from the upper deck called, "There's a crocodile in the river."

I scanned the water ahead with a telephoto lens and was confronted with a magnificent sight. Swimming across the river in front of us was, not a crocodile, it was a full-grown tiger. Mowgli got the words out before I did.

"Tiger! Tiger! Tiger!"

The golden striped one wasn't too happy to see us, or to be sharing its river with a noisy steel boat. Opening its mouth wide, enormous teeth gnashing the air, it roared its anger. The boat trembled, as if in fear. Our helmsman took us in close. Too close. The tiger made a lunge for the boat, catching it a glancing blow with one powerful paw. Steel decks offer little purchase, even for sharpened claws. With nothing to grip, the tiger fell back. Astern, enjoying a private cruise in our wooden sampan, a boatman and a nine-year-old English boy stood up to see what the commotion was all about.

Bellowing with rage the furious tiger bounced against the side of the mother boat. As the current carried it past our stern the tiger smacked its head on the sampan's tow rope. The pressure forced its head under water as a chorus of voices shouted to young Joseph to "Sit down!" The tiger surfaced and lashed out at the new adversary. Wicked claws ripped splinters from the sampan within reach of the boy. The boatman pulled him back sharply, flattening him. Clear of us, and the sampan, the tiger paddled at full speed for the river bank. With a mighty lunge it ploughed its way up the muddy bank in two strides and was gone.

The following day, in Dhaka, we described our experience to a Bangladeshi naturalist. He listened intently, occasionally interrupting with a question. When we, Mowgli and I, finished our story, the naturalist told us, "I think you probably met the man-eater of Chandpai, he has taken many people from that area in the last two years."

Mentally I ticked off one more item from my long held list of hoped for adventures. I was content.

FROG DREAMIN' PLACE

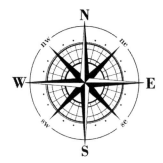

Looking down on the rock pool, from the advantage of a sandstone cliff, I scanned the depths. There were no telltale shadows to warn of crocodiles lurking on the bottom. I couldn't see anything, except water. Brad pointed to the darkest section of the pool, right below us, close to the cliff. That's where the waterfall would hit, I realized, when the rainy season sent a torrent of floodwater streaming over the cliff on which we stood. Standing baking in the dry afternoon on super heated rock, the pool looked particularly inviting.

"See, there," Brad pointed again. A kingfisher flashed across my vision in search of prey. A night heron took off from a ledge and flapped awkwardly away from our disturbing influence. I followed the line of Brad's arm. Sure enough there was the familiar shape of a crocodile rising slowly towards the surface. I had been looking forward to a cooling swim in the rock pool Aborigines call Niparmgin. Suddenly it didn't look so inviting any more. I knew freshwater crocs were harmless: I'd been told that many times. I still couldn't help wondering if the crocs really understood how benign they are.

Tom was in the water by the time we got down to his level. Brad sat on a rock, rolled a smoke and settled back to relax. I stripped off and joined Tom. I didn't get molested yet, all the time I was in the pool, I felt a tingling sensation running up and down my legs. I found I was able to swim faster in Niparmgin than I could elsewhere.

Only a few days before, I had stood beside the South Alligator River with that same Tom, Brad's boss. Tom Winter is one of those irrepressible Australian outback characters who could easily have been the role model for Paul Hogan's Crocodile Dundee. He's of medium height with fair wavy hair. He wears soft-sided hiking boots, shorts, a safari shirt, and a broad-brimmed hat made from buffalo hide. The hat, which had seen better days, was decorated with an assortment of crocodile teeth set in a thin leather band around the crown. We were talking about crocodiles, the saltwater variety. The ones whose teeth Tom likes to wear. Those that grow big, mean, bold, and usually hungry.

"You go for a swim in there, Mate, and you're dead," he told me matter of factly. "Those bastards'll have you in no time."

The idea of a swim had not, at that juncture, entered my head. I'd already seen the warning signs and deep tracks in the mud.

"Oh yeah," Tom said, as I asked about a series of deep prints in the dry mud of the river bank, "some stupid bastard was down there by the water's edge when this croc came up and took him. Just like that."

Saltwater crocodiles have a vicious reputation in the top end of Australia's Northern Territory. Each year, or so the locals like to tell, a tourist or two fall foul of the predatory reptiles. Tom certainly showed concern any time he saw people too close to the wrong spot on the wrong river. "Stupid bastards," he'd say. "They never bloody learn."

We went to Fogg Dam. As we drove over the earthen causeway the early morning mist swirled around Tom's six-wheel drive truck. He pointed out a group of wallabies among the water lilies.

"I've never seen it so dry," he sounded surprised. "Not in over twenty years."

The wallabies and the water lilies were both on the dry bed of the dam.

"There's plenty of crocs in there normally," Tom added.

It was obvious the dry season had affected more than the water level. Up in a nearby tree a Rufous owl stared silently at us with huge eyes as it waited for nightfall. Tom pointed to it.

"Don't usually see those out in daylight," he said.

We left the owl to dream of darkness and a night of hunting. Returning to the truck we examined a vivid trail crossing the dusty soil. The track was recent, very recent. It crossed over the footprints Tom and I had left only five or ten minutes before.

"That's a death adder. They're deadly," he announced with a certain amount of satisfaction. "I met one once. I was climbing up the cliff on a vine over at Barramundi Gorge to get above the water hole. The adder was coming down the vine next to me."

"What did you do, jump?"

"Nah, I leaned as far away from him as I could and tried to keep still. He didn't want to fight, he was just passing through."

I could do without the snakes and I didn't have a great desire to swim with the crocs, but I was keen to get close to the latter in the wild. Tom suggested I took a boat trip on Yellow Waters, part of the Alligator River system. He declined to join me, saying he had someone to see. As I walked the footpath leading to the sightseeing boats I saw why — crowds of tourists chattered inanely as they vied for the best seats. With a sigh of resignation I joined them.

The close to two hour running commentary from the boat's operator was good and informative. The continual chat from my fellow passengers was not. Fortunately there were plenty of exotic birds to take my mind off humans. Sea eagles streaked out of the sky snatching fish from the water. Tiny blue and gold kingfishers darted energetically from tree to tree. A great black-necked stork, called a Jabiru, strode purposefully away from the water's edge with a large black catfish in its beak. And the reptiles were out on their daily business. A monitor lizard, called a goanna locally, prowled the riverside in search of eggs — any kind. Crocodiles, no babies that I saw, were up to four or five metres long. Some lay soaking up the sun in the muddy shallows, others stretched out on the banks. One or two drifted past showing only their eyes and snouts. Known for their appetite for any creature smaller than themselves, and for their phenomenal acceleration, they stared at the boat's passengers with menace in their eyes.

"If you fell overboard here you wouldn't stand a chance," the guide intoned. I had the feeling, in spite of what he was saying, that he would have been quite open to the idea of someone taking an impromptu bath. Especially the obligatory loud mouth, without whom no group could be complete. She sat immediately behind me — a woman who had, she advised everyone without taking a breath, "... Three lovely grandchildren back in Sydney, near the Rocks, and my daughter lives in a pretty house and her husband is a good enough sort and I'm so pleased I've come all the way to the territory to see...ooh look, that one moved. He opened his mouth ever so wide. Where was I? Oh yes, she's ever so good with them. Bringing them up right she is. I do miss them."

No wonder the croc opened its mouth. It was as bored with her prattle as we were. Just one little push, I thought. One little push when no one else is looking: unless someone beat me to it.

There were no such noisy distractions on the cliffs overlooking the pool. Niparmgin is in Manyallaluk, a part of the Eva Valley in Australia's Northern Territory. Few people knew about it and no one went there without Brad or one of his other guides.

Long before Europeans trekked through the outback of Australia, the Jawoyn Aboriginal peoples lived there, as they do now. They called their home Man-yalla-luk, 'the frog dreaming place.' When the Europeans arrived they changed the face of the landscape and the lives of the indigenous people forever. They also changed the name.

For a long time, close to one hundred years, this land was known to white people as the Eva Valley Station. During that time its 3,000 square kilometres was leased for pastoral use, employing some local stockmen. Just to the west of the present community, gold, tin, and wolfram were mined. The Jawoyn supplied most of the workforce for those dangerous underground endeavours. Further away, though close enough to do harm, uranium too was mined. And healthy outdoor people became ill. Aborigines still call the region, 'sickness country.' Since 1984 the Jawoyn finally own the land again: the land they once worked for others. Some of them are still sick.

Tom's a safari outfitter, the only company allowed onto Jawoyn tribal land. Brad operates out of Tom's permanent campsite at Manyallaluk. He and a female cook, plus Tom's daughter, Julie, her husband, Murray, and their two young kids, are the only non-Aboriginal inhabitants of the Jawoyn property. Brad had spent many months pushing trails through the bush up towards the Arnhemland border. He went alone much of the time, in search of hitherto unknown Aboriginal rock paintings. The best ones were way beyond Niparmgin, and that idyllic spot was a hard drive from base camp. Only the truly dedicated, should they somehow gain permission from Jawoyn elders, would tackle that run. As with off-road trails in many countries, the track varied from easy to interesting. It was the latter which sorted out the good, the bad, and the useless.

Red soil, sandy soil, fine dust and, later, great sandstone boulders among the spinifex, were there to challenge four-wheel-drive experts. The bull dust was the worst: absolutely impossible to drive through without creating a greyish cloud all around and inside the vehicle. When you are up to your axles in bull dust, it doesn't just settle on your skin, it gets right under it!

Halfway through our journey, on one of Brad's trails, we stopped suddenly in an area where a bush fire had created more than a little mayhem. Blackened stumps of trees and spindly poles, where the bark and branches had been burned off, stuck colourfully but uselessly out of the deep red earth.

Brad grabbed a shovel and marched off muttering, "It's around here somewhere."

He soon found 'it' — a hollow tree stump with tiny native bees buzzing around it. They look and sound like flies. If we'd been anywhere else in the world we would have left them alone. In the Northern Territory we had no such need. The little black creatures are stingless. More important, they produce delicious honey. Brad was willing to share it with them, and us. At the base of the stump, inside the hollow, was the honeycomb. We stood there like kids in front of a candy store, with sticky fingers. Aborigines appropriately call the delicacy a 'sugar bag.' Brad made sure enough was left to encourage the bees to return and continue their labours.

We left Niparmgin to the crocodiles and rolled through the stony country. Brad's trail was visible but it would have been impossible to follow without a 4 x 4 with reasonable ground clearance. The two narrow identical parallel tracks wound laboriously through spinifex grass and paperbark trees.

"How old is this track?" I asked.

"I pushed this one through a few weeks ago," Brad answered. "The oldest trail around here is only about eight months old."

We crossed dried up water courses littered with boulders, struggling up and down the crumbling banks in low gear. There were no people and little wildlife. Tom indicated a buffalo shading itself in a grove of trees. It watched us cautiously until we passed. There was nothing else. We rocked and rolled over the orange and red sandstone trail towards a high cliff: the end of Brad's trail.

"We'll walk from here," he said unnecessarily.

Brad led the way up the rock wall on a narrow path, wide enough for one person at a time. I stopped at the top and looked back the way we had come. Trees and rocks covered the harsh landscape. To the north the view stretched under a deep blue sky all the way to the Arnhemland Escarpment. In between was the same vast panorama of rocks and boulders interspersed with dry golden grass and and spindly trees with thin caps of green.

"No wonder the Aborigines call this the stone country," I told Tom.

A miniature ring-tailed dragon sunned itself at my feet. It didn't scuttle away, it simply looked at my feet with enormous eyes and, I assumed, hoped I wouldn't step on its tail.

The other two strode off towards another rocky outcrop across the plateau. As I caught up with them Brad was pointing up under the rim of an overhang. The rock, sheltered from the eroding effect of wind, occasional rain and almost constant sun, was alive with vibrant colours. Thousands of years of Aboriginal history is represented in paintings on walls and in caves across Australia. Brad told me the paintings above us had rarely, if ever, been seen by white travellers.

"This one and the others up here were unknown until I found them a few weeks back," Brad told us.

We climbed up for a closer look. As one we stretched out on our backs, the better to study the natural gallery under the overhanging ledge. For a couple of hours we stayed with the ghosts of the long dead Aboriginal artists, humbled by the beauty of the paintings and the carefully chosen setting. The vivid minds and talented hands had expressed their impressions of crocodiles, kangaroos, turtles, serpents, their fellow men and, of course, frogs. Since those exceptional artists coloured the rock with their imaginations, maybe thousands of years ago, little had changed in the land. Could they only return they would know it well. We were no more than casual intruders.

"How many more studios do you reckon there are

like this, out here?" I asked Brad.

"Thousands I should think."

Brad showed us more. Anywhere there was a flat rock away from direct sunlight there was at least one painting. The plateau held enough glorious art to outshine the easily accessible galleries of Kakadu National Park. The famed rock art walls of Ubirr, Nourlangie Rock, and Anbangbang are visited by thousands of tourists each season. None could equal the remote sites in Brad's wilderness. Each with his own thoughts, we retraced our steps and our tracks. Tom's been around in the north for many years. He's an enthusiastic conversationalist and usually quite blasé about the sights he's seen. Even so, he was moved enough to remain silent for a long time.

Back at Manyallaluk we told a small group of overnight campers of our finds. They were rightfully envious. Their guide would take them to Niparmgin the next morning, but no further. We consoled them with the knowledge that there was a wall of beautiful paintings in a cave at the pool.

At night in the outdoors strange calls are heard. A soft deep 'oom, oom' intrigued me.

"What's that?"

"It's a tawny frogmouth," Tom told us "He's nocturnal, like an owl, but he's got a face like a frog with a sharp beak. There's lots of them up here."

That made sense to me. A bird with the face of a frog had every right to hunt in a frog dreaming place. Tom went on to tell us the frogmouth has feathers of mottled grey to make it virtually invisible against the bark of a tree. It lives on beetles, centipedes, mice and, of course, frogs. It occurred to me that it must have exceptional night vision to see and catch a beetle in the dark.

I went for a bush walk with Jawoyn guides one morning. Close to the camp is a lush green area of grasses and palms. I was introduced to palms which tasted like cabbage and another with a distinctly nutty flavour. Others, I was shown, were perfect for weaving baskets. The Jawoyn strip palms into thin green lengths and plait them into a variety of shapes. One, a skilled artist, painted delicate designs on bark using natural ink and home made paints. Everything he needed for his studio was right there in the wild. He held out a fine brush and a bark palette for me to try my skill. I managed to produce a reasonable facsimile of his design, without displaying any sign of his delicacy and finesse.

Murray had agreed to show me something of the wetter areas of Manyallaluk, which meant following a creek through the lowest part of the land. I invited Tom to go with us to help us get Murray's Toyota stuck, for the photographs, nothing more.

"A waste of time, Mate," he laughed. "I don't know how to get a vehicle stuck!"

We didn't get stuck either, but we did enjoy ploughing through the shallow Emu creek and forcing our way up swampy banks. Murray rarely, if ever, wears anything in the nature of shoes or thongs. His feet, the Cockney expression 'plates of meat' springs easily to mind, are obviously impervious to pain. Consequently he found himself wading knee-deep to find suitable fording points while I, the photographer, directed him from dry land. I assumed that anything noxious in the creek would flee in terror from Murray's mighty soles.

Down there, by Emu creek, while Murray was paddling up and down stream, I wondered about the earliest Aboriginal people. How did they come to call this place Manyallaluk? Perhaps, I discussed with myself, through something as simple as this encounter. While walking in the dry, as opposed to Murray in the wet, I came across a mottled green and brown frog. I didn't know its proper name, neither did Murray. There are so many varieties in Australia's north only an expert could positively identify it. The frog was half submerged in the water. Its chin rested on the surface and its mouth was closed. I could see it was alive by a tiny pulse in its throat. It looked, with its eyes half closed, as if it might be dreaming.

Maybe, I thought, I had inadvertently stumbled on the actual Frog Dreaming Place.

HIGH WINDS & ELEPHANT SEALS

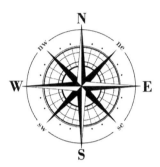

We faced each other like mismatched gladiators. He kept one eye on me. The other, weeping copiously, remained closed. I crouched lower and held his Cyclopean gaze. Without warning, or apology, he opened his mouth wide. Two brown-stained tusks reared up like poorly maintained sabres, one on each side of his lower jaw. The interior of his mouth was a large, soft, moist, rose-pink cavern. He exhaled. A ghastly stale fishy stench surged past the soft, moist, rose-pink and blasted in my direction. A deep rumbling roar bubbled up from his belly behind the smell and he charged. In the second before discretion proved the better part of valour, I took one more picture. Then I ran.

Southern elephant seals can grow to six metres in length and weigh up to five tonnes. My adversary wasn't the largest of his species, but he was well on his way to becoming a giant. Obviously camera shy, he thundered up the beach with surprising speed. His great flippers pounded the sand and his bloated body lurched after them.

I had travelled a long way to photograph that old bull and others like him: giving up was out of the question. I hurdled over three sleeping pups and turned to face his onslaught from a safer distance. Having proved beyond a doubt that he was bigger, braver and tougher than I, the seal gave a last bellow. With a sigh he settled down with his head propped on another's back. He closed his watchful eye and wrapped his whiskered mouth over his tusks. The pink cavern disappeared.

Eighteen hours in a Royal Air Force L-1011 Tristar jet may seem like a less than perfect start to an adventure. In fact, if going to the Falkland Islands from Europe — as I did, it's the best way to travel. After a brief stop at Ascension Island on the way, I arrived at Mount Pleasant Airport wide-awake and ready for anything the remote windswept islands had to offer. Being escorted in and closely observed by two Tornado fighters, one above and one below the port wing, plus a lumbering Hercules much too close behind the starboard wing, may have had something to do with my alert status.

Stanley, the capital, is home to 1,700 people: roughly 80% of the total population of the islands. Scattered across a hillside overlooking a virtually land-locked harbour, the tiny city conveys a vibrancy out of all proportion to its size. It is, and always has been, a seaport. As such it caters to sailors. It has plenty of bars, pubs, and cafes. None are far from the water.

Stanley harbour, once an important port of call for shipping rounding Cape Horn, is reluctant to shed itself of its heritage. A shore-side walking trail links a series of fifteen wrecks, said to be the most unique collection of decaying wooden sailing vessels in the world. The best preserved of the wrecks, not surprisingly, is iron rather than wood. The rusting three-masted *Lady Elizabeth* sits in full view on a sand bar in Whalebone Cove.

I sat on the beach and studied *Lady Elizabeth* through a long lens. She was on a voyage from Vancouver to Delagoa Bay, in Mozambique, carrying lumber when she fetched up on a rock at the entrance to Berkeley Sound. That was in March 1913. Badly damaged and too expensive to repair, she was left to rot in the Falklands.

As I let my imagination wander, seeing the crew battling their ship round the Horn so long ago, a movement caught my eye. To my right, the rusty brown head and neck of an Upland goose hove into view. I stayed perfectly still, expecting her to make a large detour round me. She didn't. Her brown chest, with its horizontal black bars, puffed up and she kept coming straight for me. Behind her, in perfect formation, followed seven fluffy goslings. She swayed from side to side as she led the convoy. The goslings swayed with her. Her eyes scanned left and right, looking for danger and food at the same time. She obviously perceived me as neither.

Only a couple of metres from me she altered course slightly. The babes took their cue from her and turned on the same spot. No longer aiming for my hip, the goose and her entourage avoided my outstretched legs, perhaps they were too big for the infants to climb over, and skirted my feet. Close enough to touch with my big toe, they passed silently. I moved a foot. All eight turned ninety degrees at the same instant and took to the water. The waves weren't big: no more than ripples really, but to those little goslings they must have looked monstrous. Gamely they thrust their tiny webbed feet down and back. Keeping their eyes on mother they rode up and down the swells and away from me. It looked like child's play.

The Falklands are an ornithologist's paradise. Well, almost. It's a bit too windy and cold to be compared with the final step before Heaven. Up to 185 species of birds have been recorded in and around the islands. My job was to photograph as many as possible, as well as the marine mammals.

I started out by Yorke Bay, not far from Stanley. There's a gorgeous white sand beach there, curving in a semi-circle round a cobalt blue bay. It's always devoid of people: has been for years: ever since the Falklands war, in fact. A barbed wire fence, well decorated with red and white signs bearing skull and cross-bones, warned of the minefield enclosing the beach and the bay. The signs keep humans out but don't deter some of the local residents. A Magellanic penguin waddled nonchalantly across the field, on the wrong side of the barbed wire, where angels fear to tread. I watched, half expecting to see the cocky little penguin disappear in a puff of smoke. Confidently, as if it knew a secret path through the danger, it battled on. At the beach it kept on walking, straight to the sea. Without breaking its stride it threw itself in and was gone.

"It's okay for you," I complained. "You only weigh a kilo or two."

A narrow path beckoned me up a hill. It stopped at another fence with a wooden stile. There were no warning signs of buried mines. The path seemed to continue on the other side.

"Hmm. What to do?" I wondered aloud. "Should I go on, or live peacefully on the right side of caution."

I crossed the stile and walked, one foot in front of the other, along the narrow path. As I progressed I found myself alternately leaning to left and right, trying to keep from stepping off the trail. At last I knew how tightrope walkers felt. The perceived exposure heightened all my senses.

The hill was riddled with burrows. A black face with a white band round it peered from one hole. I stopped and waited. The penguin wriggled backwards out of sight. Behind the burrow, marginally higher, two more faces watched me. Instinctively, forgetting where I was for the moment, I changed my stance to take a photograph. One foot slid sideways, the other moved in the opposite direction to assume its correct position. Both feet went off the path. There was an ominous click — and it wasn't the camera shutter.

Many years before, deep in the Sahara, a friend of mine was answering a call of nature. His pants were round his ankles as he squatted on the sand. In front of him a piece of wire protruded from the desert. Idly, having little else to do at the moment except think, he tugged at the wire. As it came free it rattled. Lawrie's brain screamed, "Oops. World War II landmine!"

He told me afterwards, once he had re-arranged his clothing, that he had expected to die, half naked, in a blaze of glory. At the time I thought the experience would probably have been beneficial to anyone suffering from constipation.

"Click."

I stood rooted to the spot, anticipating an unscheduled launch into outer space before I could blink. Time stood still with me. I looked down. My feet were still attached to my legs. That was a relief. My eyes swung round the immediate vicinity, searching for the source of the frightening sound. They didn't have to look far. Touching my left foot was a spent rifle shell. I had kicked it as I moved and knocked it against a pebble.

"Click."

My breathing, which had experimented with racing, erratic behaviour, and cessation, returned to normal. The two penguins watched me curiously.

"Well," I asked, "are there any mines up here or not?"

From somewhere inside a burrow a young penguin called, "Pee-pee-pee."

"Yeah, me too," I answered.

Photographing birds can be hazardous to one's health. On Pebble Island, while trying to get a perfect shot of an immature black-crowned night heron, I almost stepped off a cliff. It was a windier than average day, even for the Falklands: blowing a gale from the land to the sea. I had my camera and lens supported on a beanbag which was, in turn, set on a boulder. I leaned against the rock to steady myself, took a breath and pressed the shutter. I did this a few times. The framing wasn't perfect. If I moved a couple of paces to my right... Still watching the heron through my lens I side-stepped.

What is it, I often wonder, which stops us doing whatever we happen to be doing for no apparent reason.

It has to be a subconscious survival instinct. With left foot planted on the cliff, camera in hands but still on the beanbag on the boulder, I went to put my right foot down. My lens and my mind were both focused on the bird, and yet, my foot refused to obey its order. The shutter opened and shut as I looked down to see what was holding my foot up. There was nothing underneath it: nothing close by, just an abyss. A perfect void: which is what I almost did. At the bottom, a long way down, there were jagged rocks and an angry looking sea swirling around, waiting for me. In my passion for the photographs I had strayed ever nearer to the cliff edge without even noticing it. My heart rate increased without prompting from me. I stepped left instead of right and my feet worked in unison, the way they'd been trained. My sphincter relaxed a little. Oh, and the picture was a winner.

Rockhopper penguins don't seem to have any problem with cliffs. If they do it doesn't show. They can't fly and they walk kind of funny, but they sure can climb. With both feet held together the birds jump from slippery rock to slippery rock. They follow traditional routes, from the sea to the nesting colony on the cliff top. Those time-honoured pathways are worn smooth by the feet of thousands of Rockhoppers. They can be seen standing close to the top with heaving chests, taking a well-earned breather before continuing to their nests.

They're noisy birds and inclined to be quarrelsome, still they build their nests as close to each other as possible. And, often, right beside black-browed albatrosses and Imperial shags. When everyone is home at the same time it's far from peaceful. One ornithologist described the noise as the sound of thousands of wheelbarrows, all badly in need of greasing, being pushed at full speed.

Biffo took me to see the graceful black-browed albatrosses on Saunders Island. They were much bigger and considerably quieter than the penguins. Biffo is an ample lady with a smile to match. She's a well known guide in the islands. Awarded the nickname by her father at a young age, because she wore a red shirt like British comic book hero, Biffo the Bear, she claims to have forgotten her real name.

"The albatrosses are just down there," she pointed across the close cropped grass to the edge of a precipice. "Take as long as you want." She leaned back against the seat and closed her eyes.

In company with another wildlife photographer, I walked the fifteen metres or so down the slope, until a recumbent Biffo and her Land Rover were out of sight. Instead of stepping off into space as we feared, we found ourselves surrounded by uniform cones of mud and grass. Sitting complacently on most were black-browed albatrosses.

Their eyes followed our movements nervously until we made ourselves comfortable out of the wind. Once we were still they went back to the serious business of incubating their eggs. As far as we could see, in both directions along the green carpeted cliffs, there were huge white birds with folded black wings. Many more rode the air currents offshore.

An RAF tornado fighter-bomber streaked past, lower than we were and close in to shore. It was followed by the screaming howl of powerful jet engines. We jumped. Our ears protested at the invasion of their privacy. The albatrosses took it all in their stride. I wondered if they had been so confident during the 1982 war. The pilot, we felt, took an enormous risk. If he'd sucked one of those great birds into an engine intake he would have been in serious trouble — if his engine didn't blow him to bits first.

A day later Robin Lee took me from Port Howard out to Narrows Island in his small motorboat. With the engine throbbing and a creamy bow wave throwing spray left and right, we were joined almost immediately by a quartet of racing black fins.

"Commerson's dolphins," Robin announced. "They're usually out here."

I photographed the dolphins playing in our wake as Robin told me a bit about the area.

"Sometimes it gets really rough in here," he pointed

to the steep hills crowding us on each side for emphasis. "You should see the waves when a real hooligan of a gale blows in."

The dolphins left us as we approached Narrows Island. Robin indicated the north end where boulders littered the shore and tussock grass protected the higher land.

"There should be sea lions among those rocks and up in the tussock."

He maneouvred us closer. The rocks were bare. Circling above the point a flock of turkey vultures were the only visible forms of life. I went ashore for a closer look while Robin stayed with the boat. Threading my way through the tough grassy hummocks I surprised a couple of vultures, and myself. They took off with squawks and urgently flapping wings. I stood still until my heart rate settled down again. The Falkland Islands' resident wildlife seemed determined to keep my blood flowing as fast as possible.

I fought through the long coarse grass, expecting any moment to come face to face with a bad-tempered sea lion. I told them I was coming, in a loud voice. I wasted my breath. The point was deserted except for a pair of night herons. They gave me the once over, decided I was harmless and went back to their silent vigil of studying the sea for sustenance.

Charles Darwin called the Falklands 'desolated and wretched' after he visited on HMS Beagle in 1835. I couldn't help wondering about his description. I think he got it wrong. The islands are certainly windswept and, I imagine, in winter they must be desolate — but I could never refer to them as wretched. Perhaps Darwin didn't visit Sea Lion Island.

All by itself in a cold blue ocean, to the south of East Falkland, the island is home to, or regularly visited by, an astonishing variety of wildlife. Darwin would have loved it. Of course, David and Pat Grey's Sea Lion Lodge wasn't there to offer a homely haven in Darwin's time.

Leaning on the well polished bar one night,

exchanging wildlife encounter stories with a couple of other guests, I told David I still hadn't seen any of the island's Orcas. He pointed north and said, "Go down to the beach at five o'clock in the morning and you'll see them."

I'm an obedient sort at times. I did as I was told the next morning. It was raining lightly, bitterly cold, and I hadn't had a cup of tea or coffee to fuel the inner being. The wind screamed over the hard packed sand, buffeting me and increasing my discomfort. At both ends of the beach elephant seals dozed, well clear of the water. Magellanic penguins trotted cheerfully down the beach from their burrows in the tussock mounds and went surfing. There were no Orcas.

I whiled away the time photographing a friendly snowy sheathbill. Looking a bit like an overweight white pigeon, it wandered haphazardly about, constantly changing direction, pecking at something or other on the sand. It didn't seem to object to my presence or my camera. To keep some semblance of warmth in my body, I patrolled the beach from one end to the other, disturbing some of the seals. One aggressive young thing got annoyed as I stamped past trying to get the feeling back in my feet, and lunged at me with a teenage roar. His voice hadn't got past puberty but he didn't know that. From a safe distance I roared back. A few others raised their heads to see what the commotion was all about, saw it was only me, and returned to dreamland.

By six I was frozen and ready to leave. A sudden movement out in the thick kelp caught my attention. A triangular black fin broke the surface, followed by two larger ones. The Orcas had arrived. They were only an hour late.

I watched the three fins scything through the water, scant metres from where I stood. At the far end of the beach pandemonium broke out as the whales came into view. The seals raised their elephantine heads and roared their defiance, confident that they were out of reach. The deadly trio cruised effortlessly past in search of other prey.

Penguins leapt out of the sea in terror. Stumbling

up the beach to safety they turned, as if to make sure they
weren't being pursued. One sharp fin aimed straight for me.
I copied the penguins and retreated. The whale changed
direction at the last moment and showed its long black back
and distinctive white side. The penguins huddled together
near their burrows and watched fearfully as the marine
predators made another pass in front of them. Then, as
suddenly as they had appeared, the Orcas vanished. None
of the beasts on the beach took the departure lightly. Though
they all had important business at sea, the penguins and the
elephant seals waited, at least until I was out of sight. They
could stay hungry if they wanted to, I decided, I was going
back for breakfast.

There are few, if any, trees on the Falklands: none at
all on Sea Lion Island. There's some gorse, some tall tough
tussock grass, but no trees. The wind fairly rips across the
island. Westerleys predominate, except when I go out.
Then the winds become contrary, blowing directly at me,
regardless of my compass bearing.

When the skies are clear the ultra-violet light is
intense. Exposed skin, which is not protected by a liberal
application of sun block, is in for a roasting. Combine that
with wind burn and skin quickly discolours, cracks and
peels.

David drove me to Rockhopper Point, near his grass
airstrip. I planned to walk the south coast all the way back
to the lodge, a distance of about six and a half kilometres.
The wind was blowing on shore, from the southwest, when
I started. As soon as it saw me get out of the Land Rover
it veered through a large southerly quadrant to get in my
face.

I bowed my head and pushed gamely on. Beside
the rockhopper penguin colony there was a nesting site
for Imperial shags. Some had strayed over and got mixed
up with the penguins, or maybe the penguins were the
intruders. It didn't seem to matter. As soon as they caught
sight of my approaching body, both species forgot their
differences for a while and started to yell at me.

One shag, a big one, probably seventy centimetres

tall, spread its broad wings part way, thrust its sharp brown bill at me and said something rude. Malignant dark eyes, ringed with bright blue, glared at me. The orange caruncles, sitting on the bill between the eyes, looked as if the bird had sneezed its brains out. Each time I pointed the camera in its direction it opened its mouth wide and alternately inclined its head left and right. By bobbing and weaving in concert, I got some impressive shots of the inside of that bird's throat. Perhaps that's what it wanted?

On a beach of grey pebbles I came upon a sextet of Magellanic penguins having a conference in the shade of a pair of large boulders. I was between them and the sea. The boulders sealed off their escape towards land. They discussed the situation amongst themselves, their body language suggesting differing opinions. One, all in favour of calling me to account for intruding on their space, became spokesman. No taller than my knee, it leaned forward aggressively, stubby wings held out from its sides and slightly back. Its mouth opened and the sound that issued was out of all proportion to its size. A deep braying, like a lonely lovesick donkey, echoed over the beach, reminding me why the islanders refer to Magellanics as jackass penguins. I laughed out loud. That did nothing to improve the situation. The noisy one looked back at its mates for support.

Obediently they all leaned forward and stuck their wings out. Six mouths opened and they commenced a braying contest. My ears couldn't handle that. I went in search of quieter birds.

There's a freshwater pond hidden deep in a jungle of tussock grass. In one hour I counted fifteen species, on or around the pond. Two delicate little silvery grebes headed unsuspectingly in my direction. I eased myself onto a thick hummock of tussock grass protruding into the pond and stretched full length. It was a perfect spot. I, and my camera, were camouflaged by the coarse grass. Happily I collected portraits in comfort.

Tucked under the protection of another stand of tussock a night heron stood silently, unmoving, unblinking.

Eventually, its instincts told it, a fish would come along. I carefully aimed my camera and lens. A blade of grass was in the way and I leaned forward a fraction to move it. The tussock objected to my weight. Slowly, but inexorably, it tore away from the bank and began a gentle descent into the pond. I took one shot, held my camera at arm's length above me and tried not to give in to gravity. Only my feet were on solid ground. I wriggled backwards with unseemly haste as the water got closer and closer. The camera stayed dry. One hand and arm, my face and the front of my parka didn't. The water was very cold. I complained as quietly as I could.

The heron, thoroughly disgusted at the noise I made, took off for the other side of the pond. That fish was more likely to turn up over there, where it was more peaceful.

To get dry I needed a sunny sandy clearing sheltered from most of the wind, as soon as possible. I shouldered my equipment and pushed through the jungle of tussock towards the sea. The only attractive spot I found was already occupied — by a dead and decaying member of the sheep family. A squadron or two of flies had flown in from Argentina to help the clean up. I left them to it. Ten metres further on I came out onto a seashore of large round stones. Not pebbles. They were stones, bigger than baseballs. The location had two other immediate drawbacks. One, it was not sheltered from the wind. Two, a bull-chested southern sea lion was sunbathing two metres away and looking straight at me.

"Don't get up," I told it, "I'm not staying."

Ignoring my politeness the sea lion raised itself on its front flippers, so I could admire its broad chest. I took the final two frames on one film before it turned for the sea. Once it looked over its shoulder to make sure I wasn't following. I wasn't. My feet were in retreat mode, high stepping in reverse gear. I reached the sanctuary of the tussock jungle as the sea lion slid into the ocean.

I did find a spot. It was ideal for a lunch break. Clean dry sandy earth, a windbreak of tussock and a cliff to look over if I felt like getting a gale in my face. It is well known that vultures can sense a meal from vast distances. Flies too have been known to materialize in the most unexpected places when food is about. The Falkland Islands have their own scavengers, little known though they may be elsewhere.

A striated caracara, one of the rarest birds of prey in the world, fluttered down to stand on a rock, two paces before me. It wasn't there for the view. We stared at each other. I was interested in the bird. It looks rather like a small eagle and is only found in the Falklands and a few islands off the south west coast of Chile. The bird was interested in my sandwich. My snack went into my camera bag for safety. While the caracara posed for me, I shot a roll of film. Realizing the potential for a meal was limited, the raptor (the locals call it 'Johnny Rook') flexed its wings and sailed off the cliff.

A scratching on my bag warned of another visitor. Tussock birds, similar to a brown sparrow, are found only in the Falklands. Two found me. Sensing crumbs, one was upended in my camera bag while the other inspected one of my cameras.

I pulled out a packet of potato chips, without the birds getting particularly upset. Carefully I selected one flat chip and fitted it under the lace of one of my hiking boots. An inquisitive tussock bird flew over to offer a taste test. Sixteen seconds was all it took for that bird to study the problem, reach a solution and put it into operation. The chip was broken and removed before the other bird realized there was an alternate food source. We shared my sandwich too. They got the crumbs I shook off my sweater, and I kept the rest of the chips to myself.

Soon after, once my jacket was dry, I found another caracara and a tussock bird competing with each other. A herd of elephant seals sprawled on a beach, baking in the sun. Moving ponderously in from the deep ocean, a big old male let the surf slide him onto a rock shelf. There was a large star-shaped scar on his side. When I described him to David later, I learned that the scar had been there for a year or two. Perhaps, we discussed, as the result of an attack by an Orca or a leopard seal. Whatever caused it, the wound must have stung something fierce when the salt water hit it.

As the wave receded the bull lurched and flopped towards the others. Elephant seals are gregarious. They like to be together. This one was lonely, he maneouvred himself between two slightly smaller relatives and dozed off.

A tussock bird, making the most of a golden opportunity, hopped on the seal's back and attacked the scar with diligent pecks. Ripples of annoyance flickered along the seal's blubbery hide as the beak prodded the injury, otherwise it didn't stir. Within a few short moments a trickle of bright crimson blood began to flow from the fresh wound. The tussock kept digging.

Meanwhile, up front where the seal's head rested on the sand, a caracara was having a go at its nose. An expert told me later that the two were probably removing ticks. Tussock birds do it regularly, although he admitted he'd never seen a caracara pick a seal's proboscis.

I reckoned the tussock bird was getting ready for a pound of flesh the way he was working. The caracara was simply looking for a few hors d'oeuvres. If that huge seal had sneezed the caracara would have ended up with a one-way ticket to South Africa.

Elephant seals could be dangerous. I knew that. I left the birds to their chosen tasks. Nearby another bull, somewhat younger, was having an erotic dream. Oblivious to the fact that there were lady seals and a visitor present, he allowed his long thick bright pink penis to stiffen and probe the sunlight.

"That'll be sore in a while," I told him. "The ultra violet rays here are murder." My cautionary words were ignored. The seal snored happily, thinking his private thoughts. Smiling with sensual pleasure.

From the beach there was still half a kilometre to go, almost due north to the lodge. The wind had died down, or so I thought. I climbed up the bank from the beach and walked into the full force of another gale coming out of the north. It took me close to an hour to fight my way across open ground to the warmth of the bar and the company of the other guests. I was the last to arrive.

With time running out, I flew back to Stanley and took a three-hour Land Rover trip over rugged terrain to Volunteer Point. After bouncing around over deep ruts and soggy peat bogs it was a relief to get out of the vehicle and stretch my legs for a while.

In the distance a group of immaculately dressed Falklanders waited. Averaging close to a metre in height, the adults milled around me as I joined them. Their silvery grey backs and spotless white fronts contrasted beautifully with yellowish gold necks and ear muffs. I felt distinctly scruffy in my grubby denims and mud splattered parka. The king penguins, too polite to comment, pretended not to notice.

Immature versions, looking like out of date punk rockers with the remains of their brown baby down still clinging to parts of their heads and chests, clamoured for my attention. I almost felt as if I should sit down and read them a story to keep them quiet. One, bolder than his pals, kept slapping the backs of my legs with one flipper. I assumed it wanted to make friends and extended a hand in greeting. It pecked me.

My tripod and camera became the centre of their interest. My erstwhile friend with the sharp bill peered intently into the long lens. Behind him a few more youngsters lined up for their turn, like tourists queuing for a seaside telescope.

Some of the kings stood hunched over their own stomachs. Only the tips of their toes showed from under a roll of feathery white. Occasionally, as they adjusted their positions, a baby peered out to see what the world was doing. Under some warm bellies, the babies were still cocooned in hard white shells. The world would have to wait a bit longer for them.

A couple, still young adults, practiced aerobics. Or maybe it was a south Atlantic version of Tai Chi. Standing erect, with flippers by their sides, they slowly leaned back until balanced on stubby tails. Once in position, they drew their flippers up and back, like the streamlined wings on a jet fighter. With the body vertical, head slightly forward and bill parallel to terra firma, they then elevated their feet until only the heels touched the ground. I tried it. It was not as easy as it looked. Without a tail to rest on I couldn't keep my body vertical. I had to lean forward from the waist, or fall over backwards. The penguins watched my efforts sympathetically. Occasionally one whistled in surprise as I stumbled. Perhaps, if I'd had more time to practice, I might have been able to save face and show them my physical skills. Instead, I had a plane to catch.

I straightened my back, put my feet firmly on the ground and packed my cameras away. After a brief farewell I turned away. I soon discovered I wasn't alone. Ambling disconsolately behind me, flippers extended as if ready for a final embrace, my new friend shrieked at me with his musical whistling call.

Half way back to the Land Rover I stopped and looked back. He, I'm sure it was a he, was still there. A group of his furry pals had clustered around him, but he was still watching me. Without thinking, I waved. He didn't respond.

The sky was overcast and the wind, as always, was harsh. As we took off for Ascension Island and, eventually, the European winter, we passed over beaches and headlands. I wondered if one little furry king penguin glanced up as we climbed skywards over Volunteer Point. I hope so: I was thinking of him.

THE RESCUE MISSION

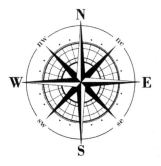

"I'm sorry Sir, we have no reservation for you," the lilting Nigerian voice was apologetic, yet definite. "The flight to Sokoto is full today."

"I was in your office in London yesterday," I retorted. "I saw my name on the confirmed passenger list."

"London does not always have the right list," the Nigerian Airways check-in agent explained politely.

Rubbish! I thought. Being In Lagos, with no way of proving my point, I kept quiet for a change. The agent handed me back my confirmed ticket with a shrug which could have represented anything from sorrow to complete indifference. I tapped the ticket on my fingers and looked him in the eye, trying to assess his worth. Embarrassed by my stare he giggled nervously. I slipped a US ten dollar bill in my ticket and handed it back to him.

"Please take another look. I'm sure there is an empty

seat somewhere."

He opened my ticket wallet. The single bill slid to his pocket with practiced perfection. Carefully he studied the passenger manifest again. Slowly his index finger worked its way down the list of names. He pursed his lips, as if showing concern. At last a glimmer of a smile flickered on his shiny face.

"Ah yes," he breathed, "there is one seat left. I will arrange it for you."

Lagos was never my favourite city. The idea of spending a day and a night there was far from appealing. I had an important job to do in Sokoto, and Sokoto was where I intended to go. I accepted my boarding pass for the flight gratefully, with a certain amount of relief. Once aboard and buckled in I noticed there were, naturally, some open seats.

On a previous visit to Nigeria I had sworn I would never return. Two years later I was back. I had been tempted with the lure of adventure.

"My son is in Nigeria and he's going to jail. Can you help?" The voice over the telephone sounded reasonably calm, desperately hopeful.

My mind, so often at odds with my mouth, shouted an emphatic "NO!" My mouth ignored the instruction and allowed a strong "Yes!" to emerge.

I had never been in a Nigerian jail and I had no desire to do so. Commonsense told me the experience would not be a happy one. A twenty-one-year-old boy from a good North American home would not, I assumed, enjoy the incarceration either.

"What's he done?"

"He was arrested for possession of marijuana. Only a small amount," his mother told me candidly.

My brain formed the words, stupid sod. My mouth said comfortingly, "Okay, don't worry, I'll see what I can do."

So, after many long discussions, I went to Nigeria, armed only with a vaguely formed plan to walk the miscreant over the border by night. All I had to recognize him by was a photograph and a description. He, out on bail awaiting his trial, knew only that a friend of the family, Tony, would be coming to Sokoto to visit and to advise him. He, we'll call him, Sonny, had no idea who I was or what I looked like.

I was the fourth person off the plane at Sokoto that hot sultry afternoon. Three Europeans, wearing comfortable lightweight safari suits alighted before me. Sonny ignored them. In deference to the winter I had so recently left behind, I wore a suit jacket — like a first time business visitor. Sonny nodded in my direction.

"Hi," he stood half a head taller than me and looked strong enough to pick me up with one hand, "I'm Sonny."

We shook hands. It hurt. I wondered what the hell I was doing in northern Nigeria planning to rescue someone bigger and obviously stronger than me.

"He's just a kid," I reminded myself, "a kid in trouble."

We talked for hours in a small hotel room. If I was to help I needed to know his side of the story. Sonny was remarkably open about his 'crime': possession of half an ounce of grass.

"I think they'd like to make an example of me," he said with a worried look on his face.

"You can bet on it," I told him. "There are two Nigerians in jail at home as we speak. Unlike you they were pushing drugs, but that won't make much difference to the authorities here."

"The trial is set for the day after tomorrow, I'd like you to be there," Sonny suggested.

I thought about that, but there were far too many potential pit-falls. I had promised Sonny's parents I would try to get him out, not watch while he was jailed for a decade or so.

"No chance. If anything goes wrong and you're convicted — and I think you will be, there's no way I will be able to help. I can't see myself physically breaking you out of jail. We'll leave tomorrow."

Sonny immediately showed his mettle. "Okay. I've

already been up to take a look at the border. I think we could cross quite safely a few kilometres to the east or west of the checkpoint."

"Good man," I was pleased to know he was prepared for anything. "We'll take a look together in the morning."

Sonny had borrowed a small motorbike from another European youth. After I slept the night, to shake off jet lag, he picked me up from the hotel and drove me back to where he was staying. I had a small pack on my back. My rolled sleeping bag dangled from Sonny's shoulder. With little thought for the potential danger, he weaved through the traffic spilling a trail of dust in our wake. En route we almost had a collision with a car, a motorcycle, and a couple of sleepy pedestrians. Actually, Sonny almost had the collision. I was on the pillion with nothing to do but try to stay on.

"That's what we have to watch out for," Sonny said over his shoulder, as if I was somehow involved in the almost mishaps. "It's the bizarre that gets you."

I soon learned that it was the 'bizarre' which got Sonny in trouble in the first place. Apprehended, for no crime other than wearing a camouflaged French army jacket, he tossed his stash of marijuana into a bush outside the police station. Unfortunately for him, his brief act of self-preservation happened to be observed by an eagle-eyed member of Sokoto's finest. I cautioned myself to watch out for anything remotely resembling the bizarre, especially where Sonny was concerned. After breakfast we walked to the market to get a few necessary supplies. We were followed.

"Do you see that guy back there on the other side of the road: the one wearing the fedora?" Sonny asked.

I looked back. "I see him. What of it? Is he bizarre?"

"He's from the CID. He's the one who arrested me."

He may have been from the criminal investigation department of the Nigerian police, but he wasn't good at tailing two healthy Canadians. Hardened criminals may have found his presence daunting. Not us: we soon lost him in the bustle of the market. Amongst the rich smells of spices and overripe fruit, amid the shouts of the merchants, the musical voices of the colourfully dressed women, the glamour and the clamour, we ducked and dived until he was out of sight. Without further discussion we went directly to the open-air bus station. An hour or so later we were dropped at the border — on the Nigerian side. Freedom was beyond the barrier. We weren't.

Sonny didn't have a passport, or any other form of identification. That was back in Sokoto, locked in a policeman's desk. Crossing the border legally did not enter the equation. Although only a dozen metres separated us from no-man's land, the dusty uncultivated strip between Nigeria and Niger, its northern neighbour, it was a world away for us. Being the only obviously white people in sight, we stuck out like whitewash on coal. Sneaking past the border guards was out. We walked nonchalantly towards the east. The road looked better that way.

The day was hot and steamy. The light reddish soil reflected the sun's rays. We were bombarded by heat from all directions. We began to sweat. Steadfastly we strolled casually on, as if out for an afternoon's walk. We said no more than a few words to each other, both concerned with conserving energy and placing one foot in front of the other. Half a dozen kilometres east from the border post, I called a halt by a large shady rain tree.

"We'll rest here for a while and go on when it cools down a bit."

We sank to the ground and each let one eye sleep while the other stayed open wide enough to spot any undesirable characters — such as policemen. Over and over again I played through half a dozen potential scenes, one of which was certain to surround us at some point during the next few hours. I began to feel drowsy.

Sonny snorted. Startled I raised my head. The eye which had been asleep opened to see what the fuss was about. The other, which had sneakily closed when no one was looking, feigned interest in a passing donkey. We were not fooled. I looked at my watch. Time was passing.

"Let's go," I stood up and dusted myself off. "If we walk straight north beside that field we should cross the border before sunset."

Sonny took the lead, placing one foot in front of the other on a narrow path. Cheerfully we greeted the few farmers and their wives working in the fields. They waved and smiled, pleased because we liked their land enough to walk on it. Wondering, no doubt, where we had left our car. We walked in single file for about half an hour, until the trail led up a slight incline — angling more and more to the right. Our shadows were lengthening, the sun hung low in the west, almost ready to spill its gold across the desert scrublands. Sonny stopped abruptly.

"Soldiers coming," he warned.

"Sit down. Quick," I ordered.

We sat on rocks as if we had every right to be out there in the imminent dusk. A uniformed soldier on horseback rode into view. Behind him, dressed in ragged civilian clothes, came two others on foot. My heart started a noisy pounding rhythm, loud enough to set a complete village tripping the light fantastic. The horseman stopped. I noticed he carried a rifle. He looked as though he knew how to use it. He didn't look like much of a dancer.

"Qu'est que vous voulez ici?" he demanded gruffly.

"We're just watching the sunset," Sonny answered, also in French, with his back to the sun's final rays.

"We've been out walking all day, from Birni'n Konni," I broke in to cover Sonny's faux pas, still avoiding English. "Now the sun has gone and we are lost."

A certain elation crept into my thoughts as I realized, due to the conversation in French, that we had already crossed from English-speaking Nigeria into the Republic of Niger. The pleasure was tempered by the possibility that the soldier, obviously on a border patrol, might ask for our passports. We had a story prepared, a flimsy one, without much strength. The soldier looked at me thoughtfully for a minute, then at Sonny. Deciding we were harmless, he pointed back the way he had come.

"There is a village back there, you can stay the night," he offered.

We bounded to our feet. "Merci, Monsieur," we thanked him in unison as he clucked his tongue against his teeth to restart his horse. Without so much as a backward glance, he and his untidy entourage wandered away.

The sun sets in the west, not the east," I muttered to Sonny as the golden orb slipped from sight.

"We made it," Sonny grinned at me in the sudden darkness, ignoring my comment. "We made it!"

"Not yet we haven't," I reminded him. "We've crossed the border that's all. We're not safe yet."

Ignoring the offer of accommodation, we went through the village without breaking our stride. A few dogs barked. Muffled voices came from the huts. Cooking smells wafted tantalizingly past. My stomach, which grumbles when my brain signals food is available, begged me to stop for refueling. We kept moving. Once clear I had a thought. Self-preservation again.

"How much Nigerian money have you left?"

"About ten Naira, that's all. Why?"

"I've got more than that. We'd better bury it," I suggested. "We sure don't want to get caught with Nigerian currency on us. That's a dead giveaway."

Sonny was horrified at the thought of burying real paper currency, even if it was Nigerian and more or less useless outside that country. He tried to argue. I insisted and I won. We scooped a hole in the earth and placed the treasure carefully in it. One day a child, or a farmer, would find it and give thanks to his or her favourite deity for the bountiful gift.

"What about the cigarettes?"

"I'm not throwing my smokes away," Sonny was emphatic.

"Okay, we'll keep the smokes. If we get caught, toss them out fast."

We walked blindly through the bush for another hour — perhaps less, always heading roughly north, until our feet touched the broken edge of a sealed road. Automatically we turned left, to the west: towards Birni'n Konni, directly north of the Nigerian border.

We soon passed a white-washed road marker. The figure 10 was emblazoned on it — nothing else. Mentally we noted we had a ten-kilometre walk ahead of us. In short order we passed another marked 9. Then 8, 7, and 6. We didn't seem to be walking that fast. Perhaps the darkness had us confused as to our pace. I worried over the problem for a hundred steps or so, knowing there must be a solution.

My mind clicked into gear at last. We passed 5, 4, 3, 2 and 1. The next marker boldly showed 10 again. I started to laugh.

"I'd forgotten the roads here have kilometre markers in bold figures and each hundred metres in between are marked in smaller figures. We've only come one kilometre, not ten."

"Shit," said Sonny and lengthened his already considerable stride. I stretched my legs as far as I could to keep up.

The world was quiet when we finally saw the lights of the town ahead of us. No cars or trucks had passed. We had spoken a few words, smoked too many cigarettes, and kept walking.

"There will be a checkpoint across the road, just outside town," I warned Sonny. "Throw the rest of your Nigerian cigarettes away and let me do the talking."

We saw the road barrier, a long red and white pole, stretching from one sentry hut to another on the opposite side of the road. We walked in silence, hardly daring to breathe. On the left side a guard sat on a stool, his head on his chest, a rifle cradled in his arms. He was asleep. We walked round the barrier on tiptoes. He woke up as we passed on the far side of the road.

"Moment," he called sleepily. "Papiers, s'il vous plait."

We ignored his request. I turned and called some inane pleasantry at him as we vanished into the night. His head fell back on his chest. A nasal rumble suggested he had lost interest in us.

Before leaving Nigeria we had arranged to stay at a particular house in Birni'n Konni, if we got that far. Rented by two Americans, they were half expecting us at some time. This week. Next week. Sometime. We searched the dark streets until well after midnight before we finally found the gate we were looking for. It was securely locked. No lights showed beyond the high mud-brick walls.

"Give me a boost," Sonny said quietly. "I'll go and wake them up."

"If they have a guard dog, you'll be back over the wall in a flash," I told him, my bared teeth the only visible evidence of my humour.

With a little help from me, Sonny slid over the top. I stood outside in the lane in pitch-black silence for ten minutes wondering what was happening. I was about to attempt scaling the wall myself when a creaking and metallic squeal broke the silence as a rusty bolt was drawn. The gate opened. Sonny stood there holding a flashlight and beaming at me.

"Come on in, there's only one old dog."

Our hosts, who had been asleep, made us a large jug of fruit juice. We downed it without much of the liquid touching the sides of parched throats. By this time we were both rocking on our heels. Sonny elected to sleep in the house where there was an old stuffed couch. I chose the open courtyard, fresh air, and a rickety camp bed.

Somewhere between then and daybreak, while the stars still kept their watch, I was rudely awakened. I had been dreaming of lions: wild lions: hungry lions. My dream and reality merged abruptly. Breathing heavily into my face, while straddling me with four hairy legs, one of the characters in my mind licked my face with a long wet tongue. Trapped in my sleeping bag, with no possibility of escape, I screamed.

The terrible beast was not put off. Taking my cry as a signal of approval for more affection, it gave me another rasping lick. I was so glad I'd gone to the toilet before going to bed.

I reached up and grabbed the shaggy creature by the throat. One of its feet slipped off my cot and a large smelly body flopped on mine.

"Get off, ya great berk," I yelled as I struggled to get out from under the monster. It licked me again before jumping to the ground. Slithering into the open, I stood up. Expectantly my erstwhile adversary sat and waited patiently for me to do something interesting. I told the passionate golden retriever what I thought of its parentage, and its halitosis-laden kisses. Shocked by my language it retired, with tail between its legs, to its own bed in a far corner of the compound. There was no more sleep for me that night.

Daybreak came and Sonny emerged from the house. "Sleep all right out here?" he asked. My reply echoed what I had said to the over friendly guard dog earlier.

As soon as the PTT, or telephone office, was open we walked into town and made a call to the capital. "Stay put," we were told. "We'll pick you up in a few hours."

We went back to the house and waited. With nothing to do, apart from watch the clock, we slept. Much too soon, still in the morning, there was a sharp knocking on the door. I recognized, with some alarm, that our transport could not possibly have arrived from Niamey so quickly. Before I could stop him Sonny had opened the door. A Canadian voice announced its owner was looking for Sonny. I sagged with relief.

"How did you guys get here so fast?" I asked. "I didn't expect you until this evening."

"Oh, we were up at Tahoua, not so far away. We were told by radio to pick you up."

Gratefully we loaded ourselves into a pale blue Toyota Land Cruiser and settled back for the long drive to Niamey. Our adventures though were not quite over.

Sonny's preoccupation with the 'bizarre' came back to haunt us as we drove through Dogondoutchi. Crowds, three and four deep, lined each side of the gravel road. They were not there for our benefit.

"The President of Niger is coming through later

today," our driver informed us.

A little girl, no more than five years old, ran across in front of us without warning. Our driver braked violently and swung the steering hard to the left. The child's red and green print dress hooked on our front fender, unravelled, spun her round. The heavy vehicle brushed past without touching her, leaving her standing almost naked in the road.

"Don't stop," I yelled. "She's okay. Just keep going."

"It's the bizarre that gets you," Sonny intoned from the back seat.

Sometime that night, in the comfort of a private office in Niamey, I phoned Sonny's father in Toronto.

"Hi," I said as his voice answered, "it's Tony. I'm in Niamey."

"When do you expect to get to Nigeria?" he asked.

"I've already been there," I replied smugly. "I have a present for you. Would you like to speak to him?"

I'm sure I heard a sob from far across a desert and an ocean. As Sonny talked with his father, then his mother, I sat back with my booted feet on a fine carpet and stretched luxuriously. We were free. Now all I had to do was to get him the rest of the way home. I wasn't too worried about that part.

ACKNOWLEDGEMENTS

I am deeply indebted to the many editors and publishers around the world who chose to include my words and photographs in their publications. Without their support over many years this book could not have been written. The re-writing of each story for this book has, for me, been another adventure and a labour of love.

Aside from the editors and publishing companies, there are many other organizations which also deserve my thanks for helping me in my far-ranging travels. Foremost among them are: Air Mali, Air New Zealand, Bangladesh Parjatan Corporation, Biman Bangladesh Airlines, CBC-TV (Ottawa), Discovery Expeditions (Belgium), FIGAS (Falkland Islands Government Air Service), The Guide (Bangladesh), GulfAir (Bahrain), Kaisosi Safari Lodge (Namibia), Kessler 4 x 4 Hire (Namibia), Lufthansa Airlines, Namibia Tourism, Northern Territory Tourist Commission (Australia), Norwegian Tourist Board (now Innovation Norway), Oman Air, Oman Discovery, the Royal Air Force, and Travel Manitoba.

Among my fellow authors, my thanks for their continued support are owed to Matthew Bin, Steve Crowhurst, Suzanne Harris, Margaret Hume, Bernice Lever, Anita Purcell, Lawrie Raskin, Arlene Smith, Patrick Taylor and Peter Vassilopoulos. Thanks also to the Starkman family for many years of friendship.

Finally, I must thank Robert Morgan of BookLand Press for taking on this project. It has been a pleasure working with you every step of the way, Robert.

ABOUT THE AUTHOR

Anthony Dalton is an adventurer, author and public speaker. In the 1970s and early '80s he led regular expeditions into and across the Sahara, through the deserts of the Middle East and into the mountainous terrain of Afghanistan. In 1984 he travelled hundreds of nautical miles along the Arctic coast alone in an inflatable speedboat. In 1994 he joined twelve members of the Cree First Nation on a traditional York boat voyage on the Hayes River between Norway House and Oxford House. While canoeing the second half of the Hayes River from Oxford House to York Factory in 2000 he participated in a television documentary on great Canadian rivers for the Discovery Channel.

Dalton has written five non-fiction books and collaborated on two others. His illustrated non-fiction articles have been published in magazines and newspapers in twenty countries and nine languages. He is currently working on two television documentaries based on his books.

Magazine assignments have taken him to the Australian Outback, Bahrain, Bangladesh, Falkland Islands, Malaysia, Namibia, Netherlands, New Zealand, Norway, Oman, Saudi Arabia, Vanuatu, and to Arctic Canada and the Manitoban shores of Hudson Bay. He has sailed in the Mediterranean, Atlantic, Baltic and North Seas as crew on the mighty windjammers of the Russian and Ukrainian tall-ship fleets.

Anthony Dalton is a Fellow of the Royal Geographical Society, a Fellow of the Explorers Club, a Member of the Welsh Academy and National President of the Canadian Authors Association.

ALSO BY ANTHONY DALTON

Alone Against the Arctic
ISBN 9781894974332

Baychimo: Arctic Ghost Ship
ISBN 9781894974141

J/Boats: Sailing to Success
ISBN 9780760321706

Wayward Sailor: In Search of the Real Tristan Jones
ISBN 9780071440288

The Best of Nautical Quarterly
Volume 1: The Lure of Sail
(with Reese Palley)
ISBN 9780760318201